ALSO BY
PHYLLIS GROSSKURTH

John Addington Symonds: A Biography

Leslie Stephen

Gabrielle Roy

Havelock Ellis: A Biography

Melanie Klein: Her World and Her Work

Margaret Mead: A Life of Controversy

The Secret Ring: Freud's Inner Circle and the Politics of Psychoanalysis

Byron: The Flawed Angel

ELUSIVE SUBJECT

A Biographer's Life

PHYLLIS GROSSKURTH

MACFARLANE WALTER & ROSS
Toronto

Macfarlane Walter & Ross
37A Hazelton Avenue
Toronto, Canada M5R 2E3

Canadian Cataloguing in Publication Data

Grosskurth, Phyllis
Elusive subject : a biographer's life

Includes index.
ISBN 1-55199-036-9

1. Grosskurth, Phyllis.   2. Biographers – Canada – Biography.   I. Title.

CT34.C3G76 1999 920'.007'202   C99-932014-9

Macfarlane Walter & Ross gratefully acknowledges support for its publishing
program from the Canada Council for the Arts, the Ontario Arts Council,
and the Government of Canada through the Book Publishing Industry
Development Program.

Printed and bound in Canada

For my sister, Joan Kerrigan.
She and I share much of this story.

CONTENTS

ACKNOWLEDGMENTS

I wish to thank my friend Ruth Rendell, who first suggested that I write this book.

I am also grateful for background material provided by Jacalyn Duffin in *Langstaff: A Nineteenth-Century Medical Life* (University of Toronto Press, 1993) and to the Hon. Henry N.R. Jackman for the history of the Empire Life Insurance Company, which he wrote for its fiftieth anniversary in 1973.

In Jan Walter, my editor, I have been fortunate to have the kind of supportive, professional help every author dreams of. In the last stages, Barbara Czarnecki has provided a probing eye for errors and lack of clarity, for which I have been truly grateful.

INTRODUCTION

Biographers tend to speak of their "methodology" in self-congratulatory terms. They approach their subjects, they claim, with complete objectivity and detachment. In writing about myself, I intended to assume the same cool distance: I would pin my life to the wall like a butterfly specimen.

It hasn't turned out that way. It was impossible to be detached. Many incidents were a joy to summon up, some were a source of misery. I had to be circumspect about the feelings of certain individuals, and there were times when I would writhe in embarrassment about my own behaviour. Most painful of all were small kindnesses neglected and cruel words that should never have been uttered.

One of the satisfactory things about writing a biography is that one can provide a beginning, a middle, and an end. But this wasn't the case in writing a memoir. I was confronted with the accumulated chaos of everyday living. I am fully aware that my imaginative memory has edited, abridged, and truncated experience out of shape, omitting longueurs and accenting highlights. And during the year I spent recalling my past, relationships changed, dear friends died, and the future looked somewhat different from when I had first put pen to paper. Almost every day, in some subtle way, we adjust to new circumstances.

Above all, there is no tidy ending because, it appears, I am still here. If the reader tends to ask, "Are we there yet?" my reply is, "Not yet, please."

Phyllis Grosskurth
Toronto, July 1999

1

ROOTS

Occasionally, when I have difficulty falling asleep, I count the houses in which I have lived in various countries. There are strict rules: I don't include Continental summer villas, boarding houses, or friends' homes. Even so, I think the correct number is forty although my mumbling usually reaches only thirty-seven or thirty-eight before memory fails and I have to start all over again. Sometimes I cannot recall the proper sequence of the homes in which we lived on Hudson Drive, Nanton Avenue, and Blythwood Road in Toronto when I was a child, though over the years it has been an obsessional habit to revisit many of them. Have you ever stood across the street from a house where you once lived and had the unnerving sensation that it was rejecting you? No, that is not precisely the word I want. To say "rejecting" implies that the house is responding to you. "Impervious" or "indifferent" is more what I mean, as though the house has transferred its allegiance to the new occupants. It is an experience I have known many times in my life.

I cannot imagine how a permanently settled life might have changed me, but sometimes I play with the idea. I have always been fascinated by a story that the people of Königsberg used to set their watches by Immanuel Kant's daily walk, so predictable was his presence and his routine. The British politician Alan Clark speaks scornfully in his diaries of people who have to buy their furniture, and I found myself more interested in that remark than in all the accounts of his

1

sexual shenanigans. It is hard to conceive of an existence where one lives in the same fully furnished house all one's life, never having to save up for carpeting nor buying china on the instalment plan. Does it mean that one's mind is filled with more important things? Does it suggest that one can move through the world with a certain ease, a sense of entitlement, because a permanent residence has been reserved – and maintained – for one in the scheme of things? Of course I envy those people, and yet it must also mean that they are deprived of other experiences such as the satisfaction I derive every time I enter our newly renovated bathroom, knowing that it was built from the royalties of one of my books. A bathroom is something most people take for granted, but mine has a certain well-earned magic to it.

I was a March baby, the eldest daughter of Milton and Winifred (née Owen) Langstaff, born on my mother's birthday in the decade referred to as the Roaring Twenties, although I don't think they roared so loudly in prim Toronto. My earliest memory is of one of those uninteresting Moore Park brick houses with a side entrance. Here we lived until I was three years old. When I was about two, there seems to have been a ritual each afternoon when my mother held me up to the window to watch the baby across the street. I was fascinated by that child. My mother would say, "Now her mummy is tucking her into her carriage. Now she is going to have a little sleep." One day I was devastated to see the mother alone, sweeping her front walk. Where on earth had she left the baby? All alone in the house as she obliviously carried out her task? Did I identify with her abandonment?

I must have been an appealing child because two older neighbourhood girls, Alice and Isabel, would regularly come to the door and ask if they could take Patsy for a walk. No one ever called me Phyllis, the name I shared with my mother's favourite sister. Since I was born close to St. Patrick's Day, my Uncle Fred said I should have an Irish name. Nowadays I squirm when anyone calls me Patsy and I dislike Phyllis almost as much. It wasn't until I was at university that I managed to persuade people to call me Pat. I have at least two friends who are called Phyllis and contentedly so, whereas I always feel like something of a fraud with this pretentious, unfamiliar name. (Incidentally, these two Phyllises grew up in the same houses all through their childhoods. I may be labouring the point, but I think it's worth considering.)

My only other memory of that remote period is of one summer evening going for a walk with my father. How lovely to think that my father and I actually strolled together, that he was relaxed enough to do this. We passed a brightly lit house in which a very jolly party was taking place. I was determined to join in and I pulled and tugged at his hand, while my big red-haired father protested laughingly that we hadn't been invited, and you couldn't just barge into other people's houses. Years later when I was in therapy my analyst would often refer to that image of a three-year-old girl feeling excluded from a happy group.

My father laughed a lot then, great choking gasps while he waved his arms as though he were brushing away swarming mosquitoes. It is marvellous to hear one's parents laugh. Dad was delighted by absurdity, and read and reread his favourite Dickens. One afternoon a very affected friend of my mother's sent him into such spasms that he had to go out and walk around the block to control himself. My sister Joan and I once laughed like that when one of us had the collywobbles at Easter service in Grace Church on-the-Hill.

Those early years on Heath Street were a sunny time in Dad's life. He and my mother hadn't been married very long and his financial star was rising on Bay Street. He had founded an insurance company, Empire Life, in 1923; by 1927, thanks to its growing success, my parents were poring over architectural blueprints of a much grander mock-Georgian house on Rosedale Heights Drive overlooking

Rosedale. In those days Moore Park was the residence of respectable new money, Rosedale that of old money, not all of it respectable. The whole area was crisscrossed with wonderful ravines, and the streets lined with elm trees, long before anyone had ever heard of blight. It was a quiet, peaceful, smug haven in a city that was still very much an overgrown colonial town, a place with deeply repressed inhibitions and guilty secrets.

Children don't like upheavals in their lives, and I lay on the edge of the lawn kicking and screaming when my mother tried to coax me into the newly completed home. In time I grew to love that pretty white house with its green shutters and curved entrance with silver fittings, although I never liked the scratchy pebbled stucco of which so many houses were built at the time. Much later, when I was in university, I had a summer job working in the book department of Simpsons. A woman and her daughter (about my age) ordered a book to be sent to 257 Rosedale Heights Drive, and I exclaimed, "But my family built that house!" They looked at me doubtfully and turned on their heels. A salesgirl in Simpsons living in *their* house!

My initial hostility to the new home must have been associated with the fact that Mother was pregnant at the time. She gradually grew heavier, and I was very suspicious one day when I accompanied her to her doctor's office and she emerged with a mysterious smile on her face. I was sullenly furious about the fuss that was being made over decorating the back bedroom, adjoining the master bedroom. Especially hateful was the elaborate point d'esprit bassinet. I hardly remember Joan as a baby, but I watched her being nursed and developed an antipathy towards my mother's breasts – and eventually towards my own.

My parents possibly realized how traumatic the appearance of this little intruder was to me, for my father took me off up north on a trip to a lodge in Muskoka, which Dad loved for its lakes and rocky landscape. I haven't the slightest idea where we stayed but it was the closest thing to paradise I'll ever know. We were probably there for only a long weekend, but every day we went canoeing – there exists a curled-up snapshot of a little girl sunk in the depths of a canoe – and once a miracle happened. We found floating in the water a miniature canoe with a carved Indian figure sitting in it. When my children were young they all loved the classic story *Paddle-to-the-Sea*. It might have been the very same Paddle whom I had been permitted to hold for a brief period during his Odyssean voyage.

I was about four when we went to Muskoka as a family. One day while I was wading, the bottom suddenly dropped beneath me. Submerged, I was terrified when I couldn't reach the surface. Suddenly Dad grabbed my hair and pulled me to safety. He then taught me to swim. For years I had nightmares of being sucked into a whirlpool like those in the Niagara River. Just the same I have always loved swimming as much as my father did, and I cherish very special swims – a quiet pond surrounded by New Hampshire hills; fighting the surf at Saint-Jean-de-Luz; and best of all, allowing myself to be borne along by the swell off the coast of Cephalonia in the Ionian sea. It was such an ecstatic experience that I never wanted it to end.

Mother didn't own a bathing suit and never showed any interest in swimming. She did things on her own terms and had her own enthusiasms. Rosedale Heights was very much her house – feminine with lots of chintz, flouncy curtains, and Chippendale reproductions. Dad's room was the library. There was a big table in the middle with a humidor and many brass ornaments. The bookends were replicas of the lion of St. Mark's, his paw resting on an open Gospel. On the table were copies of the *Strand Magazine*, a British monthly, and other publications to which Dad subscribed. On the back cover of the *Strand* were pictures of deliciously coloured puddings like jam roly-poly, and I longed to go to England where I could eat such scrumptious food. The walls were lined with dark bookcases containing sets of the classics – Macaulay, Carlyle, all the great nineteenth-century novelists. The chairs were large red leather recesses into which a child could sink. My father had been a great reader and collector, but by then his reading seemed to be confined to Dickens and the mystery writer Edgar Wallace.

Each evening when Dad came home, he would seat himself comfortably in the corner of the library, cut off the end of a cigar, and open the newspaper. I sat partly on his shoulder, partly on the high wing of the chair, chattering incessantly. Once I said pertly, "I can twist you around my little finger." "Oh, you think so, do you?" he replied. Within a week he had pulled down my drawers and given me the spanking of my life for some transgression while I wailed in pain and humiliation.

It was in this same chair that I confessed I was a thief. I often passed a drugstore whose window displayed a beautiful golden treasure chest filled with chocolates. I desperately wanted to give it to my mother. It cost $5, an enormous sum for a child who probably possessed a dime at most. I brooded incessantly about that chest – the most desirable thing I had ever seen – and one day nervously opened Mummy's handbag and extracted a $5 bill. I triumphantly presented my trophy to her, concocting some cock-and-bull story that the uncle of a school friend had given it to me. My parents exclaimed over his generosity. My mother said that she must telephone and thank him. In a panic I explained that he had been in Toronto only on a visit. Partly because of the threat of exposure but more through agonies of conscience, I was compelled one evening to confess to Dad. His main reaction was deep disappointment that I had been able to lie so convincingly. He would look at me from time to time, shaking his head sorrowfully. One of the cardinal rules in our house was that we were never to lie or cheat.

Dad had been born in a beautiful house in Richmond Hill, a

small town north of Toronto. His father, the local physician, had been educated at Guy's Hospital in London. He was very emancipated for a country doctor, probing the significance of dreams before psycho-analysis made such theories popular; Margaret Atwood used him as the model for one of the characters in *Alias Grace*. After the death of his first wife he married a young teacher at the high school; she bore him three sons and a daughter.

My grandmother had achieved honours in maths and languages in her matriculation, but women were not yet admitted to the university. She was an early advocate of the vote for women and headed the temperance movement in Richmond Hill. Twenty-seven years younger than my grandfather, she was hardly older than her stepchildren, who very much resented her, and I think their descendants still regard her as the wicked stepmother.

Dad often told us about sitting on his father's knee when he was two and of being suddenly thrust onto the floor as his father clutched his chest and died on the spot. Apparently a will in favour of my grandmother was missing, and she and her four little children were obliged to get on the train and head for Toronto. There had been lots of entertaining during the marriage, musicals and garden parties, and small towns being what they are, I imagine there was some nasty rejoicing at her downfall. I have been inside the Richmond Hill house only once – and that was just a few years ago because of the continuing feud – but it became a familiar sight to us as we passed it driving north to Muskoka. The car would slow down, and Dad would point to the pump beside a smaller house where they had moved after Grandfather's death. "That's where I sat and said, 'I am five years old today.'" I was so impressed by this that on my fifth birthday I sat at the top of our stairs and repeated the same solemn words. I was dramatic from an early age.

I believe my grandmother owned some property on Queen Street in downtown Toronto, but life in the big city was a struggle for economic survival. And there was the constant preoccupation of legal battles with her stepchildren after the last will was finally discovered. As a boy Dad delivered milk in the early morning and papers in the late afternoon, casting longing glances at the baseball diamond as he passed on his rounds. Nevertheless, he managed to become an award-winning athlete. He entered Harbord Collegiate at the age of twelve and at seventeen graduated with three scholarships, including the highest in the province, the Prince of Wales. He never related any of this in a bragging way, nor did he want us to feel sorry for him, but I did and thought he was heroic.

Dad hadn't been able to go to war because of poor eyesight, but his adored older brother, Miles, was killed at Vimy. Miles had persuaded Dad to leave university in his second year to enter the insurance business with him. Their plan was to become actuaries and found a company of their own. They would get up at four in the morning to study for their actuarial exams, which they both passed brilliantly. After Miles's death I think Dad must have expended a lot of energy compensating to my grandmother for his loss as well as for the death of his only sister, Clara, from tuberculosis, and I expect he felt proud when he could buy Grandmother Langstaff a nice house on Huron Street and provide her with a housekeeper.

Our own home on Rosedale Heights spoke of his success. The garden was half an acre, the area directly behind the house well tended, with beds of peonies and iris and forget-me-nots, separated at the end by a wide spirea hedge. Bleeding hearts poked through the fence from the garden next door, and I loved them so much that I swore I would have them in my garden one day. Beyond the cultivated section was a wild garden where I played. People said that if you dug deep enough you would reach China. With my little shovel I set out with ambitious intentions but would give up after about ten inches. (Little did I know that my one true love was living in China at that very moment, and that we would find each other after many wrong roads taken.)

The wild garden plunged into a ravine, and at the bottom was a high chain-link fence – it must have cost a fortune even then – where the dogs were kept. My father was crazy about bull terriers. He liked their scrappy nature, and at one time there were as many as ten barking their heads off. The dogs had a little house divided into rooms. It was perfectly ridiculous. I hated those dogs, except for lame gentle Jack, who was the only one allowed into our house. The neighbours were always complaining, and I didn't blame them. The dogs particularly disturbed me when they were in heat. It was my first experience with that mysterious thing called sex. I only once saw my father naked, and that thing hanging between his legs was as distressing as – and even more puzzling than – those panting dogs.

We never seemed to fit into the neighbourhood, or at least that was how I felt. Several of the people living on that street were doctors, and once Dr. Charles Best, co-discoverer of insulin, who lived partway up the hill, tried to persuade Dad to sell our house to him. Everyone was well-to-do, but perhaps we seemed a good deal more so and even a bit flashy. Two expensive cars, a Packard and a Hupmobile, were parked in the driveway. For a while we had a Scottish nanny called Margaret, impressive in a white starched uniform, in addition to an all-purpose maid. We never seemed able to keep maids long. Even in days of deep unemployment I think they found Mother difficult to work for. In my teens I read a book called *A Good Home with Nice People,* about the humiliations maids had to endure, and I experienced a horrible shock of recognition when I thought of the narrow life those poor young women must have led in that tiny room in the attic. Innumerable times I heard Mother on the telephone talking to the employment agency about her requirements for someone who could make "simple milk puddings."

When it came to children, Mother had fixed ideas about pro-
nunciation and posture, and she was obsessed with diet and hygiene.
No self-respecting middle-class woman in Toronto at that time would
dream of taking her children to any other pediatrician but Dr. Alan
Brown, whose words of wisdom were cited by all the neighbourhood
mothers. Undoubtedly he was a very able doctor since he had invented
Pablum and was responsible for the physical welfare of the Dionne
quintuplets. Nevertheless, he was adamant on the subject of tonsils. To
him they were like original sin, and he would point at a child, thun-
dering, "Tonsils out!"

As a result of Dr. Brown's influence, we were never allowed to
eat white bread or fried food, and I wasn't permitted to go to school
until I was seven and a half so that I could get plenty of fresh air. The
local children started at Whitney Public School at least a year before I
could venture into the world. Mother didn't approve of public schools
so I was sent to a small private school in Rosedale. We stayed until one
o'clock, and as I walked home along Edgar Avenue, which bisected
Rosedale, I would stare at the houses and wonder about the lives of the
privileged people who lived in them. By the time I climbed Maclennan
Hill and made my way along the ridge behind Whitney it was early
afternoon, and the other children would be back in class. After lunch
I'd listen to soap operas like *Helen Trent*, the story of a noble woman
battling a hostile world, and *The Little French Princess*, who had an
adorable accent and an adoring American husband. Then I'd roller-
skate all over Moore Park or, after I received my first bike, ride through
Mount Pleasant Cemetery. A lot of the time, too, I was curled up
reading in one of the deep leather armchairs. Even though I had a
younger sister it was quite a solitary childhood.

The school I attended was run by Miss Railton, an English
woman of indeterminate age, who had a lot of hair imprisoned
within a net. She was extremely well informed about foreign affairs,

and I particularly remember her passionate conviction that the Allies had imposed cruel reparations on the Germans after the First World War. Although children seldom remember much about early lessons, I think our enthusiasms are awakened then. Certainly she made history sound fascinating. I wish Miss Railton had been able to awaken some interest in math in me, but perhaps I was too thick. Later I had extra lessons with her, and while I would assume an expression of intense concentration my mind was elsewhere. My parents were simply throwing away money which by then they could ill afford.

As I grew older I played more often with my Rosedale schoolmates than with the Whitney School gang, although I loved it when I was allowed to join kick-the-can or hide-and-seek. However, my particular enemies, June and Bubbles, who were next-door neighbours, usually tried to exclude me. I don't know why they hated me so much. Outside my family circle I was a very shy child, but bullies have an uncanny nose for the natural victim. I think these two must have suffered from a limitation of imagination; their most exquisite pleasure in life seemed to be in making me cry. Even in Rosedale I wasn't safe from them. We used to skate in the park off Maclennan Avenue, and my greatest torment took place within the hut where we changed our skates. I would be subjected to a barrage of insults about the size of my feet and the fact that my bottom apparently stuck out. I never told my parents; I simply assumed that everything they said about me must be true, and that I was a pretty miserable specimen. On the way home the two collaborators would walk close together, sniggering about me, while I trailed forlornly half a block behind them.

But I could be pretty cruel myself. There was a chubby little girl around the corner on Inglewood Drive who had a gorgeous head of red curls. I loathed her beauty. I would stand ingratiatingly on the pavement in front of her house, trying to persuade her to come over to my place to play. For a long time she sensibly refused, but one day I broke down her resistance. It had taken so much energy to lure her off her property that I hadn't worked out any plan about what I was going to do next, but I was effectively kidnapping her. We entered the vestibule and I pushed her into the double-doored cupboard with its little silver knobs. It was hard work holding two doors closed while she pushed and banged and hollered blue murder. Mother eventually heard the uproar and in bewilderment opened the inner door of the house, and instantly released the child. I could give her no explanation for what I had been doing. After that, whenever I passed down Inglewood, the terrified girl would run and hide within the safety of her own home.

In those days my home too was a haven, especially as my mother and aunts encouraged me in thinking I was very clever. I developed what the child analyst D. W. Winnicott would describe as a "false self," conforming to their expectations in order to win their approval. I took ballet and elocution lessons, although I never learned how to breathe properly from my diaphragm. I was pretty, but skinny and pale, and I hated it when Mother pinched my cheeks before I appeared in public. Photographs of the time show me with a ghastly artificial smile. There exists a shame-making home movie where I ham it up, teeth gleaming, toes pointed out, in a white rabbit coat and beret. It is mortifying to realize one was so awful. I developed a whole repertoire of poems to recite to rapturous applause at family Christmas parties and gave a particularly emotional rendering of "Crossing the Bar." My mother would plead unavailingly for me not to continue with another poem, which ended:

Too busy with dusting and sweeping to play,
And now they have silently wandered away.

I, the observing self, watch a series of tableaux such as this which I extract from some deep well of memory. This self-conscious little girl is apparently someone with whom I shared a past. Joan must have found me a terrible pain in the neck.

Mother adored both New England and the southern states. On either side of the matrimonial bed hung two large pictures of the Old South entitled *Honeymoon Departure* and *Honeymoon Return*. The bride was in a crinoline in both, and in one she was climbing into a coach and in the other she was descending from it. The live oaks, festooned with trailing moss, remained the same and the porticoed antebellum house hadn't changed in her absence. In both the bride remained expressionless. I often used to stare fixedly at these pictures trying to detect the difference between the two.

I spent my fourth birthday in South Carolina. On the journey down I sat in the back seat with Aunt Phyllis, surreptitiously masturbating, under the illusion that she was oblivious to what was going on. I became more and more reckless about it, and finally she suddenly pulled down my dress sharply, asking me if I was itchy. This discomfiting incident is juxtaposed in my memory with the first argument between my parents that I vividly remember. When we arrived at the hotel in Charleston, there was shouting and doors banging. I felt very confused, and Aunt Phyllis told me not to pay any attention. Not many years later the noise of their battling was so awful that we were asked to leave a hotel in northern Ontario. It was dreadfully humiliating, with people staring as we children, miserable and flushed, climbed into the car.

I don't think I ever carried around any transitional object – that is, the beloved possession that (theoretically) most children refuse to be parted from. I certainly had no desire for a teddy bear and I scorned baby dolls: what were you supposed to do with them? However, I was rather fond of a large china replica of myself with long ringlets whom I called Rosemary. After seeing the film *Little Miss Marker* I was determined to have a Shirley Temple doll in that cute coin-dotted dress, but I soon lost interest in her.

Even in childhood books and houses were my main interests. One could say that a book is a form of house in which one finds a world with characters and furnishings all its own. I often played with a large white dolls' house I received for Christmas one year. I spent even more time cutting out pictures of houses from magazines, complete with all the requisite furniture. The entire carpet of my bedroom was covered with streets – a whole model village. It says a lot for my mother that she didn't nag me to clean it all up.

On the whole, I think I was treated indulgently as a youngster. Once, at the dinner table, I felt that some awful injustice had been done to me – it could have been that I wasn't allowed a piece of cake – and I announced that I was leaving home. I went up to my room and wrapped some belongings in a towel, then stalked out in high indignation, with my parents agreeing amiably that they could see that I had no other alternative. It was a windy autumn night and by the time I reached the edge of the lawn I was suddenly terrified with the realization that I had nowhere to go. Not a word was said when I slunk back ignominiously. I cannot think of any episode when my parents behaved more sensibly in unison. Undoubtedly they had been in gales of laughter peeking behind the curtains.

A good deal of the time I seemed to be ill, specializing in hives, bronchitis, and bilious attacks. I was pampered with ginger ale and fussed over by Mother. She was strikingly pretty, with large blue eyes and a retroussé nose, and for years I was proud that she looked so young for her age. She was like a mature version of my doll Rosemary. Mother was much more elegant than the other women on the street, and I remember her in one particularly stunning pale blue suit with a long jacket trimmed with fox fur dyed to match. I thought she looked incredibly beautiful until my enemies, Bubbles and June, made nasty remarks about her being a show-off.

Why is it that I can remember her clothes vividly but didn't comprehend the unexpected and increasingly frequent changes in her moods? Once she played store with me on the back veranda, and no child could have had a more enchanting companion. (She was wearing a sort of rustic red-and-white gingham dress with bands of white organdy.) But the next time I asked her to play she sullenly refused, and I was bewildered by her intractability.

Dad was ten years older, and I considered it peculiar for a man to marry at the advanced age of thirty-five. Apparently he met Mother at a dinner party and was so infatuated that he bombarded her with roses. She was on the rebound from someone else. In later years she sometimes spoke tenderly about a beau called Jock. I don't think I should have been told that she had travelled to New York, where she and this mysterious man had had an intense discussion in a hotel lobby, and that she had wept all the way back to Toronto in the train. Such information only added to the confusion of my perception of my parents' relationship.

I was very jealous of Dad and used to watch closely to see whether he was attracted to other women. There was no doubt that he fancied Mrs. Brandon, who would sometimes come to our garden fence to call her children to dinner. She was a pretty, good-natured woman. His face would light up when she appeared and he would follow her out to the street. I remember staring at him warningly and then turning my gaze up to the bedroom window as though suggesting that Mother was watching. Little sneak that I was, I told Mother that he had been flirting with Mrs. Brandon, and the ensuing row effectively ended that budding romance. For days afterwards I was too ashamed even to look at my father.

I never saw my parents kiss or embrace or call each other by any endearment. I never thought Mother was in love with Dad, although I am now sure she did love him. For a long time I was convinced that he must hate her, but apparently he didn't, and I subsequently learned that they had a very active sex life. Marriages are a mystery that will never be solved.

I sound as though I was a watchful child, but most children are. So many impressions are impinging on their consciousness that they have to be on the alert constantly to make some sort of order out of a mass of data. Not long ago I noticed one of my grandsons scrutinizing an affectionate greeting between his grandfather (my first husband) and myself. He had never before seen us together, and he was trying to create a context for this unfamiliar scene. As we grow older we learn to sift and winnow; otherwise we would be overwhelmed by the pressures of a chaotic world. Long ago I heavily scored a passage in the conclusion to Walter Pater's *The Renaissance*: "Experience seems to bury us under a flood of external objects, pressing upon us with a sharp and importunate reality . . . Every one of those impressions is the impression of the individual in his isolation, each mind keeping as a solitary prisoner its own dream of a world." We must each create a world that makes sense to us.

THE WORLD OF BOOKS

During the first few years in Rosedale Heights I think my mother was reasonably contented. I desperately hoped that she was. She had a lovely singing voice (which her children didn't inherit) and she loved sentimental songs like Al Jolson's "Mammy" and "Sonny Boy." She often sang around the house until she believed that she no longer had anything to sing about. She had a baby grand piano which she played occasionally and of course we had the obligatory piano lessons, but music didn't play as great a role in our lives as I would have wished. She liked soulful novels like Warwick Deeping's *Sorrell and Son* but also enjoyed Booth Tarkington's Yankee humour. She, too, loved Dickens – especially *Our Mutual Friend* – so she and Dad shared some interests.

But I don't want to minimize her sharp intelligence. It was she who alerted me in the early 1950s to someone I had never heard of: Marshall McLuhan, whose groundbreaking *The Mechanical Bride* she was reading with great enthusiasm. At the same time she was enraptured with Thomas Mann's *Buddenbrooks*.

Mother belonged to a charity called the Big Sisters and played bridge in the afternoons. The only entertaining my parents ever did occurred during that period, when they gave an occasional bridge party. I remember little silver dishes of nuts placed on the baize table. Both parents had a horror of alcohol (the temperance movement was highly influential in those days), so I suppose they drank tea. Toronto was filled with cake shops and tea rooms and Mother was addicted to teacup reading. There were two places I especially liked as treats. One was the Diet Kitchen, a pleasant house set back from the street on the northwest corner of Bloor and Bay, where we sat under an apple tree in the summer, and in the winter had our tea and crumpets swimming in butter in one of the warren of rooms. Sometimes on Sundays we would take the Bloor streetcar to the end of the line and walk to the Old Mill. I adored the stone floors, and especially the winding staircase lined with cases of mounted butterflies.

My parents were typical Toronto bigots of their time. Both despised Baptists and Methodists (all were hypocrites, in their opinion), were highly suspicious of Catholics (whom the kids called "Micks"), but never spoke disparagingly about Jews. That was left to my gentle Uncle Fred, who would become almost apoplectic once he got on the subject. Fred disapproved very much of my Uncle Mac, who was vice-president of Tip Top Tailors and therefore worked for Jews. I didn't know any Jewish people except Shirley Katz, who also attended Miss Railton's, and who lived on Edgar Avenue. She was a gifted pianist and was very sweet to me when I made some terrible sounds on her piano, pretending that it was a famous concerto. "That was your own composition, wasn't it?" she asked kindly, without a trace of sarcasm. From the way Uncle Fred talked, Shirley must have been an exception to this vile race.

Every Sunday my mother attended St. Paul's Church where she venerated Canon Cody, who later became president of the University of Toronto. She was always repeating lines from his sermons like "There is no royal road to learning." My father had been brought up as a strict Presbyterian, forced to attend church three times a day, but now he never darkened a church door. They also differed in politics. My father voted Liberal and my mother's family were staunch Conservatives. Nana Owen considered John A. Macdonald, the nineteenth-century prime minister who created a nation out of the Canadas, a saint. (She clearly knew nothing about his drinking habits.) She used to say that it was the duty of the rich to look after the poor, and was very disturbed when I showed socialist tendencies in my teens.

There was a strong allegiance to the monarchy and to the "Mother Country" in Canada in those days. I can remember choking with emotion when we sang "God Save the King," and I was very interested in the little princesses, Elizabeth and Margaret Rose (when did *she* change her name?). When the Wallis Simpson affair broke, Mother and her sisters could talk of nothing else. (On the other side of the world, in China, my husband's father cancelled his subscription to *Time* because it had leaked the affair, whereas the British press maintained a self-imposed censorship.) An English actor who used to visit us occasionally described Mrs. Simpson as an adventuress who was "very limited." Mother was beside herself with delight. And the excitement when the new King George VI and his charming queen visited Toronto! It was a small enough city then that we could rush from place to place to see the royal pair graciously gesturing to us as we waved our little flags and cheered. Dad seemed totally bored by the whole thing.

Dad was a skeptic in many ways but he respected his stern mother's piety, and as long as she was alive I attended morning Sunday school at the Presbyterian church on the corner of Bloor and Huron. Afterwards I would walk up to Nana Langstaff's, where her house-keeper, Mrs. Stirton, always served me lamb chops, mashed potatoes, and some overcooked vegetable. Then I would mount the stairs to my grandmother's sitting room, where she awaited me, erect in a chair, a pince-nez perched on the end of her nose and a lace collar around her throat. I don't remember her ever hugging me, but she was a splendid grandmother and one of the great influences in my life.

It was Nana Langstaff who taught me to read. I vividly remember our hours together with *Robinson Crusoe*, *Pilgrim's Progress*, *The Swiss Family Robinson*, and *Alice in Wonderland*. I sat on a little stool beside her and was enraptured by these dramatic stories. She also had albums of Old Master prints, and years later in various galleries I recalled where I had first seen reproductions of Hogarth's *Shrimp Girl* and Hobbema's country road lined with tall poplars. Occasionally I ventured into her bedroom, where I would sniff from the neat bottles with glass stoppers containing rosewater and similar essences which were lined up on her dressing table. Even more rarely, I entered the parlour whose spindly ornate furniture Mother spoke of with contempt. (My mother loathed Nana Langstaff, and I believe Nana thought my mother very frivolous.) I would peer into the mirror wondering if I could climb through like Alice. When she was old enough, Joan also came along, hovering shyly in the background. I don't doubt for a minute that I made her feel *de trop*.

In addition to the Sunday sessions with Nana Langstaff I read a lot at home. I felt angrily frustrated until I could decipher those signs on the page for myself. Mother, who owned a complete set of the works of J.M. Barrie, introduced me to *Peter Pan*, and I used to crawl out on the steep ridge of the garage and try to work up the courage to fly. Once I could read by myself, I developed strong likes and dislikes. I didn't like animal stories, but I devoured the whole Bobbsey Twins series, the saga of a perfect family, Bert and Nan, and Freddie and Flossie, with her mop of curls. But generally I was addicted to stories of suffering orphans. There was Cedric, Little Lord Fauntleroy, whose English father dies when he is tiny and leaves him as the protector of his mother, whom he addresses as "Dearest." Then he learns that he is the heir of the Earl of Dorincourt, and that he must go and live with him. But Dearest (since she is a vulgar American) is banished to a cottage on the estate. The illustrations of Cedric with his curls and slender feminine legs made him look a lot like my doll Rosemary. Of course Cedric is the most appealing little chap in the world, and it is inevitable that he wins over the heart of his gruff grandfather, who comes to see what a treasure Dearest is too.

Elsie Dinsmore was even more of a tearjerker. Her father has departed for Europe shortly after the death of Elsie's mother, and she is left in the hands of her cruel and unjust Southern relatives. Eventually her father returns, but life becomes even more unjust when he clearly prefers her cousin. Elsie is almost too saintly to be true, finding constant solace in the Bible, so I skipped all the religious bits – there were plenty of them – in order to learn whether Elsie's father ever appreciated her true worth.

My all-time favourite was handed to me on my tenth birthday by Mother; she had loved L.M. Montgomery's *The Story Girl* when she was young. *Anne of Green Gables* never appealed to me much, but I liked the *Emily* books, and I remember the last line of the one about Marilla, who has a lisp. Her love returns from the war and asks, "Is it Marilla, my Marilla?" "Yeth," says Marilla. But none of these girls was a patch on the storytelling Sara Stanley, another orphan, who holds all the children on the farm transfixed with her tales – delicate Cecily who nearly dies one night after having cucumbers and milk, gawky Dan, and

Felix who is besotted with the beautiful Felicity who makes him very unhappy. (Girls with beautiful hair have that power.) I must have read *The Story Girl* a hundred times. Another special favourite was *Coral Island,* which prompted my first fan letter to an author. I wondered why he never answered, unaware that R.M. Ballantyne had died in 1894.

It was around this time that I decided that I would be a writer when I grew up. I had originally planned to be a detective, but reading changed my ambitions. I wrote a novel called "The Daring Messenger" about the Cavaliers and the Roundheads. Naturally I was on the side of the Cavaliers; now I would favour the Roundheads, apart from their desecration of churches and the execution of the king. Part of the manuscript of this early work is lying somewhere in the basement with all the other accumulated detritus from which I cannot bear to part. Too many things have been mislaid with the passing of the years.

As my reading became more sophisticated I turned to the books above me on the shelves in our library. I was lucky enough to start with *The Mill on the Floss.* It was heartbreaking how poor Maggie Tulliver is treated so cruelly by her brother Tom, who finds her love burdensome. Next I discovered Dumas and fell into historical fiction. *The Three Musketeers* never appealed to me as much as *Le Vicomte de Bragelonne,* and I assure you that I read all three volumes. The Marquise de Maintenon was referred to as the "mistress" of Louis XIV, but I didn't know what a mistress was; besides, she was the sweetest, gentlest thing and they were so in love. It wasn't until years later that I was astonished to read that she had schemed to supersede Madame de Montespan in the king's affections, but other writers claim that she was devout, sensible, and cultivated. Whatever her qualities, this was one of the books that awakened my passion for France. Generally I was given unlimited liberty to read what I wanted, but occasionally Mother would sweep down like a censor from the Inquisition and snatch away a book, such as one about the wives of Henry VIII. I was furious because she hadn't even read it, and I argued unavailingly that it was history. She tended to be particularly self-righteous when she behaved irrationally.

CRAZY RELATIVES

My mother was far too engrossed with her eccentric relatives, although I enjoyed their boisterous company and loved listening to grown-up conversation. I remember their all being present for Christmas one year when we were seated in the elegant dining room. Mother was wearing an exquisite dress of stiffened green tulle with a flounced skirt embossed with garlands of flowers. It was sleeveless and the V-neck revealed the curve of her breasts. My Aunt Dots's husband, Uncle Mac, was sitting beside her and kept glancing down her front. I hated his fat smug face and felt that my father was demeaning himself when he laughed uproariously in an artificial way at his feeble jokes. My childish judgment was correct, for right from the beginning of their marriage Mac had been cheating on my aunt. She once caught him outside the Uptown Theatre with his current mistress and hit her over the head with a great swing of her handbag.

Aunt Phyllis was the most interesting of the group. Apparently she received regular visitations from her dead husband, Oliver, who would suddenly materialize to warn her that the RCMP were on her trail because she hadn't paid her income tax. I remember him (that is, when he was visibly alive) as the mildest of men with a habitual expression of anxious astonishment. In the other world it seems he underwent a transformation of personality, and was keenly alert to evil forces like the Mounties, who expended considerable manpower pursuing his widow, even tapping her telephone. If so, they overheard a lot of family rows.

We treated such stories as amusing and endearing foibles.

Nevertheless, Phyllis Johns was a shrewd businesswoman who was the first to introduce to Toronto the fad for old pine furniture. She would collect pieces while touring all over Quebec in her little car and have them sent back home to be stripped by her workman, Bowles, then sold in her Bloor Street shop. Aunt Phyllis lived in an apartment above the shop. She had marvellous taste and could make any room attractive with little touches such as hanging red ball fringe on heavy natural wool curtains. Mother and I spent many evenings with her, drinking countless cups of tea and listening to accounts of Uncle Oliver's most recent visits.

Phyllis had a large serene face with features so lovely that they looked as though they could have been traced on with a graphite pencil. On one occasion years later she and Mother lay asleep in the grass in the lakeside park at Niagara-on-the-Lake. I sat scrutinizing and comparing their faces. Phyllis's was the image of serenity; Mother's was pinched as though she were suffering from tortured dreams. It may seem strange that this calm aunt suffered from harmless delusions, but it was so – even though she conducted her life in a perfectly rational way.

Nana Owen could not have been more different from Nana Langstaff. A tiny person, she used to joke that she was "going down like the cow's tail," but she still had enormous vitality. She loved to laugh, and I would often drop in to visit her in her house on Cottingham Street, which remains today as wide and shady and tranquil as it was then. She made me feel that I was her special grandchild and always served my favourite sausages and pineapple. Later on I would voluntarily bring my boyfriends to meet her, eager for her approval.

I loved Nana's pretty sitting room, which was filled with interesting things to examine. She and I would frequently sit and chat on the curved sofa that fitted into the bow window. In order to impress her I once asked her if a certain family was "common," a favourite word among the Owens. She sniffed disdainfully that the grandfather had been a grocer. I would question her about my forebears, but she would become stubbornly silent. Not long ago Joan triumphantly claimed that she had discovered that Nana's own father had been a butcher.

Grandfather Owen died when I was about five. His father had been a doctor in England, and when he died of cholera the older son disappeared with the inheritance and his widow migrated to Canada with my grandfather and his brother. In Toronto Grandfather became a tea-taster for the Salada Company. When I knew him he was an old man with a white goatee. I think he could have been a gifted painter (a talent Aunt Phyllis inherited), and I would give anything to have his painting of a young girl tenderly holding a bird's nest, but my greedy cousin Georgie swept into the house after the death of Bea, the youngest sister, and spirited everything away to Winnipeg.

Grandfather and I would often sit companionably in his rose garden as he puffed away quietly at his pipe. One day we climbed up the steps to the house, and suddenly Nana appeared at the top. She said something biting to him with a dark expression I had never seen on her face before. Whatever it was, he turned around and returned to the garden. My very strong sense was that he was being banished, excluded from the inner circle, and indeed I don't remember his being present at a single family gathering. After his death whenever my grandmother sallied forth in public she assumed elaborate widow's weeds, regal in a long black lace dress and a high hat.

It was very much a matriarchal family, as though the women were so vibrant that they sucked all the life out of the men. There were five girls and one brother, Uncle Fred, who was the oldest. I heard that he had tried to get married, but when my grandmother got wind of it she flew to the church and broke up the ceremony. He lived all his life at home in a room on the top floor piled high with crumbling copies of the ultra-conservative *Evening Telegram*. A sweet, passive man, he drove my grandmother and the "baby," Bea, wherever they wanted to go. I believe that he worked in the office of a lumber company. I once heard him, like Chekhov's Uncle Vanya, lamenting his limited life to Aunt Phyllis. She turned to him briskly: "Fred, look at it this way. When you were young you had a wonderful time. Now it's over. Can't you be content with that?" Poor Fred looked more miserable than ever. A boyfriend of Joan's once saw him on the streetcar late at night reeling drunk. Perhaps he was an alcoholic – perhaps even my grand-father was – which would account for the family's aversion to alcohol.

Each of the five sisters would phone my grandmother every morning, always with a complaint about one of the others. The entire morning seemed to be spent in accusations and counter-accusations and the forging of secret alliances. Receivers would be banged down in tears and threats. I well remember my mother wailing, "Mama, if you take Gladys's side, I'll never speak to you again!" My Aunt Gladys's husband, Uncle Hughie, used to laugh about the "Owen family Christmases" when everyone became lovey-dovey for a single day in the year.

My mother loved my grandmother extravagantly. There was a dramatic scene at her funeral when Mother leaned into the open casket and smothered Nana's gnarled hands with kisses. I, too, adored my grandmother so much that it was years before I could acknowledge that she was a power broker, basking in the neurotic dependence of her daughters.

I sometimes stayed with my various older cousins. Aunt Dots's daughters, Georgie and Dottie, lived in a spacious house in Lawrence Park where I particularly liked the fish pond in the garden. Since I was so much younger they treated me with great condescension, but I tagged along when they visited their friends and danced to records with each other. They attended Havergal College, later transferring to Bishop Strachan, both very snobbish schools. Once they played truant from school and let me go to a movie with them. It was terribly grown-up, with Joan Crawford fainting on the floor of a bathroom (I believe this was to convey that she was pregnant). I was sworn to secrecy about their skipping school and I had every intention of keeping my mouth shut, but I have always had trouble with secrets, and I spilled the beans. No wonder they always considered me a sneak. I was.

I preferred the more bohemian atmosphere of Aunt Gladys's cottage in Bronte, which in those days was considered some distance out of the city. She made the most wonderful stew with lots of pepper which I have never been able to duplicate, any more than I have been able to imitate my late mother-in-law's marvellous pastry, even with exactly the same ingredients. Once after I had been put to bed – I must have been very little – I found a box of needles and set about meticulously threading the blanket with them. By the time Aunt Gladys discovered this, the blanket was almost too heavy to lift, but she laughed merrily and repeated the story for years. There was a pebbly beach across the road where one day a big boy accosted me and asked if he could kiss me. Suddenly my older cousin Billie loomed up ominously and scared him away. He said that I was to tell him if anyone ever tried to kiss me and he would beat up the culprit. Billie was lovely, but he ended up a sad alcoholic.

I wonder what year things within my own family started to go really wrong. If I knew the date when the Lytells, our next-door neighbours, moved away, I could pinpoint it. Before they relocated to a mansion on Avenue Road, I spent a fair amount of time in the Lytells' house, which I sensed was founded on far more solid money than ours. The attraction was Mary Louise, the Lytells' niece, who had come to live with them. She was two years older and I worshipped her. It was she who initiated my first sexual experience. We got into bed one day; I don't know what we did, but it was delicious. The next day I suggested we do it again but she said no, we might get caught. She was referring, of course, to her grim-faced nursemaid, Elsie.

Mary Louise's bedroom was opposite our library. One day she said to me, "I heard your parents fighting last night." I vigorously denied it, although I knew only too well that it was true. The fury of their row had easily penetrated the wall of my bedroom. When this happened night after night I was too embarrassed to play with Mary Louise any more.

I began to feel that we were the only family that wasn't "normal." Up at the top of the hill I sometimes played with a boy called Buddy Tisdall whose parents were social acquaintances of my mother and father. For some odd reason I was invited into their bedroom one morning, probably a Saturday. Mrs. Tisdall was very striking and even at my age I could see that she was extremely sexy. She was stretched out on a chaise longue in a negligee and Mr. Tisdall was still in his dressing gown. They were exceedingly, unexpectedly sweet to me, and then suddenly Mrs. Tisdall asked, "Patsy, are your parents still fighting?" "No, of course not," I replied. I remember vividly how the pair exchanged amused, knowing glances. Do grown-ups have any idea how cruel they can be to helpless children? Youngsters do not have the words to reply: "If you prick us, do we not bleed? If you wrong us, shall we not revenge?" Revenge never crossed my mind, simply abject humiliation. If people at the top of the hill knew too, it must be universal knowledge.

There was no point in trying to drown out the sound of those nightly arguments; the screaming, which went on for hours, could not be avoided. Also I suppose I listened to try to make some sense of what it was all about. The Depression hit us relatively late, probably about 1932. The first I understood that we were in financial trouble was when Mother sent me to Quinn's Grocery Store on St. Clair Avenue with a list of items to bring back. Fat Mr. Quinn leaned down across the counter and said angrily: "Tell your mother that I am not extending any more credit to her." I walked home in a state of confusion. When I reported the conversation to Mother her reaction was aggrieved indignation.

Again and again I would hear Mother reproach Dad for having bought "on margin" – that is, purchasing stocks using a partial payment, without sufficient reserve to pay the whole amount if demanded. Repeatedly she harped on the fact that he had shown poor judgment in the quality of the men he had appointed to the board of his insurance company. Everything seemed to be reduced to personalities. According to Mother, the particular enemies responsible for Dad's downfall had the names of Fell, Foster, and Matthews. Matthews (who later became lieutenant-governor) was particularly suspect because he was a Baptist, and hence totally untrustworthy. We once drove past Matthews standing outside his house in fashionable Forest Hill, and Mother let loose a stream of vituperation against him for having ruined our lives. Another of the scoundrels, Charles P. Fell, became president of Empire Life in 1933 and led the company for thirty-four years.

Mother might have been absolutely right in all her reproaches, but never did I hear a word of support for Dad in his time of travail. What I subsequently learned was that in the months before the stock market crash, Dad had committed his company to a heavy program of acquiring Canadian common stocks. They plunged in value after the crash but in 1930 the company continued to invest in them to take advantage of the "all-time lows." Dad's optimistic expectation of a rebound in the market was shared by thousands of businessmen. A board of directors decision had limited common stock investments to 20 percent of total assets (much higher than the industry average), but by the end of the year that percentage had climbed to 40 percent. Expansion into British Columbia and the prairie provinces only added to the problem: too much outlay for too little income. Policyholders had difficulty meeting their monthly payments, and for many the cash in their policies was all the money they had left. Unfortunately Empire Life was still a young company with insufficient capital behind it in accumulated reserves.

The dissatisfaction among members of the board that had been slowly growing over the previous two years came to a head at a stormy meeting in 1932. A policy of retrenchment became necessary to save the company and Dad tendered his resignation. He stayed on as salaried general manager for a year and then moved to another company where he felt that he could do better on commission. Dad's unshaken belief in the long-term growth of equities was no doubt reflected in his personal investments, and it seems that he was using our house as security for his share purchases.

He was undoubtedly a remarkable man both as an actuary and as a salesman, an unusual combination. To achieve what he did required courage, optimism, determination, and the ability to take risks. Yet his predicament was serious: other desperate businessmen were jumping to their deaths from the tops of buildings. (I later knew two girls at St. Clement's School whose fathers had done precisely that.) Dad might have overextended himself because Mother expected a certain standard of living; she was very eager that he take her to Europe. All I understood at the time was that she was making a hell of our home, and I was bitterly unhappy. One day I sat at the crest of the ravine and wrote down an account of my sufferings and how much I wished that I were dead. I buried this note in the ground, like sending a note for help in a bottle out to sea. It was at this point that my attitude towards Mother entered a state of confusing and permanent ambivalence. It seemed my glamorous and loving mummy had been transformed into a witch.

Joan was at home when the bailiff arrived. (I might have been riding my bike in the cemetery because I tried to be out of the house as much as possible.) My sister has described the scene so many times that I can visualize it. A very embarrassed man handed Mother a summons repossessing the house; even a child could see how uncomfortable he felt executing his duty. Across the road Colonel and Mrs. Royce worked tranquilly in their rock garden. It was early summer and the sun continued to shine with brassy radiance. Life went on for the rest of the world.

By the time of this calamity, two more children had been added to the family, a third daughter, Virginia, and a son, Garry, hardly more than a baby. (I overheard Aunt Bea remark bitterly that Dad had kept Mother pregnant until he secured his much-desired son, an observation that made me shakily re-evaluate my own place in the family.) Dad had lost his business and his home, all his assets, and had five mouths to feed. Today he would have walked away with a golden handshake, but at that time he had to start again from scratch. The humiliation of his descent from wizard of Bay Street to ruined failure must have been devastating, but he soldiered on and lived until the ripe old age of eighty-seven, handsome and reasonably hearty in his last years.

I could never persuade him to tell me the whole story of the loss of Empire Life. He was like a man who had been in the trenches and could not bear to relive painful memories. I was recently invited to attend a celebration marking the seventy-fifth anniversary of the company, whose present board includes a former prime minister. I was moved when the current president, Christopher McElvaine, described Dad as an icon to the rest of them. He told the story of how Dad had once made a wager that within a month he personally could bring in more business than all the branches combined – and he easily won. How ironic it all was.

Joan and I cannot remember the weeping and wailing that must have erupted following the visit of the bailiff, or even actually leaving the house. This suggests that we were immediately farmed out to the various aunts until we moved into a home that had been rented in

Hoggs Hollow, then north of the city limits. It was to be the beginning of a life of perpetual wandering. For many decades my favourite book has been Homer's *Odyssey*. I used to ask my students, when we were discussing it, what the word "home" meant to them, and I was always intensely interested in their answers. I have searched for my own answer to that question much of my life.

Before I left Toronto in 1976 to live in England for some years I bought myself a little cottage in Cabbagetown, a gentrified area once occupied by Irish immigrants. There were all sorts of difficulties in being an absentee landlord, but I could not bear to part from it because I had a deep need to have a nest somewhere. Not everyone shares this nesting compulsion. My friend the feminist writer Ann Jones is a free spirit. Sometimes she is riding in the Gobi Desert or in Patagonia, or bumping through the heart of Africa in a Land Rover. Once I rang her by satellite in the Arctic. Nomads like Ann are content to fold up their tents and move on. But others, like myself, need the reassurance of roots and routine. Just like those people in Königsberg setting their watches by Kant's daily walk.

2

GYPSIES

Occasionally I fantasize that a skinny child of ten is standing in the hall at Rosedale Heights again. Slightly to the left is a short flight of stairs leading to a landing. At the far right of the landing the stairs ascend to the second floor. If I turn left along a passage I pass the telephone where Mother spent so many emotional mornings. Beyond it, to the right, is a large cupboard, always a jumble of rubbers and galoshes, a symbol of the hidden mess of our domestic life. I could go right through the house this way, describing almost every feature. Despite its vicissitudes, that house represented a certain early security. Ever after we were gypsies.

None of the many houses in the next ten years of my life are remembered in such graphic detail. They are broken pieces rattling around inside my head, a door here, a room there, a window seat, a sense of airiness or of gloom. I have no idea why it was necessary to move quite so often. Applying the arts of the biographer, I have searched vainly for a pattern to this stage of our family life. The cartography of my adolescence is a serrated landscape of peaks and valleys. Alternating between happiness and misery, our existence was governed by the erratic course of our parents' circumstances.

Actually the house in Hoggs Hollow was extremely pretty, and, strange as it sounds, there was an air of festivity as we moved into it. I loved the sunken living room, and the garden beyond led to a secluded stream where Mother encouraged us to sunbathe in the nude. (What

33

on earth had got into this prudish woman?) It was in this house that I taught myself to cook, and I can remember proudly presenting the family with frosted cupcakes.

At summer's end we enrolled at the local public school, Baron Renfrew. Here an extremely disturbed male teacher reduced me to tears with insults because I had attended a private school, launching into a diatribe to the class about the dangers of such institutions. Apparently I was one of its unfortunate products. This monster was also given to suddenly hurling pieces of chalk at erring pupils. He was such a good shot that he could hit targets in the back row.

The torment lasted until spring. Dad had moved to Winnipeg to work for another insurance company, and in early May we joined him and made a slow trek by car to the West Coast. The first place I remember was the Wascana Hotel in Regina, where we stayed for some weeks. We ate our lunch at the soda counter of a drugstore, where we always ordered a grilled cheese sandwich and fruit salad for 35 cents. To pass the time we would haunt libraries and second-hand bookshops or climb on the trolley and ride from one end of the line to the other.

These were the bleak years of the dust bowl, and we drove for mile after mile along miasmic dirt roads accompanied by rolling tumbleweed. When we reached the Rockies, everyone screamed at Joan to take her face out of *Black Beauty* and look at the scenery. Garry, a toddler, stood between Mother and Dad in the front. They doted on this tiny blond messiah, a shining light in the darkness of their misery. Mother always referred to him – even when he was grown up – in a voice of tremulous pride as "my boy" – little knowing what hell lay ahead.

In Vancouver we rented a house for the summer in the seaside area of Point Grey, within walking distance of a nice beach. I can recall a painting of a beatific Saint Cecilia, hands clasped in ecstasy, which hung above my bed, and the masses of sweet peas in the garden.

When I was a child in Toronto it was very rare for backyards to have anything in them except grass, so it was only gradually that I accumulated a list of flowers that have been among my greatest pleasures. Small details like these delicate flowers left far more memory-traces than Stanley Park or Capilano Canyon. Memory doesn't unfold itself like a travelogue.

The quarrels between my parents had started in earnest again. One night Dad came home in a jovial mood after attending a boxing match; I regarded him apprehensively. Did he not realize he was courting trouble by appearing happy? Sure enough, within an hour all fury had erupted. Mother was particularly incensed about the man he was working for (I believe his name was Tweed) because she considered him a crook. Dad kept repeating, "We have to build up a reserve," and another line which he would often utter through the years: "You think I am indestructible."

By fall we were back in Toronto. The first house we occupied was on Hudson Drive, only a block away from the home where we'd lived until I was three. Money went so much farther in those days that it was possible to rent a substantial house even in our reduced circumstances. This one had a sort of minstrel's gallery over the main hall and, apart from residences in England, was the coldest house I have ever lived in.

My main preoccupation at this time was collecting. I sent away for everything that had a coupon – movie star pictures, miniature lipsticks, merchandise of all kinds. I also developed a passion for telephone requests. I would ring the wallpaper and fabric departments of Eaton's and Simpsons and tell them in a quavering voice that I was a cripple confined to bed, and would they kindly send me samples of velvet or bits of flowered wallpaper. Then I would go through the Yellow Pages and repeat the process. Only in the Depression could one get away with this. I loved the arrival of the postman with my useless treasures, but the day of reckoning was inevitable. One day a man came to the door and asked for Miss Langstaff. My puzzled mother called me from my room and I sheepishly slunk to the top of the stairs, clinging to the banister. The man looked up at me in astonishment. Apparently I had been ringing travel agencies, inquiring about brochures on cruises.

The next house seems to have been on Nanton Avenue in Rosedale, memorable for its gloomy dark panelling. The only good thing about living on Nanton was the skating rink directly behind us where the boys let me play goalie, especially as I would volunteer to go after the puck when it flew out to the street. I was sickeningly ingratiating because I loved playing with boys, who seemed to have so much more fun and freedom than girls. The rink was particularly attractive because of the presence of Alan Percival, my first great crush, who tolerated my adoring presence. He later became a player for a minor-league hockey team, the Marlboroughs.

Despite the upheavals and occasional emotional explosions, Mother coped admirably with the material alteration in our lifestyle. She was a splendid seamstress and made practically all our clothes. She served us real Depression food – overcooked liver, flank steak, mackerel, and stuffed heart. She was not an enthusiastic cook but she made the best macaroni and cheese I have ever tasted. (Since this was Dad's favourite dish, it may have been one of the reasons he didn't leave her permanently.) The contrast between our comparative poverty and the accoutrements of our life was ludicrous. Meals were still served on Wedgwood plates and we ate with sterling silver cutlery. On important occasions Mother brought out the Dresden with a cut-out pattern around the rim. Sadly, though, Dad sold off most of his collection of books, especially the more valuable editions.

Movies were our year-round Saturday afternoon entertainment. I don't think I missed a single Ginger Rogers–Fred Astaire musical. In the middle of the Depression the public basked in their characters' lavish lifestyles, never questioning the economics of the fairy story. We went to the Hollywood, where for the student rate of 10 cents we could see two features, a cartoon, a newsreel, and coming attractions. It was usually dark when we emerged from this fantasy world.

We could no longer afford cottages in Muskoka, but we more than made up for it by regular excursions to Niagara-on-the-Lake, which Mother loved passionately. She would rouse us very early, make a picnic, and then it was down to the docks by streetcar where we would board the steamer *Cayuga* for the trip across Lake Ontario. There was always the tormenting decision as to whether we would stay on board at Niagara-on-the-Lake and take the wonderful trip up the river to Queenston, or disembark to spend the day just in Niagara. In those days before erosion, there was a beach where you could swim in water warmed by the Niagara River. Mother was at her best on these occasions, when Dad was far away. She treated us and me particularly as companions; she was a delight to be with and able to laugh at herself.

The summer following the year we lived on Nanton Avenue, we took rooms for the season in Niagara-on-the-Lake so that we would be away from the terrible polio epidemic of 1937 in the city. We had our meals in a restaurant opposite the park. The two indistinguishable bachelor brothers who ran the pharmacy on Queen Street (now a museum) ate their meals there as well – in total silence. Not long into the summer while we were lingering over our dinner, Garry ran across the road to the park and was hit by a car, fracturing his leg. Mother had to take him back to Toronto to the Hospital for Sick Children. At thirteen I was left to look after my younger sisters in solitary bliss. Dad would visit us at weekends, and he was a fun-loving father without Mother around. He took us to movies in St. Catharines, and on the bumpy road back to Niagara we would scream with joy as the car swooped up and down like a roller-coaster.

Without any supervision, our time was spent very pleasantly.

From the library in the Court House I borrowed musty books such as the autobiographies of Ellen Terry and Sir Henry Irving. I attended the Sunday school, also held in the Court House, until the teacher expressed her horror that a girl of my age had read *Gone With the Wind*, and it was made clear that my presence would contaminate the class. The nice woman who ran the restaurant, knowing that I loved books, lent me a novel of Jack London's. Towards the end the heroine is escaping from some building with her clothing ripped so that one breast is exposed. I was shocked, and when I returned it and was asked if I liked it, I replied no, embarrassed to tell the puzzled woman why. I had a real fixation about breasts.

We sisters shared Mother's love for that tranquil early nineteenth-century town, entirely different from the Disneyland atmosphere of today. I for one was perfectly content just to walk its streets, savouring the deep grassy ditches, the tall trees, and the lovely old houses, few of them tarted up except for those owned by rich Americans. Queen Street would often be completely deserted. There were two doctors in town, and in the early evening one of them sat placidly on his porch simply rocking back and forth.

In the fall the family was reunited – this time in Hamilton, in one of the darkest, most depressing houses I have ever known. To add to my misery I was sent to a convent where many of the nuns turned out to be as sadistic as the teacher at Baron Renfrew. However, as a non-Catholic I was fascinated by the ritual. I loved crossing myself before every class, and the poetic words "Hail Mary, full of grace, Blessed art thou among women" were music to my ears. On my way home I passed a second-hand bookstore which sold old copies of architectural folios for next to nothing. Starved for beauty in that grim, provincial city, I cut out my favourites and pasted them in a scrapbook. I was particularly fond of graceful bridges and stairways. It was not until August 1963 that I saw the Spanish Steps for the first time on a visit to Rome. It was noon and no one else was stupid enough to be out in the stifling heat. The elegant flow of moulded stone, devoid of people, poured down from the Trinità dei Monti into Bernini's playful overflowing boat. I could hardly believe that there was a reality to all those pictures in my scrapbook.

Yet another move back to Toronto. What is amazing is that we children seemed to accept these constant changes so readily. Wrapping cups and plates in newspaper, then packing them into cardboard cartons became routine. What it was doing to us subterraneously was another matter. This time it was an old farmhouse set far back from Bayview Avenue. A farmer across the road (at what is now the busy corner of Moore Avenue) could be hired for sleigh-riding parties. Every Friday afternoon there was a mad dash to cash the $50 cheque that arrived from Dad, now working out west again. Was there time to get down to the Canada Permanent on lower Bay Street before closing? The rent for the house was $40 a month, so the remainder had to stretch a long way.

Children do not want exotic, unsettled, or interesting childhoods. They want life to be predictable, repetitious, and respectable. I was fortunate enough to attend two schools which provided this stability. The first was the Model School (which Mother had also attended) attached to the teachers' training college on the grounds of what is now Ryerson Polytechnic University. I was there for two years – when I was eleven and twelve, perhaps. Then, at fourteen, I was sent to St. Clement's School in north Toronto. It was a long walk in winter along Moore Avenue to catch the streetcar on Mount Pleasant, but it was worth it.

As far as I was concerned, there were some advantages to Dad's losing his money. If he had not done so, we undoubtedly would have been sent to more expensive and snobbish schools. St. Clement's occupied a small building surrounded not by lavish grounds but by simple basketball courts. E. Gordon Waugh, the headmistress, reduced the modest fees because she thought I had promise. A large imposing lesbian, Miss Waugh was a woman whose shining integrity inspired awe. Every morning we met in the basement gym for prayers and to sing the school song, "To Be a Pilgrim," followed by a little talk by Miss Waugh, whose religion was deep and sincere.

The standard of teaching was excellent and the teachers were superb – in particular Miss Winspear (German), Miss Sale (French), Miss Macdonald (French), and Miss Steele (history and English). A high level of performance was expected, and I was in my element because I loved studying. The majority of the girls came from families of moderate incomes, and since we wore tunics, there was no competition among us. For the first time in my life I had a group of real friends. We played basketball and bridge and had tea parties. Although Mother was increasingly moody, I could still invite friends home on Sunday afternoons.

I also started to meet boys and be invited on the occasional date. I had been comfortable playing hockey with boys when we lived on Nanton Avenue, but they remained disturbing and mysterious to me, and I didn't know how to act or what to say to them. I was still much more comfortable with girls, but I envied those with older brothers who had friends who took them to wonderful dances at Upper Canada College. I used to fantasize that I had one of these incredibly supportive brothers.

Before the end of the last term of that first year at St. Clement's we were told that Dad was moving to the West Indies to set up branches of an insurance company, and that we were to pack up and join him. I had very mixed feelings about this. It sounded glamorous but I didn't want to be uprooted from the first place in which I had felt really happy. It was some consolation when Joan and I were each given a steamer trunk with drawers on one side. Since we were expected to dress for dinner every night on the ship, at fifteen I had my first evening dress, demure white organdy with puffed sleeves.

We arrived in Boston in the middle of an August heat wave, and I tottered around in agony in my first pair of high heels. Once aboard the *Lady Nelson* it felt as though we had entered that Ginger Rogers–Fred Astaire fantasy world. Dad met us at Bermuda, after which we headed for Barbados, where we were to live for an unspecified period. The ship stopped at all the islands – St. Kitts, Nevis, Montserrat, Antigua, St. Lucia – and I wanted to go ashore and see everything while the ship loaded provisions. Dad said sourly, "This isn't a pleasure cruise, you know." I became friendly with a girl from Washington and we went dancing every evening. One night, feeling frightfully sophisticated as we stood chatting with two flirtatious married men, I saw Dad suddenly rear up: "Patsy, it's time you were in bed." Murder was in my heart.

On board I did meet a boy my own age from Barbados called Perry, who developed a crush on me. As a result, when we arrived in Barbados he introduced me to a crowd of young people. Life suddenly became as exciting as any teenager could dream of. We rented a house in St. Lawrence Gap, a few miles out of Bridgetown. It stood proudly on a point from which a wide sweep of beach curved around a bay surrounded by palm trees. It would have made a perfect picture for a tourist brochure, except that in those days few tourists visited the islands.

I was enrolled in a little dame-school during the mornings and learned absolutely nothing. I could hardly wait for the early afternoon when I got on the bus and headed for the Aquatic Club in Bridgetown. By then I had ditched Perry and acquired a handsome and fun-loving new steady, Maurice, five years older than me. We were soppy about each other, especially when the band played "Deep Purple." Life was sheer bliss – swimming, sailing, and later tea dancing. In a pink bathing suit with a pattern of bow-knots, I thought I was the bee's knees, and before stepping into the water I would pause so that everyone could admire me. For one brief period in my life I was proud of my body.

I was vaguely aware that late every afternoon a large group of worried-looking men gathered in the lounge of the club to listen to the radio, but I was so self-absorbed that it came as a shock when I heard that war had been declared. Young people began to talk about joining up – but not yet. We were all too busy playing water polo, going to formal dances (always with dance cards to which a tassel was attached), and organizing beach parties. Every Sunday a privileged group of us sailed off for the day in a schooner. It was Lotus Land, populated by young people with a sense of entitlement, the boys in blazers and white flannels, the girls in flowery prints. Like all my new friends, I never questioned the existence of a colour bar in that closed society. Influenced by the prevailing prejudice, Mother got into the habit of locking up the pantry so that the cook couldn't steal anything. I loved driving between the fields of sugar cane from one lovely plantation to another, never questioning how they were maintained.

Mother approved of Maurice, and there were no domestic battles because Dad was away establishing offices in the other islands. She seemed pleased that I was enjoying myself, stepping out night after night, and I never gave a thought to her loneliness as she sat playing solitaire hour after hour. She had no friends in Barbados, and she must have missed the daily drama of her sisters' lives.

After just six months of paradise Dad reappeared with the news that we were moving to Trinidad almost immediately. As the ship steamed out of the harbour I lay on my bunk sobbing. Maurice had promised to come to Trinidad for Carnival, yet that seemed small compensation for what I was leaving behind. And the reality proved far worse than my apprehensions.

From bustling Port-of-Spain we seemed to drive for miles through jungle – or was it rainforest? Whatever it was, it was infinitely dismal. At last the road came to an end at a hamlet called Macqueripe. A posh hotel stood high on a bluff overlooking the sea. No, we weren't going to stay there. We were to live in one of the small cramped cottages on the side of the hill. We were permitted to use the hotel's beach, but the sand was dark and muddy. There was a tennis court where Joan and I played; Virginia and Garry seemed reasonably contented with each other. There was not another person of our age in the place.

St. Clement's sent me textbooks to study on my own, but what teenaged girl would have the self-discipline to apply herself systematically to Latin without supervision? In addition to missing the heaven I had left behind, every day I would examine myself fearfully in the mirror to see if my tummy was expanding. Maurice had kissed me – my first kiss – and I worried that this was how one became pregnant. Anything to do with the reproductive system was a forbidden topic in our family. Sex was always treated as something ugly and dirty.

If I was discontented, my misery was nothing compared with Mother's. Now Dad was home almost every night, and the fights within that confined space became horrendous. For a time Mother sported a black eye. The residents of the other cottages complained to the hotel management, and we were told we would have to leave unless the noise stopped.

Yes, Maurice came for Carnival, but the cost of the taxi back and forth from Port-of-Spain made me seem like a ball and chain. The romance didn't exactly flower. The only good memory I have of that awful place is of the spicy crab cakes made by the grim-faced cook, who always wore a man's fedora on top of her bandana.

Was it eons or only months we stayed in that hellhole? Eventually Dad moved us on to Jamaica. After the bleakness of Trinidad, its colourful beauty was bewildering, yet I couldn't enjoy it because of the constant family tension. During an awful fight in the car, I screamed at Mother, "I wish you were dead!" Everyone including Dad turned on me in horror. While the others went into the hotel in Kingston where we were staying, I walked round and round a scruffy vacant lot in a state of despair.

Help was at hand. It was decided that Joan and I should have some formal education once again and that Mother would take us back to Toronto and leave us to board with a friend from St. Clement's. The voyage was dangerous because of German submarines and we had to maintain a strict blackout. We passed the *Queen Mary* carrying troops along a southern route to evade the U-boats. But oh, the welcome sight of Montreal! The first thing I did when we reached Toronto was to make a beeline for St. Clement's. My friends thought I had been through an incredibly exotic experience; I didn't disabuse them.

EDUCATION RESUMED

It was good to be with Joan and on our own. Even though there was more than three years between us, in many ways she took the role of the mature older sister. I was the volatile one, she the sensible centre of calm whom the rest of the family treated with respect. From an early age she stood aloof from sibling rivalries. What do sisters talk about, I wonder? Are they silent or do they chatter incessantly? How strange it is that I can recall so few of our conversations.

Every Saturday afternoon we attended a matinee of a touring production at the Royal Alex. I particularly remember *The Pursuit of Happiness*, a play about the American Revolution. Francis Lederer played a Hessian mercenary quartered with a New England family. The crucial scene was centred on a bed with a bundling board where couples kept warm. Joan said sternly, "If they get into that bed, we walk out." Naturally Lederer and the leading lady, Joan Bennett, did exactly that, and with a self-righteous air Joan marched up the aisle, with me trailing reluctantly behind her.

Miss Waugh let me skip a grade so that I could remain with my friends. This was what I wanted, but it meant that I had to cram in order to catch up, and I had to drop German, which proved a real handicap in later life. It wasn't quite so bad when Mother was in Jamaica or after the family moved again to Winnipeg for a while, but once she returned to Toronto the pressure to achieve became terrible. If I didn't come home with a dazzling report card there was hell to pay. Mother didn't seem to realize the handicap of having missed so much school.

My classmates remember me as nervous and always anxious that I might fail an exam, although somehow I managed to be among those at the top of the class. I was supposed to be popular as well. "I noticed that you didn't receive any valentines this year," she remarked. "Mother," I replied patiently, "at our age we don't exchange valentines." I loved the school itself and developed a passion for basketball. But walking home – at that time we lived on Blythwood Road – I would slacken my pace, apprehensive about what Mother's mood might be. She had become not only demanding but totally unpredictable.

In the summer of 1942, a friend of mine, Marion MacNish, won a *Mademoiselle* bursary to Sarah Lawrence. I will never forget the look Mother threw me after Marion rang with the news: a mixture of malice and contempt for the failure I was in comparison.

There was no question but that after high school I would go to Trinity, one of the federated colleges of the University of Toronto. It was an Anglican institution, we were Anglicans, and my school friends took it for granted we would register as a group. (I was going through a deeply religious phase and would attend evensong faithfully at St. Simon's Church, which was within walking distance of our house.) My friends' mothers sent their daughters to university in the expectation of finding suitable husbands, but marriage was the last thing Mother wanted for us. We were to become qualified for interesting careers, the precise nature of which was never clear. Nonetheless, in many ways

Mother was a woman born before her time, a curious blend of conventionality and ardent feminism.

I didn't know what to make of Trinity and its faux Gothic building in the heart of downtown Toronto. From the outset I didn't feel that I quite belonged. As freshmen we were forced to wear large signs around our necks bearing our names. It was utterly humiliating to cross the campus to the catcalls and whistles of the engineers. I wore the traditional garb: saddle shoes and bobby socks, a full skirt, a twin-set or an oversized "sloppy Joe," and a string of pearls. My long dark hair gleamed from brushing a hundred strokes a night and washing it in vinegar – as Mother told us to do.

Eventually the hazing came to an end, and I threw myself into the work of an honours English language and literature program. The first class I remember was Bertie Wilkinson's European history course in Room 149 of University College. He was a great ham, and on our first day he shouted, "You have come here to seek truth!" I was in a state of ecstasy. Professor Arthur Barker's course in American literature was so mesmerizing that I couldn't take a single note. He told us how clever Henry James was in conveying the atmosphere of a relationship, citing the passage in *The Portrait of a Lady* when Isabel grasps the truth on entering a room and seeing Madame Merle leaning against the mantelpiece while Gilbert Osmond lounges on the sofa. Until then no one had ever analyzed the psychological nuances in literature for me like this. Mother listened eagerly to accounts of my classes, but she was disturbed to hear that the sexologist Havelock Ellis's *Dance of Life* was a prescribed text on a philosophy course. I was being exposed to influences beyond her control.

In hindsight her criticisms of me are less mysterious: she had been denied the opportunities and excitement that I was experiencing, and while she had no concrete idea of what kind of future she wanted for me any more than I did, she envied my youth and the world of possibilities that lay ahead for me. At the time, however, her outbursts left me in a state of confusion. She became especially suspicious of my sexual activities, which were in fact just about non-existent. As a child I had been her cherished pet. As an adolescent I was her girlfriend. Now I was developing into her rival, and the fury and violence that had once been focused exclusively on Dad began to shift to me.

Ever since childhood I had learned how to compartmentalize my life. I enjoyed making friends at Trinity, and I don't think anyone had any idea how unhappy I was at home although friends told me later that my hands used to shake. To add to the turmoil, I fell in love with a second-year student in history. His name was Bob McMullan, and there was a certain glamour attached to him. He had been brought up in China and educated in England, and his father had been killed in a Japanese prison. He was tall and handsome and had the sexiest eyes I had ever seen. I used to position myself in the library so that I could have a clear view of him when he entered. We went out occasionally and I once did a terrible thing: I stood up a date when Bob asked me to something only hours before I was to go out with the other boy. I don't know what excuse Mother made to him but she was quite shocked by my behaviour. Nonetheless, Bob was one of the few boys who won my parents' approval.

My taste in Bob was justified, but I was generally extremely naive. Among my ill-judged acts was to date a young man who had been thrown out of the air force for bad "attitude." If I had been as smart then as I am now, I would have recognized Mike as a dangerous psychotic. My parents distrusted him intensely and once actually locked me in my room to prevent me from seeing him. The more objections they raised, the more stubborn I became, even though I didn't like him particularly. Mike was on the short side, slight, with wavy chestnut hair. He was a loner with a whiny voice and a perpetually sneering expression. But there was a certain desperation in my stubbornness too, since fewer and fewer men remained as the war continued. After a time he started to talk about "going all the way," while I was adamant that a girl shouldn't "do it" until she was married.

I had my first glass of sherry at a Trinity dance when I was eighteen. Prohibition still prevailed in Toronto to the hypocritical extent that people were not allowed to drink in public. It was customary when a group of university students attended dances at the Royal York to book a room in the hotel where they could drink in private. Shortly before Christmas in my freshman year Mike invited me to one of these parties. In all innocence – or foolishness – I accompanied him to the room, although my suspicions were aroused when, instead of knocking on the door, he inserted a key in the lock. He pushed me inside and it was immediately apparent that he intended to rape me. I didn't dare scream because I was so ashamed. There was a terrible struggle as I whimpered and pleaded with him to leave me alone. I can still recall the pain as I lay on the floor while he sadistically banged my head against the pipes of the radiator in order to subdue me.

We eventually emerged in the small hours of the morning. I stood on the mezzanine overlooking the lobby while he paid the bill. I was overcome with humiliation as I saw the house detective eyeing me suspiciously. The following day I was black and blue, and in order to explain my bruises and torn clothes I told Mother that I had fallen down the stairs at the hotel. I suspected that she didn't believe me but didn't want to know the truth.

I wanted to expunge the whole sordid episode from my memory, but my ordeal had only begun. Mike began an obsessional pursuit of me, following my steps around the university and beyond. He even managed to steal my prayer book. My only ally was a friend from St. Clement's, Daphne Glynne-Jones (later Crawford), who was also enrolled in English at Trinity. Daphne knew that I wanted to drop Mike, but I couldn't bring myself to tell her the real reason. She simply assumed he was crazy. Before and after classes Daphne would go out to the corridor to check whether the coast was clear. Many a night I would arrive home to find my tormentor waiting on the doorstep. On one occasion there was a tussle with a very nice naval rating, George Ronald. George came into the house with me, puzzled because I wouldn't go to my father or call the police. Worst of all, Mike threatened to reveal all to Bob McMullan, and I lived in dread that Bob would discover my guilty secret.

This harassment continued until early spring. By then perhaps Mike had found another victim. Bob McMullan started to invite me out more regularly so I assumed he had heard nothing, and I began to feel comparatively safe. There were certain girls who were considered "fast" and I was a little in awe of them, but I certainly didn't want to be one of them.

Bob and I went to movies and dances, and took long walks. Those strolls were extremely awkward because I never knew what to talk about. Sitting beside the reservoir above Summerhill Avenue one afternoon, I tentatively broached the possibility of a hereafter or some other deep subject. Bob jeered at my pretentiousness. A worse occasion was a dance at the house in Hoggs Hollow where Daphne, who was British, was staying, far from the Blitz. During the evening, Bob decided that he preferred the company of one of my friends from St. Clement's. He asked me if one had to have supper with the person one had brought to the party. I replied that that was the usual custom. He sat in sullen silence all through the meal. When the dancing resumed he partnered the other girl for the rest of the evening. She had never particularly liked me, so she looked like the cat who had swallowed the cream, while I sat there trying to appear completely disinterested. One of Bob's friends, Blair Seaborn (later a senior officer with External Affairs), took pity on me. "Pat, I can't apologize sufficiently for McMullan. His behaviour is absolutely disgusting." Bob escorted the other girl home, while Blair took me under his wing, but we all had to pile into the same car.

I was so besotted that I continued to see Bob despite this snub. His mother, who had been repatriated from China, clearly liked me. On one occasion we three attended evensong together and returned to their apartment for supper. Over tea she said delicately, "I have to go somewhere next Sunday. If I prepared the supper, would you like to have it here together – that is, if you think you know each other well enough?" I sat in agonizing suspense while Bob mulled this over. Finally he replied, "I don't think we know each other well enough."

Our next date was a movie at Shea's (on the site of the present City Hall). Bob was unexpectedly sweet to me and I thought we were on the right track at last. Then, a day or so later, a friend informed me gently that he had given his pin to another girl – and not the one from the earlier dance. I suppose I thought my heart would break. But I also concluded that it was inevitable. I had such a low opinion of myself that I wondered how someone like Bob McMullan could ever be interested in me. Looking back, I realize that I was too needy, too unsure of myself. Bob preferred assertively confident girls. He joined the army shortly after our last date and we went our separate ways.

By now the family had moved from a house on Binscarth in Rosedale, which Mother had fixed up and sold for a profit, to a grander residence on Russell Hill Road in Forest Hill. (Mother had hit on the idea of buying houses, repairing and redecorating them to her refined taste, and then selling them to appreciative buyers as a way of supplementing the family income. She was successful at it and, again, ahead of her time.) I remember it vividly, partly because that is where Bob used to pick me up, but mainly because it is associated with a particularly awful period at home. That first summer in the new house I often sat on the wide window seat in my bedroom, longing for a congenial boyfriend. But I didn't spend all my time feeling sorry for myself. Within the university, small by today's standards, there were countless interesting individuals, and the people to whom I was attracted were originals. These special people seemed to seize life, determined that it should be as full and fascinating as possible.

I had started skipping a lot of my Trinity classes for others at University College. Here I met Dorothy Cameron, tall, vivacious, well-coiffed, dressed far more maturely than the rest of us. She came from a wealthy family but was totally unpretentious. She was the most glamorous person I had ever met, and she was genuinely passionate about poetry. She wasn't a scholar, but her intuitive grasp was outstanding. I fell completely under her spell, and we often spent summer evenings discussing and reading poetry together.

Towards the end of my first year, an elegant fourth-year student began to take an interest in me. Originally from Jamaica, Peter Conacher was blond, with an aquiline nose, brown eyes, and a Noël Coward air of sophistication. He was bisexual, but an unlikely friendship developed between us. I was impressed beyond words by the fact that he could recite from memory the passage describing the *Mona Lisa* from Walter Pater's *The Renaissance*: "The presence that rose thus so strangely beside the waters, is expressive of what in the ways of a thousand years men had come to desire." Peter was determined to make a sophisticate out of me and set about trying to teach me how to smoke. I was hopeless. "Practise in front of the mirror," he would cry in exasperation. He told me that Pater advised men to live with a hard gemlike flame. No one at St. Clement's had ever talked about hard gemlike flames. I replied that I wanted to taste all experience before I was thirty. "Well, then," he remarked dryly, "you will be completely knocked out."

In that second term at university I learned more about modern literature from students like Dorothy and Peter than I did from my professors. I began to read Virginia Woolf, Aldous Huxley, T.S. Eliot, and

Proust. My hunger for books was insatiable. As I approached the lending library on leafy St. George Street my heart would actually beat faster in anticipation of the riches ahead. I lost one of my first summer jobs because of this obsession.

During the war it was easy enough for a girl to find summer work – it was necessary in my case to cover my fees, which came to about $180 a year. I made at the most $25 a week, out of which I had to save for tuition, books, and clothing. One of the first jobs I took was at British American Motors on Avenue Road, where I was trained as a switchboard operator. Unfortunately there had been a mix-up at the manpower office. The accountant had asked for an economics major and they had sent an English student by mistake. I was also supposed to do the bookkeeping, and as I had never seen a journal or a ledger in my life, I nearly drove the accountant crazy. His face would flush with dark fury at my ignorance. Finally he found a reason to fire me. One day I was so immersed in Irving Stone's *Lust for Life* that I was oblivious to the flashing red lights on the switchboard. I took my dismissal philosophically and immediately found another job as a switchboard operator where I was careful to read only during my lunch hour.

I spent hours stretched on my bed totally lost in other worlds. To me reading has always been the most private, most treasured of pastimes. One evening I was deep into *War and Peace*. Pierre Bezukov was dying on the battlefield, looking up at the sky in a state of joyous harmony with the universe, when Dad suddenly appeared at my door. "Patsy, you are completely unsociable. Come down and join the family." He was probably right, but I felt aggrieved. When he was my age he had been just as voracious a reader. Mother had told him to fetch me, of course, and he was learning that life could be a lot easier if he accommodated her every wish. I sulkily joined the superficially happy family group. What were we supposed to do? Exchange pleasantries? Dad had taught us to play bridge when we were very young so that he would have partners, but by then we were beyond even that harmless recreation.

I was becoming increasingly detached from my family, beginning to question not only their values but those of the middle-class conventional world I was supposed to enter. This included Trinity. In my second year I was elected to the board of the *Trinity Review*. During meetings, I sat knitting formless socks – my contribution to the war effort – barely opening my mouth. However, I began to publish what I describe as my "juvenilia." These included a short story which Hugh Kenner (later a famous critic) praised in the student newspaper the *Varsity*. I expect it was only slightly better than my poetry, which was intended to suggest that the quiet knitter had unexpected depths of emotion. Many years later my teenage children found a pile of old copies of the *Trinity Review*, and they fell about laughing as they read aloud the poetic effusions of one Patricia Langstaff. A work entitled "The Brimming Cup" they found particularly hilarious.

It cannot be.
This joy is too intense; its bright beauty
Is stifling in its ecstasy.
My fingers are dogwood blossoms.
My eyes are lilac poems of spring.
My mouth is the kiss of April.
For I have dwelt in sky, and sun and stars –
I have walked in violets.
And scattered spendthrift beauty
On my way; I taste the tender tang
Of earth, and stir the smoky depths
Of dreaming pools.
It cannot last. I must school
This quivering flamingo dance of joy.

All I can say is that none of the others was worse than this.

My main criticism of Trinity was that, like Toronto itself, it was too complacent. "We are the salt of the earth / So give ear to us / No new ideas shall ever come near to us," the Trinity students sang, only half deprecatingly. Did they have reason to be so smug? Apart from Arthur Barker, the calibre of the professors in the English department at Trinity was far inferior to that at University College, headed by the formidable Milton scholar A.J.P. Woodhouse. I especially recall that Mrs. Mossie May Kirkwood, the dean of women, was a lamentable teacher. She disliked me intensely after I persistently argued with her contention that Stalin's purge trials were "necessary." Such sympathy for the Communists was probably far more widespread among the faculty than any of us realized.

At University College I was meeting young Jews for the first time in my life, and I have subsequently found that my Jewish friends are among the most stimulating of all the people I know. (Mordecai Richler says they are not smarter, just more alert after centuries of persecution.) One such student was Henry Kreisel, a German refugee who had been confined in an internment camp on his arrival in Canada. He seemed to feel no bitterness towards the country that had treated him so disgracefully. Year after year he topped our English course, yet there was not a trace of arrogance in him. He used to give me helpful hints about writing exams: "Address yourself directly to the specific question asked." He later became an academic and drew on his wartime experiences in two novels, *The Rich Man* (1948) and *The Betrayal* (1964).

When I was invited to be the after-dinner speaker at the fiftieth anniversary of Trinity's class of 1946, I could not bring myself to indulge in soppy nostalgia. I mentioned the smugness at Trinity that I had found so distasteful. Had they been aware, I pursued, that while we were students there had been a quota on Jews in medicine and dentistry faculties? I asked them to look back on themselves with affection and tolerance, yes, but to take more pride in what they had survived through life. There were some scowling faces, but also a startling number of people who came up and congratulated me warmly, assuring me that they had felt the same way about Trinity when they were students.

My allegiance was not to Trinity but to the whole university, which offered every delectation I could desire. I sat in on classes in economics, art history, and political science. For a time I thought of transferring to fine art. The history department was particularly strong. In my second year I worked like a beaver, preparing a seminar on the Fabian movement for Professor Frank Underhill. As we were leaving his office one of my male Trinity colleagues pompously remarked: "I didn't think you had it in you." In third year we were permitted entry into the stacks which formed the actual library. (Until then we had to submit request slips for specific titles at the desk and wait for a librarian to deliver the volume; now we could roam the shelves at will.) This was magical, the same rush of adrenalin I experience every time I am confronted with unpublished papers or allowed to handle original correspondence when researching a biography. I staked off a corner for myself, and there I experienced real joy while reading Dr. Johnson's *Lives of the British Poets*. I still quiver at the audacity of his description of the Metaphysical poets: "The most heterogeneous ideas are linked by violence together." Those afternoons in the stacks were the high point of my university career.

ESCAPE

The war hardly impinged on that self-contained world. Sometimes a rumour would circulate that a shipment of silk stockings had arrived at Eaton's and we girls would make a mad dash to grab some. Boys in uniform drilled on the playing field above University College, and gradually there were fewer and fewer men around the campus. But I was too busy studying to read the newspapers. In the summer of 1941 I did make an effort to follow the Russian campaign with the aid of a map: Rostov, Smolensk, Vitebsk, Minsk, Kiev, Pskov. It was too confusing to understand and the only word I retained was "attrition." I do not think I was more self-absorbed than other students, but I had reason to retreat into the world of the university.

I was beginning to develop independent and sometimes flamboyant tastes of my own. There was an awful argument when I declared at the family dinner table that I preferred the French Impressionists to English landscape painters. My clothes became unconventional – in the autumn I wore a yellow Harris tweed coat, in winter a purple plush one. Sweaters were selected for their striking colours, and this somewhat dramatic wardrobe may have been misleading. Many people didn't realize how seriously studious I was.

In fact, the university provided me with a refuge. The family residence effectively ceased to be "home," and old buildings like University College and Baldwin House became my surrogate emotional base. This is not to say that I worked all the time. I was dating more, and there was hardly a weekend I wasn't out dancing, a gardenia tucked in my hair. This was the era of swing – "The Sunny Side of the Street," "Don't Get Around Much Any More," "Take the A Train," "You'll Never Know" – and what was to become the signature song for me forty years later, the Mills Brothers singing "I'll Be Around." Could there be anything more joyous in the world than dancing the night away at the Palais Royale or Casa Loma? And who needed drugs when one could jitterbug? It was all sweetly innocent. Dad described me as "the dancing fool" and remarked mordantly, "You'll get over it" – as though it were some kind of disease. I never did. That period of my life still holds a lot of nostalgia, and that I am not dancing – even by myself, as I used to do – is an unwelcome reminder that I am growing old.

Every boy I went out with was subjected to intense critical scrutiny. A young man whom I met in Wakefield, Quebec, where Joan and I stayed in the summer of 1941, had to correspond with me secretly because my parents disapproved of Catholics. This prejudice was nothing compared with their attitude to blacks, reinforced by their sojourn in the West Indies. A gorgeous mulatto from Montserrat, Fred Kelsick, invited me out. The mayhem that would inevitably ensue made it impossible for me even to consider a date. I arranged to meet him in the rotunda of the library to explain the situation. I was so cowardly that I couldn't force the words out, but he graciously got the point.

My academic performance was also constantly criticized. Why didn't I get a first? How was it that Henry Kreisel consistently headed the course? As a little girl I had been praised as clever. Bewilderingly, I was beginning to be regarded as a failure, and both parents began to transfer their narcissistic frustrations onto Virginia.

Virginia was now thirteen years old, so much younger than Joan and me that we hardly paid any attention to her. As a child she had a little monkey-face and we treated her in a rather jokey manner. Suddenly she was a ravishing beauty, and the boys hovered around her like bees around a honey pot, yet Mother imposed none of the dating restrictions on her that she had with us. Not only was Virginia gorgeous, she was brainy. Compared with her older sisters, she had had a relatively uninterrupted school career and her marks were spectacular. She began to emerge as the favourite daughter and I felt angry and abandoned. The competitive atmosphere within the family created a tension between us, a sad residue that was never to be fully resolved.

Mother seemed to regard me with contempt, as though I had become her enemy, and to the barrage of invectives hurled at me, she now added physical blows. I had been so indoctrinated by the attitude that one never answered back to one's parents that I simply lay weeping and cowering on my bed. In an attempt to regain her approval and love I would scour the house when she was out from top to bottom, the bathroom and kitchen floors washed and waxed, the silver and brass gleaming. I went through that house like someone possessed. Occasionally she would express pleasure; more often she would ignore my efforts. It seemed nothing would satisfy her.

Finally I turned to Dad for help. One evening he was stretched on his bed reading a detective story when I tearfully pleaded with him to intervene. He didn't even look at me, calmly continuing to turn the pages of his book. Better that the wrath be directed elsewhere. He had totally withdrawn from the storm around him.

I was desperate for some way to escape. In my third year Professor Philip Child at Trinity unexpectedly offered to arrange a fellowship to Bryn Mawr after graduation. How different my life would have been if I had had the gumption to take up his suggestion. Instead, I was dissuaded by the fact that even with a fellowship, there would be additional expenses. Bryn Mawr was an impossible dream. The only solution to the intolerable situation at home seemed to be marriage. I was so beaten down that I never considered any other alternative.

That year I became involved with Bob Grosskurth, an engineering student a couple of years ahead of me. He was a Big Man on Campus, managing editor of the *Varsity*, and a popular personality with masses of friends. My old tormentor Mike still lingered in the corners of my life. "BG," as I later came to call Bob, was comfortable to be with, and he was the first person to whom I confessed the whole sordid story. One Sunday evening we attended a concert in Hart House and spotted my nemesis in the audience. We were sitting in the gallery, and as people filed out Mike glanced up at us. BG glared down at him threateningly. I knew at once that I would marry this man: he would look after me.

I received a Sigma Chi pin and then an engagement ring. Of course there was hell to pay at home, and BG and Mother had a number of noisy confrontations. In one particularly stormy episode Mother told my intended that I had been brought up "with great trouble, expense, and inconvenience," and that she wasn't about to hand over such a valuable commodity to the likes of him. An awful snob, she considered his family inferior to ours. He found this remark hilarious and repeated the story to all his friends. I couldn't see the humour in it. Indeed it sometimes troubled me that he didn't seem to grasp the depth of my misery and was puzzled when I would lapse into depressions. Only once – when we were dancing at Casa Loma – was I overcome with horror that I was making a mistake, but I stifled the feeling. Was this a moment of real choice, or had my life already hardened into a series of wrong decisions from which I would have to extricate myself?

Just before I entered my final year Mother sold the Russell Hill house (again making a profit), and we moved out to a beautifully pro-portioned farmhouse at the end of a lane off Scarlett Road in Toronto's west end. Buses ran infrequently from the junction of Dundas and Weston Road, and the last one left the city at eleven, which meant an early end to any evening activities. Dad (who was frequently travelling on business) had the car, and in any case Joan and I couldn't drive. Trapped at home, we found the atmosphere even more fraught, particularly as Garry, now in his teens, was exhibiting the first evidence of emotional trouble that would escalate in the years ahead.

Since Garry was seven years younger, I had always ignored him or simply regarded him as a pest. He had frequent temper tantrums as a child, but no one took them seriously. In adolescence he began to show signs of erratic behaviour, and there were violent incidents at school, where at first he seemed to fit in well because he had inherited Dad's athletic prowess. In addition to these developing problems, he must have been going through a sexually ambivalent stage. He met an older man, a dentist, who gave him a photograph of himself. The man called on Mother, and she was so charmed by him that she ignored my warnings, flattered that someone appreciated what a treasure Garry was. Dad was away at this time, and when he returned he overheard the dentist make a remark at the YMCA pool, "something that no decent man would say." And that was the end of the dentist. These events served only to heighten Mother's anxieties.

If lithium or Prozac had been available then, Mother might have been helped, but I am convinced that only a long and deep analysis could have probed the depth of her psychological problems. Aunt Bea suggested to Mother that she see a psychiatrist but she angrily rejected the idea. Dad confided in me that she was suffering from the "climacteric." I scoffed, not even knowing what the word meant. He was obviously very earnest about this, but it did not explain her erratic behaviour over so many years.

Around this time Dad did something rather odd: he secretly wrote a novel in which Mother figured as the leading character, a character who suffered from a Freudian-like sexual frustration. (Dad had never read Freud.) He urged me to read it. It wasn't very good, but I have often wished that I had paid more attention to what he had to say, particularly as he must have been trying to create some kind of understanding between us. More than I realized, he was attempting to understand the strange psychology of a beautiful creature who could become a raging harridan at the slightest provocation.

I threw myself even harder into my studies, determined to graduate with a first. During final exams, however, there were daily tirades at breakfast before I left home. My best subject was "Nineteenth-Century Thought," but when I got into the examination hall my hands were shaking so much that it was twenty minutes before I could hold the pen steady. Once I pulled myself together I knew I was writing an outstanding paper. Afterwards, pleasurably rereading the exam questions, I realized that I had answered only three of the four required questions, thus automatically losing twenty-five marks. As a result I didn't graduate with my cherished first but stood first in the seconds. It has only recently occurred to me that perhaps I unconsciously missed the fourth question in order to hurt Mother, to show her how she was ruining my life. It was the only act of rebellion I could muster.

I could stand it no longer. Soon after, when she was out one night, I packed a suitcase, and BG took me to his house. His mother was extremely kind but firm that it would be unseemly for me to stay there.

I rented a room on St. George Street which I shared with another girl. Following graduation I took a job editing the Red Cross magazine, which of course paid very little. One night I was standing at the corner of Bloor and Bay when the family car swooped around the corner. Mother got out and I was reluctantly persuaded to return home. Everything was forgiven, she said. She understood that I was really in love with BG, and now wanted to get on with plans for the wedding – a white wedding, of course. We went over to Buffalo, then considered a shoppers' paradise, where I bought a few clothes for my trousseau. On the return bus I smuggled them across the border by wearing them all.

BG had been working for Bell Telephone for a year or so. We decided that we had to get as far away from Mother as possible. Having served in the naval reserve as a student, BG joined the regular navy as a sub-lieutenant, although neither of us had any inkling of what naval life would entail. The pattern of flight as a solution to various predicaments – a wild rush towards the unknown – was now established. But even mistakes can be put to some use, or at least I'd prefer to believe so.

On September 7, 1946, making the ritual journey to Grace Church on-the-Hill, Dad and I sat together in the limousine in uncomfortable silence. The bridesmaids – Joan, Virginia, and Marion

MacNish – looked lovely and the bride appeared radiant. Mother's mouth was a taut line, something like the Queen's when Princess Margaret married Anthony Armstrong-Jones. In the vestry, the rector asked the newly married pair who would act as their witnesses. BG indicated his father, while I replied automatically, "My mother." I'll never forget the reproachful look Dad turned on me. My thoughtless response was the result of Mother having taken on the role of the only parent who mattered. For years Dad had been an increasingly remote figure.

The reception was held in the garden of the Scarlett Road house, after which the bride and groom left for a New England honeymoon in BG's father's car. We spent the first night at the Roycroft Inn in Aurora, New York, for no other reason than that Mother had been a great fan of Elbert Hubbard, the American Arts and Crafts disciple of William Morris and founder of the Roycroft Press in that town. It would take more than distance to exorcise her influence on me.

3

JUNIOR WIFE

Emotional maturity, like teenage height, comes in spurts. Looking back over my life, it seems there have been long periods when I lay fallow, when there was no discernible change. (Of course this is a view I have picked up from applying a developmental structure to the life of a biographical subject.) The twelve years when I was an active naval wife were such a period, undisturbed by Sturm und Drang, though in fact I was gradually moving towards a comprehension of what I wanted in life and what I didn't.

To say that I lay fallow simply means that my writing life was in suspension. I was not one of those women who, like Sylvia Plath, felt compelled to write. Part of her frustration, I am sure, came from wanting it all: career, children, the lot. So did I – eventually – but I sometimes thank God that I belonged to that generation, only slightly older than Plath's, that was content for a time in motherhood.

My children were born in the years between 1949 and 1955. Just as my mother had been an ardent follower of the pediatrician Alan Brown, I in turn was reassured by Benjamin Spock's sensible *Baby and Child Care*. "Trust yourself," Dr. Spock told young mothers; "you know more than you think you do." Until I had children I had never loved another human being completely. I loved them anxiously, I loved them tigerishly. If there was one thing, one precious moment, that could be granted to me again, it would be to hold one of my babies close to me. It is easy to be sentimental about motherhood, but how can one not be overwhelmed by the miracle of birth, the thrill of that first tooth, and the excitement attending the first faltering steps? I would not trade those early years with my children for anything, and yet if I were a young woman today I realize that I would be faced with an agonizing choice.

Perhaps I accepted the naval life because it involved so much movement – a familiar sensation. The children, born three years apart, emerged from hospitals in Ottawa, Halifax, and Victoria. We traipsed (usually by car) across the continent again and again, through every province and almost every state. We could have passed Jack Kerouac on Route 66. The first year of our marriage we changed cities four times, living in rooms where I cooked on a hot plate. And I enjoyed it. Friends in Toronto groaned when they heard that BG's first posting was Halifax, but I was attracted to the city from the moment I saw it. Unlike almost any other city in Canada, it had atmosphere – it was old-fashioned, self-contained, comfortable with itself. I loved the steep citadel rising from the harbour, the bow-fronted houses, and the quiet, tree-lined streets.

Just as I was writing these chapters, I heard that a friend from those days had died. Unexpectedly I found myself grieving deeply, not just for Don Smith, but for a period when I was young, expectant, and enthusiastic. I had seen Don only a few months before on a nostalgic visit to Halifax. His ebullience hadn't been tempered by a long stint as Agent General for Nova Scotia in London. "There you are," he boomed, "the bloom of youth on your cheeks, and the cheeks of youth in your bloomers."

Don was courting my friend Elsie Guildford when I first met him in Halifax. From the beginning of my marriage I realized that the only way to avoid being swallowed by the navy was to have some friends who had no connection with it. Otherwise, I was the dutiful wife, slow to realize that one restrictive milieu had been exchanged for another. I thought I was free and I thought I was important – a Married Woman. And at first I was intrigued and mystified by the navy's oddly stratified world. With each new posting the naval wife, in gloves and hat, called on the wives of the senior officers, leaving one card of her own and two of her husband's on a silver salver. One corner of the husband's had to be folded down to indicate an apology that he hadn't accompanied his wife.

Every afternoon the naval wife's house had to be spotless, she had to look fresh, there had to be cookies or banana bread available, because each of her calls would be returned – and there was no warning when the invasion would take place. Furthermore, there was a rigid pecking order. There were wives of admirals who could strike terror into one's heart. There were wives of commodores who turned one into a blithering idiot. Even my high school math teacher could not reduce me to such an infantile state. As the wife of a very junior officer I was a very junior wife, the lowest of the low, especially as I didn't come from a well-to-do family, which seemed necessary even to survive in the service financially. I was not living with the intensity of the hard gemlike flame recommended by Walter Pater, nor was I likely to taste all of experience before I was thirty.

Nevertheless, the constant house-hunting was exciting and challenging in those days of severe housing shortages. I always refused to live on the base, and my greatest coup occurred when BG was posted to HMCS *Cornwallis* on the Digby Basin in Nova Scotia. We drove past a large white frame house with which I immediately fell in love. I traced the owners to Kentville in the heart of the Annapolis Valley, and there I talked an elderly, slightly bemused couple into renting us their summer place for year-round occupancy.

I was very proud of having snared the prize. The work involved in looking after the house was tremendous, but I enjoyed cooking porridge on the wood stove on cold mornings, and in the summer I weeded the long, curving flowerbed with Brian in a playpen beside me. "Mum sure loves living in the country," his older brother, Christopher, remarked one day.

After we had moved on, the owners died, and I heard that a motel had obliterated the delphiniums and foxgloves. I saw the house once again on a soft June evening forty years later. It was heartbreakingly derelict, and the smooth lawns had turned to chin-high hay. The climbing roses around the front porch had completely disappeared. Empty windows frowned on the world, full of blank sky and oddly arranged trees. Craning on tiptoe, I peered through the windows, trying to detect some of my past through a distorted reflection in the glass. There was the very spot where Brian had triumphantly made his first staggering steps. Feeling sad, I returned to Annapolis Royal, where we were spending the night. The following morning, on our way to catch the ferry to New Brunswick, we stopped again. Roofers were busy hammering away; they told me that a rich Texan had bought the property. *Gaudeamus igitur.*

Decades later my daughter, Anne, asked me if, during those years, I could have identified with the dissatisfied wife in Marilyn French's *The Women's Room*. She was surprised when I said no. I loved the smell of fresh laundry when I pulled it in at the end of the day. I polished the silver every week. I learned to be a gourmet cook inspired by attractive pictures in *House and Garden*. I sometimes baked bread. I was gregarious, too uncritical in my eagerness to make friends. I went to innumerable tea and coffee parties, and I never stopped smiling amiably. The perfect *Ladies' Home Journal* wife.

I recall no conscious resentment of the fact that I was bowing to societal pressures. "Togetherness" was the buzzword of the time, and what society expected from women penetrated family life. One couldn't simply enjoy doing things with one's children without feeling also that one had fulfilled a universal moral obligation, that one was behaving like a good member of the community.

Yet there was much kindness among the junior wives. We would exchange maternity clothes, look after children when one of us was in hospital with a new baby, take casseroles to the latest arrivals. In contrast to the bizarre world of my own family, I believed that I had finally found normality. In addition to our love for our children, BG and I spent comfortable evenings reading. Without other distractions I absorbed a vast amount and variety of literature – as though, somehow, I knew deep down that I was preparing myself for something else. This was what I regarded as my secret life, a part of me that no one in the navy knew anything about.

BG's long absences were very difficult. During the Korean War he was away for a year. As well as loneliness, I was left with very little money. I did not have enough to pay the rent on the house in Victoria and we couldn't afford to live on the base, so Christopher and I moved back east where I threw myself on the kindness of my in-laws, who lived just outside Toronto. I managed to get into the city occasionally to visit Aunt Phyllis, who would pace the floor, ranting and raving about how shockingly destitute I was.

I was a long time acknowledging the fact that the officers were well off on these sea duties, while I had been left to fend for myself. This neglect was not deliberate on BG's part; he simply didn't waste time wondering how we would manage. Joan and her husband, Hal Rogers, then living in Kingston, took us in for a while. For a month we joined my parents in their rented apartment on the Battery in Charleston, South Carolina. It was a lovely break because Mother was at her best in this her favourite city, and because Garry hadn't accompanied them. I had earlier stayed briefly with them in London, Ontario, where they had moved when Garry entered medical school there. As far as I know, he never attended a class. He would go for long walks and return with a dark, frightening expression. After he angrily pushed

Christopher off the piano bench, we left in a hurry. It was apparent that he was sinking deeper and deeper into serious mental difficulties.

Christopher was about a year and a half old when BG left for Korea, and the two of us were constant companions during all those months. I often scrutinize pictures of his little pixie face in his plaid dressing gown or his smart miniature trenchcoat. His father's return wasn't all that welcome to him. ("When's Daddy going away again?" he asked.) Nor was the arrival of his brother, Brian, less than a year later. But in his early years he had more of my exclusive attention than the other children. Occasionally now when I talk to my witty, sardonic son, I think, Did I once actually change his diapers? More important, did I almost lose him?

Not long after I knew I was pregnant for the first time I started to hemorrhage on the tennis court at the Rideau Club in Ottawa. All one day blood poured out of me. BG was told to scrutinize the contents of the pan for a fibrous thing that could be the fetus. At one point he said, "I think we can take it that you have had a miscarriage." "No," I replied firmly, "I want this one." To keep the baby I had to stay in bed for the rest of the nine months, passing the time by reading the four volumes of Churchill's *A History of the English-Speaking People*. I was ecstatic when a healthy little boy was born, but I had developed a tumour in my breast – the first of my many breast problems – and was unable to nurse him. We brought him home to our renovated attic in Sandy Hill, a happy place full of light, in a pleasant older section of Ottawa.

I would like to think that my children led fairly stable lives despite all our moves. Determined to be as unlike my mother as possible, I was careful never to impose unrealistic expectations and to treat them as fairly and lovingly as possible. "The trouble with this family," Brian once remarked, "is that each of us thinks we're the favourite." Perhaps, but they could not have been more different from one another.

Before Christopher was born I had an image of Christopher Robin confiding in his teddy bear. What I was given was a dynamo, so active that mothers would tremble if they heard I was bringing him to tea. Crawling at six months, by nine months he was walking and creating havoc. He was curious about everything, bombarding me with an endless stream of questions. Unusually charismatic, he would draw children to linger around our house from the first day he attended a new school. Brian, on the other hand, was quiet and imaginative, with a rare empathy from an unusually early age. Anne was energetic and resourceful, fuelled by her eagerness to keep up with her brothers. Nevertheless, there was a vulnerability in her, a deep craving for love. In our peripatetic life the children lacked the presence of aunts and cousins, and especially of supportive grandmothers like those who had played such an important part in my early life.

The children's world was their family, and they certainly weren't aware of those aspects of the navy that I gradually began to question. As a young bride in the Ward Room in Halifax I made the tactless remark that the officers were like a lot of little boys playing with swords. I soon learned to keep my mouth buttoned. The navy was a self-contained universe. With few exceptions, no one talked about anything but postings and promotions, and none of the wives worked. Before the children were born I occasionally took a temporary job in the jewellery department at Birks or as an aide in a day nursery. Even if a profession had been acceptable for a navy wife, no one would hire a woman who might move at a moment's notice.

Then there was the constant preoccupation with appearances. We had to go to a great many balls – which required evening dresses. Once while BG was away at sea I ordered a red chiffon gown from a dressmaker. When BG returned he reacted as though I had been a naughty child, refusing to pay the $75 bill. I would have to find the money myself, he declared. I had no money of my own and went tremblingly to the local bank manager. For years I used to break out in a sweat whenever I entered a bank, a residue of the terrors of the bailiff repossessing our house. My nervousness wasn't assuaged by the manager, a very odd bird indeed, who pulled a revolver out of his drawer. "I always keep it there," he whispered conspiratorially. I fled with my $75.

In order to repay the loan I stretched the family budget with Kraft Dinner and other thrifty meals. A senior officer's wife remarked facetiously that our money would go farther if we bought our clothes at Eddy's, a discount store. I flushed because I was already paying Eddy's $5 a week for my wardrobe. It is true that we had little money, but BG also had a joking reputation in his family as a tightwad, and once to my dismay he flew into a tantrum when I bought Christopher a snowsuit. This flare-up was one of the first apparent cracks in the marriage. There were to be many similar incidents.

My great salvation during the years we spent in Victoria was the University Women's Club. I joined the architecture and literature groups, and met a number of remarkably interesting, well-read women. We each gave papers which involved a good deal of preparation. I volunteered to give one on William Faulkner and became so intrigued by him that I read almost every one of his books. He appealed to me partly because the Southern Gothic atmosphere was so far removed from the conventional life I was leading, but more because of his sensuous relationship with words.

Following Anne's birth in 1955, BG was posted to a ship which followed a pattern of being away four months, back a week, and then at sea again. This continued for almost a year, a year in which Brian developed rheumatic fever, followed by a heart murmur, and had to be kept in bed. I was in a state of constant exhaustion. I developed a cyst on my breast that required surgery and was warned that eventually I would probably develop cancer.

Then suddenly Garry appeared on my doorstep. My parents had sent him out to stay with us – without consulting me – in order to avoid facing the fact that something had to be done about him. I was beside myself as he taught Christopher the goose step or flew into sudden rages and broke the china. It was the beginning of a long, acrimonious struggle with Mother to secure psychiatric help for him. Joan had long since given up the fight; indeed she and Mother had been estranged since shortly after my marriage. With my departure, Joan became not only the victim of Mother's rages but the target of Garry's violence. When I protested, Mother defended him against all reason: "He is only standing up for me." Joan too left home, never to return.

The personal difficulties of that difficult year on my own and my interest in Faulkner were closely related. I realized that my brain was atrophying in the constrictive atmosphere of the navy. Ironically my liberation began with the acquisition of a clothes dryer, which meant that I no longer had to spend hours ironing. I can remember walking to the postbox with a letter to BG, telling him that I wanted to return to university and become a professor. He was entirely amenable to the idea. He was more emancipated than most men of his generation, and he also saw the advantages of an extra income.

It is odd how a strangely quiet period can precede a storm. In the summer of 1956, after the children were put to bed, I spent my evenings happily rereading the Greek dramatists. In late August BG returned from sea duty. My instincts have always been extremely acute and I asked him if anything had happened when he was away. He openly confessed to an amatory episode. He realized that it had been stupid and was truly remorseful – but I was totally unforgiving. For me every issue was black and white, a tendency it has taken years to modify. A trust, an intimacy, had been broken and there was no way we could restore what we'd had. Perhaps we might have been able to patch up the relationship if we hadn't already been growing apart through constant separations. Perhaps I was unconsciously looking for an open fissure between us. Part of me felt terribly sorry for BG, and my heart turned over when I noted that a crease had developed between his brows. Standing one evening in our darkened garden, he pointed to our cozy book-filled living room. "Do you want to sacrifice all *that*?" he asked. No, of course I didn't; nor did I want to separate the children from their father.

The episode, however, triggered periods of deep depression. BG was irritated by my moodiness. "Who cares if a little housewife is unhappy?" was his exasperated response. I had not been able to trust my mother, and had placed complete faith in my husband. I had a haunting dream during this period: Dad was lying very ill in a tent in Antarctica. I went out into the blizzard to try to find some food for him. Suddenly a white stoat leaped up and sank its teeth into my neck. I suppose I felt that I had been keeping the home fires burning, only to be rewarded with a sudden blow. These periods of depression – linked to a fear of abandonment – were to continue for the next twenty-five years. I couldn't seem to control them, and my guilt over how they might be affecting the children only made the situation worse.

Band-Aid measures kept the marriage intact for an extraordinary length of time. At this crucial juncture BG was posted to Ottawa – which meant that I could return to university for graduate work. There was also a strong possibility that we would eventually be moved to England, a dream we shared.

Despite a general unhappiness I hadn't ceased to enjoy life altogether, nor were my aesthetic responses entirely dead. On this last cross-continent motor trip, we stretched out the journey as far as we could. In those days Burma Shave's rhyming billboards lined the highways, the kids had ice cream cones at Howard Johnson's, and we stayed at the kitschy motels immortalized in old movies. We dipped south to Texas into the rolling hill country with its little scrub oaks. There we stayed one night at Ozona, which had marvellous air as well as a fully armed sheriff. We passed the great rivers, the Mississippi, the Missouri, and the Ohio. We made a detour to Oxford, Mississippi, to see the home of my hero, William Faulkner. I peeked in the windows of his rather seedy antebellum house to glimpse a much-lived-in room spilling over with books. I have no idea what I would have said if he had suddenly confronted me. We also visited the Great Mammoth Cave in Kentucky, where BG inhaled spoor from bat droppings that later caused him to endure an unnecessary operation for suspected lung cancer, when what he had developed was a benign fungus.

After we had settled into a house on the edge of Rockcliffe, I enrolled in the master's program at the University of Ottawa. Since Anne was less than two I took evening classes. Professor Brian Robinson was assigned as the supervisor of my thesis on Faulkner, which was to concentrate on "Snopesism," the redneck mentality of his fictional Yoknapatawpha County.

I did everything backwards. Instead of starting my thesis after I had completed my courses, I launched in on it immediately. I was immensely proud of the first section handed in to Professor Robinson and was devastated when he tore it to pieces. I wept all the way home after he spared me nothing in his comments about my stream-of-consciousness style of writing. The fact was that I simply did not know how to organize material. Robinson's bluntness was the best lesson in writing I have ever had, enabling me to approach the much more difficult task of a doctoral dissertation a couple of years later. I did well in all my courses, and particularly in the gruelling oral comprehensive which covered all of English literature from Beowulf to T.S. Eliot. In my second year I was given a fellowship which allowed me to hire someone to look after Anne one day a week while I worked in the library. I was beginning to realize that my wide reading was my entrée to the intellectual life I had always craved.

My brother's condition continued to haunt us. By now he had been diagnosed as schizophrenic and an alcoholic. After electric shock treatments he could be utterly charming and thoughtful for about four or five weeks until the effects wore off. Then he would get into fights and my father would be constantly bailing him out of jail. On one occasion he took a rifle to the zoo and shot a bear because he imagined that bears were taking over the world. On another we were having Sunday tea when suddenly he rushed across the room and started to throttle me. The children were terrified, and for days Brian went around the house checking that all the doors and windows were locked. I told Mother that I could not subject the children to this kind of thing. She was angrily defensive of Garry, claiming that he was soon to take on an important job. In fact, he never held a job in his life.

Work had always taken my mind off personal problems. Professor Robinson suggested that I take a part-time job teaching English to two colonels in the Russian embassy who had requested an instructor. It seemed that whenever I entered or left the embassy, Mounties – disguised as telephone employees – were working on the lines outside. Was I hallucinating like my late Aunt Phyllis? Several times I drove past on other days to see if they were there but apparently it was only on Thursdays that the lines needed repairing. I grew very fond of my burly colonels and we even discussed politics frankly. Not long after we left Ottawa, Professor Robinson sent me a wad of newspaper clippings: my colonels had been expelled from Canada for spying! "You see how well you taught them," Robinson commented. Aunt Phyllis and Uncle Oliver must have been beaming down at me from the Celestial Control Room.

I was still very much the proper housewife who felt obliged to bake a pie every week. Nevertheless, I was distancing myself more and more from navy life, determined never to make another formal call. Some thought me eccentric but I was beginning to care less about what other people thought. In June 1960 I received my M.A., BG had been promoted to commander, and we sailed for England on an Italian ship to the strains of "Volare." I had already been accepted by the University of London, where I was to be supervised in a doctoral program by the eminent scholar Geoffrey Tillotson.

FOREIGN POSTING

Our first priority in London was to find a house. I told the estate agent that I wanted central heating, and he replied that there was one available with "background heating." When I demurred, he urged us just to have a look at it. This 1795 Georgian house, in an exquisite street in Chelsea, St. Leonard's Terrace, was the most beautiful home I ever lived in. Each window had flower boxes and these were to be my pride and joy – daffodils in the spring, geraniums and trailing lobelia in the summer. Every time I approached the house across the gravel fore-court, I pinched myself, scarcely believing that we were living in so grand a setting. Life was unfair: why should I, and not Mother, who took such pleasure in houses, have had an opportunity to live like this? The house was let to us for 30 guineas a week.

We couldn't take possession until late August, so the children and I spent the summer in Broadstairs and Eastbourne on the south coast. But first I went to Birkbeck College to introduce myself to Professor Tillotson and tell him that I wanted to write a thesis on Matthew Arnold. Arnold appealed to me because he asked that crucial question: How does one live a humane life? The professor was irritated because I had disturbed him at his own work during his seasonal holiday, a serious breach of British academic protocol. He had a par-ticularly withering way of gazing at students over his rimless glasses, and after hearing me out, he sneered that he failed to see how I could pos-sibly add anything to what had already been written on Arnold.

Instead, he suggested a number of lesser-known critics. One was John Addington Symonds, a nineteenth-century English man of letters whose name was completely unknown to me but who was renowned for his seven-volume *Renaissance in Italy.*

A week or so later BG and I were browsing in a second-hand bookshop in Broadstairs. BG picked up a copy of a biography of Symonds, published in 1895, a couple of years after Symonds's death, by his literary executor, Horatio Brown. I bought it and sat up most of the night totally engrossed. A victim of tuberculosis, Symonds had left England for Switzerland, but he escaped frequently to Venice. There was a mystery to Brown's book and the detective in me was aroused. The work comprised extracts from Symonds's autobiography, linked with commentary by Brown, who presented Symonds as a man tormented by religious doubt, a common phenomenon in the nineteenth century. Why, I asked myself, did Brown not simply publish the autobiography complete?

The summer passed pleasantly enough. Each morning, curled up uncomfortably on the pebbly Broadstairs beach, I would read the *Times,* whose letters page was filled with correspondence from people arguing about such arcane topics as what precisely was wrong with Lord Byron's foot. I discovered the area's stately homes, and almost every afternoon the children and I would climb on a green bus and tour all over Kent and Sussex. Firle Place was the first of these wonderful houses, and I was so enchanted by it that tracking down every residence in the National Trust guide became something of an obsession. In the evenings we played miniature golf.

Back in London we settled into our exotic new life. We hired an Italian au pair, Luisa, whom the children adored. BG worked in offices in Grosvenor Square and the boys were enrolled in Hill House, where Prince Charles had been a student. Anne was to attend a very snobbish girls' school where most of the children were picked up by uniformed nannies. Her schoolmates had their birthday parties in grand places like the Dorchester, to which they wore satin-lined velvet cloaks. I could never afford such a garment for Anne, but she looked adorable in her blue Harris tweed coat and matching velvet beret.

The time came to confront Professor Tillotson again. He was in a mellower mood. "I've been thinking," he said. "If you really have your heart set on Matthew Arnold I have no objection." "No," I replied, "I have changed my mind. I'd like to work on Symonds." Life is a series of strange coincidences. At the very moment I was making this crucial decision, Melanie Klein lay dying in University College Hospital only a block away. I had never heard of Melanie Klein either, but Symonds would indirectly lead me towards eventually writing a biography of the leading woman in the psychoanalytic movement.

I tried to explain to the puzzled professor the reason for my abrupt *volte-face*, telling him about the Brown biography and my conviction that the full autobiography still existed somewhere. He scoffed at this idea, arguing that Brown had probably thrown it into the wastebasket after he had extracted the bits he needed. Nevertheless, he signed my application form to the reading room of the British Museum, and thereafter I was on my own to sink or swim.

While reading through Symonds's work chronologically, I went about my search for the autobiography, visiting rare book dealers like Quaritch and Maggs. I placed an ad in the *Times Literary Supplement* requesting information about any papers or letters relating to Symonds. In the meantime I attended Professor Tillotson's weekly seminars on nineteenth-century poetry. He didn't know what to make of me. I think he viewed me as a dilettante, a mistake a lot of people have made. Now in my mid-thirties, with blue-grey eyeshadow and coiffed hair, I didn't look like the average graduate student, and he subjected me to a barrage of anti-American remarks. I determined to show this bastard what I could do.

There was a suspicious competitiveness among the graduate students, who had been selected from universities all over the world, and I felt very lonely in the impersonal atmosphere of the University of London. In our seminars the students would vie to impress the professor and chortle gleefully when someone said something stupid. The British-born students were smart enough to be silent.

Within a surprisingly short time I received responses to my inquiries about Symonds. I paid a visit to Hatfield, north of London, where the family of Graham Dakyns, Symonds's closest friend, had a trunk full of extraordinary letters – some very personal indeed, a good many from famous nineteenth-century literary figures. Then somehow I discovered that the University of Bristol had acquired a cache. They were stored in cardboard boxes in a kind of cage, and I was literally hopping up and down with excitement as the librarian fumbled with his keys. These papers proved to be every bit as revealing as those in Hatfield, and in those pre-photocopier days I had to reproduce them by hand. The Dakynses were generous enough to lend me their collection for some weeks. I arranged them in a chronological procession snaking around the bedroom floor.

Finally there came a note from the librarian of the London Library requesting that I pay him a visit. Stanley Gillam, a charming man, explained that he actually possessed the original manuscript of the autobiography – and it was right there, in a safe in his office. There was, however, an embargo until 1976 – but since I was a bona fide scholar I could have access to it. (E.M. Forster was one of the few others who had been allowed to read it.) I have dealt with many archivists in my time, but Mr. Gillam and later his successor, Douglas Matthews, were the most civilized I ever encountered. It is a profession, I have discovered, that tends to attract possessive, anal types. Neither of these men fell into that category.

In that wonderful private library, one of whose founders was

Thomas Carlyle, I mounted the stairs every day to read through Symonds's memoir. It revealed something I had already begun to suspect: it was the tortured account of his secret homosexuality. Brown had been as circumspect in protecting Symonds's reputation as John Cam Hobhouse had been when he encouraged the burning of Byron's memoirs some seventy years earlier.

I went back to report my findings to an amazed Professor Tillotson. Furthermore, after I handed in the first fifty pages of my thesis, his attitude towards me changed completely. The other students noticed it. "He's afraid of you," one of them whispered.

Each morning I would order the groceries before setting out for the British Museum. Just getting there and back every day was an adventure. I had a choice between three buses – the 19, the 22, or the 11. The first two were the more direct: up Sloane Street, along Piccadilly past Green Park, then around the Circus to Shaftesbury Avenue. The 11 was much longer, dipping down to Whitehall and through Trafalgar Square. Whatever the route, I tried to get the front seat on the upper deck for one of the most scenic trips in the world.

I adored the BM's circular reading room with its leather desks and soft lamps. I particularly loved the huge cumbersome catalogues with new entries pasted in them. It was wonderful to pass the hours in that hushed atmosphere, where Marx, Shaw, and so many other scholars had bent intently over some esoteric subject. Learning to fend for myself, to organize and distill a vast amount of disparate material, was the best possible preparation for the kind of biography I would eventually write.

I more or less worked office hours, sometimes arriving home in time to pick up Anne at school. I cooked dinner as I had always done. The children suffered the usual childhood diseases. We had a general practitioner whom BG compared to G. Aubrey Smith as he made his rounds in Chelsea, tall and military in bearing. One time I went to him to have a diaphragm fitted. He took an interminable time inserting it, panting and perspiring as he did so. "Does this have to take so long?" I asked nervously. I was shaking as I left his surgery. What should I do? Report him? His best feature as a doctor was that as soon as I rang when one of the children was ill, he was at our house in a flash. Nevertheless, I simply found another family doctor.

We attended the occasional naval event, like a grand ball in the Painted Hall at Greenwich. At a dance at the fashionable nightclub Quaglino's we shared the floor with Princess Margaret and Lord Snowdon. (She blatantly sized up my strapless turquoise silk and lamé evening dress.) I didn't have time to make many close friends, but we had regular dinner parties. Luisa taught me how to make Mont Blanc: a mixture of puréed chestnuts, cream, chocolate, and kirsch to bubble for a time, then poured into a bowl and chilled until it was firm. Just before serving I would invert it and cover the rich concoction with a snowy topping of whipped cream.

The sixties were a marvellous time to see the theatre in London, and during the week BG and I attended innumerable plays and operas. The Mermaid and the Royal Court were incomparable. The former's rendition of *'Tis Pity She's a Whore* was so powerful that a woman in the middle of the row threw up the night we were there. There was the brilliant zaniness of *Beyond the Fringe,* with such skits as Jonathan Miller playing the unctuous clergyman who wants to take violence off the streets and bring it into the churches. Young Judi Dench was Juliet, and an intense Albert Finney was a mesmerizing Billy Liar. I took the boys to Joan Littlewood's *Oh, What a Lovely War,* and Anne – rightly – has never forgiven me for leaving her at home with Luisa. When she attended *Peter Pan* she sat fiercely silent when Tinker Bell pleaded with the children to clap if they believed in fairies. "Anne, why aren't you clapping?" "I don't believe in fairies," she replied through clenched teeth. The play that made the greatest impression on me was Pinter's *The Caretaker*. Elizabeth Taylor was in the audience, and I overheard her whisper to Eddie Fisher, "I don't like it, do you?" Neither did I after the first act, but during the second act I realized its sheer brilliance. I returned twice in the following fortnight to gain yet more insights from its terrifying portrayals of bullying power and cringing subservience.

I heard lectures by George Steiner, Angus Wilson, Herbert Read, and William Empson, whose *Seven Types of Ambiguity* had been something of a bible to me at the University of Ottawa. A friend, the antiquarian bookseller Timothy D'Arch Smith, took me to auctions of original manuscripts at Sotheby's. At the weekends with the children we explored museums and art galleries. Those were the glory days of the Whitechapel Gallery, where I first saw the work of Rothko and Rauschenberg. The Tate had Manzu's stony cardinals and Bacon's screaming popes. The children were just as enthusiastic about art as we were. I remember asking Brian after one exhibition whose work he had admired most and he replied, "Soutine." An odd choice for a little boy, but I think both Soutine and Rothko had an influence on his own later work as a painter and art historian. It was a day of mourning in our house in 1970 when we heard that Rothko had committed suicide.

During the school holidays we would take motor trips or rent apartments or villas on the continent. The first time we arrived in Paris I screamed with joy in the taxi. At the age of eleven Brian had learned Latin in such a vivid way that as we travelled through Italy he gave us a running commentary on Hannibal's campaign. I do not think any family could have sucked sweeter juice out of the experience. We lived with an intensity made all the sharper by the fact that we never knew when BG's posting would come to an end. As a result, I probably set a record in finishing my thesis within two years.

The navy was still very much a part of our lives. Once a visiting senior officer from Ottawa came to our house for dinner. Sitting in the drawing room afterwards he silently beckoned to me. Puzzled, I crossed the room and he pulled me down on his lap. It was a disgusting show of the power he had over us. I was disappointed in BG for saying nothing; I was more furious with myself for permitting this arrogant man to cuddle me.

Incidents like these reinforced my conviction that I had made the right decision in taking control of my life. The thesis was an academic exercise, with innumerable footnotes, and of course I could not use all the personal material about Symonds's homosexuality that I had discovered. I had never contemplated writing a book, but various publishers got wind of the incendiary information I possessed. I had an interview with John Guest, the senior editor at Longman, at the company's elegant offices off Grosvenor Square. Guest was a refined aesthete but also a hard-nosed businessman. At that first meeting he scrutinized me appraisingly. "I'd like to commission you on the spot," he said, "but we don't know whether you can write." He suggested that I provide him with a sample chapter as well as a synopsis. This meant blood, sweat, and tears because I had to free myself from writing in a dry academic mode. The manuscript was sent off, and within ten days I received a letter from John that Longman was commissioning a full biography.

This was an extraordinary coup for someone who had never written a book, and I later learned that John had many sleepless nights about the rashness of what he had done. Moreover, while I was thrilled by the prospect of authorship, I had never particularly cared for biography. We were about to go off to Spain for our holidays, and I took with me a small suitcase containing various biographies to decide what I considered good biographical writing to be. Whilst sitting on the beach acquiring a tan, I decided that I liked graphic detail, defining moments, and a sense of period in which the subject is firmly placed. But biographies were not my only models. Of all the books I have read, Barbara Tuchman's histories, with her method of weaving together disparate threads, have best demonstrated the platonic ideal towards which I have always striven.

Back in London I was faced with blank foolscap paper. In a TV interview I heard the historian Hugh Trevor-Roper say that he always wrote six pages a day. Aha, so that's how one does it – and six pages a day continued to be my habit for years. Some days it was an effort to reach page 6; on others I would force myself to stop. Nowadays I am more flexible, but this discipline enabled me to finish the book in nine months. (Actually it was a sensible method because writing is like a muscle that must be kept flexible through daily use.) I wrote most of the book in bed in order to keep warm during the terrible winter of 1963. (The "background heating" the estate agent had referred to was two radiators. We tried – unsuccessfully – to keep warm with electric heaters, and for the only time in my life I developed chilblains.) Ours was one of the few houses on the fashionable street where the pipes didn't freeze. The neighbours' maids had to fill pails with water from a faucet on the sidewalk. It was the winter that Sylvia Plath committed suicide, and although I am an avid newspaper reader, I saw no notice of her death in February, so little known was she at the time.

I experienced some difficulties with Symonds's relatives, particularly his granddaughter, Dame Janet Vaughan, the principal of Somerville College in Oxford. My great ally was another granddaughter, Kitty West, who arranged a lunch with her cousin to try to win her approval for me to use the family's materials. Dame Janet sat stiffly throughout the meal and left with the same disapproving expression on her face. Eventually she realized that I did not intend to sensationalize Symonds's homosexuality and she relented, graciously inviting BG and me to spend a delightful weekend with her at Somerville.

Since this was my first book, I had no expectations of what the publishing process would entail. Few editorial changes were made to the manuscript submitted, and the forthright title – *John Addington Symonds: A Biography* – was mutually agreed. (In the United States, Holt Rinehart insisted on calling it *The Woeful Victorian* despite my strenuous objections.)

While the book was being edited and printed I taught a course in modern literature to a continuing education class for a group of women in Hornchurch, in east London. Early in 1964 BG received word that he was being posted back to Ottawa in early July. Jungians would call it synchronicity, for at about the same time I received a letter from Munro Beattie, the chairman of the English department at Carleton University, offering me a teaching position.

On the June Saturday night before the book was to be published my editor, Peter Carson, was having dinner with us. He remarked that one could go down to Fleet Street at about three a.m. and pick up copies of the reviews in the weeklies hot off the press. We chatted into the night, then ventured out. The tired typesetters were sitting on the curbs with their pints. The first paper I opened was the *Observer*. The lead review was by Philip Toynbee, and I gasped when I saw a large photograph of Symonds. As I quickly scanned what he had to say I realized that he loved the book. We picked up paper after paper, the ink still wet. In every one of them my book received the lead review – and what reviews! When we showed them to Christopher after he woke up, he kept exclaiming, "Oh Mum! Oh Mum!"

The book had the particular impact it did because it was the first frank biography of a homosexual. Its author was an unknown Canadian woman who did not seem driven by any polemical purpose. The recommendations of the government's Wolfenden report were not to be implemented until 1967; sex between consenting adult males remained a criminal offence until that year. The book made me something of a heroine to the homosexual community, and I am told that it was regarded as a small catalyst in changing attitudes.

Nana Owen: Loving grandmother and indomitable matriarch,
she ruled a family of five feuding daughters and one obedient son.

Mother: Exquisite, elegant,
and seemingly fragile.
I knew another side, and so did Dad.

Father: Tenacious and vigorous at
the peak of his financial career.

Mother with her first baby, yours truly.

Rosedale Heights Drive: The house built
on soon-to-be-shattered optimism.
All changed when the bailiffs came.

Patsy and Joan: Sisters, allies,
and finally friends.

An unnamed friend, Virginia,
Joan, and Patsy with my first love,
Maurice, in Barbados, 1940.

Bob McMullan, just after joining
the Canadian army in 1943.
He was callow, sarcastic, and sexy.

The girls of English Lang and Lit graduating in 1946,
one of them hogging the limelight.

Marriage to Bob Grosskurth, September 7, 1946:
An escape from home to the restrictive life of a navy wife.

With navy friends at a ball at Cornwallis naval base, Nova Scotia, 1953.
Despite our tight finances, a wardrobe of formal dresses was required.

Happy family: Brian, Anne, and Christopher in Victoria in 1955 in outfits knitted by their mother.

St. Leonard's Terrace, Chelsea, where we lived between 1960 and 1964. These years in London were the turning point in my life.

Heavy research work on a Spanish beach in 1962
for the biography of John Addington Symonds.

Receiving the Governor General's Award from Georges Vanier
for *Symonds* in 1965, homophobic parents conspicuously absent.

With second husband Mavor Moore in 1970, at one of innumerable social events.

Hippie Brian, glowering, with Fiona and Christopher
just before they set off around the world in 1974.

With Jorge in New York during the romantic summer of 1977.

Ian Scott-Kilvert, stalwart companion and dear friend, in 1978.

Professor Tillotson was stunned, and I think not altogether pleased. "I have never seen a first book have such a reception," he remarked in astonishment. I also began to learn something of the headaches that seem inevitably to be attached to life-writing. A librarian in Liverpool, claiming that I had stolen material from his M.A. thesis, wrote a letter of complaint to the chancellor of the university, who happened to be the Queen Mother. Two American academics who were editing Symonds's letters had tried to persuade the Dakyns family not to permit me to publish the letters in my biography because that would affect their chances of finding a publisher for their work. Through the years I was to discover that such problems were a predictable part of the territory, but by nature I wasn't tough enough to slough them off easily.

At a symposium on Symonds at the University of Bristol thirty-five years later (in April 1998) I told the audience that after rereading the book I thought it stood up remarkably well, except for my endorsement of Freud's pathological explanation for the etiology of homosexuality. I confessed sheepishly that while I had made authoritative references to Freud, in truth I had hardly begun to read his work.

After the publication of the book, I became a mini-celebrity – my fifteen minutes of fame – and all sorts of offers suddenly appeared. The novelist Graham Greene wrote urging me to write a book on Walter Pater for Bodley Head, with which he was then associated. Just as life was opening up to me, the prospect ahead – that is, of returning to Canada – seemed to foreclose all my opportunities. To add to the irony of the situation, BG was not to go to Ottawa after all, but to sea – which meant that the children and I would be living alone in Ottawa.

I recently discovered a journal in which I had written sporadically during those four years in London. How I wish I had then – and subsequently – kept a daily journal as I have been doing since 1990. In diary writing I have always favoured the intriguing vignette, the conversation in which unexpected nuances of character are revealed. Most of these entries were written on holidays and contain descriptions of places we visited and analyses of books I was reading. There is an entry for May 31, 1961, when we attended the Derby at Epsom. A gypsy read my palm. "You have three children. You don't want any more and you're not going to have any more. Your husband has been very sick with a chest complaint. You have a sister-in-law who is jealous of you. More than anything else you want happiness. You're going to have it."

That last year in London I feared I might be pregnant. I confided in Daphne Seaborne-May, a friend who was an actual card-carrying member of the Communist Party. We sometimes shared picnics in the sculpture garden of Battersea Park. Daphne went to a great deal of trouble finding the name of a doctor who would perform an abortion. Fortunately it was a false alarm. In those days I was terrified of being dragged back into the maelstrom of total domesticity.

Life was busy and stimulating, but I was not coming to terms with my own unhappiness. An entry appears for September 1962 which describes sitting on the terrace of a pub with an American who was in England doing psychoanalytic training. "Well, talk," he says to me. "What's making you so unhappy?" My answer is not recorded. He goes on to say, "I doubt whether you have the temperament to break away." No, I didn't have the temperament to break away. I was still conventional and dependent, and to leave BG would break me, I was sure. We were companionable when doing things that interested us both, yet there was not the meeting of hearts that should form the basis of a marriage. I had married him for the wrong reasons, and now we were both suffering the consequences. In my solipsistic depression I was unaware of how unhappy he was as well.

In this vulnerable state I had fallen into a relationship with a writer whom I had met at the British Museum. I soon realized that I disliked him intensely. He was, however, obsessive about me. In order to escape from him I was forced to work in the library of the Senate House or the London Library. Even so, he would track me down. When I was on holiday in Italy he went to the woman who was typing my thesis to tell her that I had asked him to pick it up. This ruse was a total fabrication, but it would force me to go to his flat to retrieve it. Knowing one day that I had an appointment with my publisher, he phoned John Guest and asked to speak to me in order to embarrass me in front of John. A stalker is a terrifying figure because he is determined to cause pain. This man's presence hung like a dark cloud over my life, making me feel deeply ashamed. This terrible secret was the only reason I felt relief at leaving England.

ANOTHER LIFE

For four years the navy had allowed us experiences beyond our means, made possible with extra pay and allowances. We had grown completely accustomed to cultural riches, and suddenly all this was taken away from us. Yet I was a Canadian whose roots were ineradicable. During our last year in London we saw a National Film Board short of wild Canadian scenery with a voiceover reciting Archibald Lampman's "Morning on the Lièvre." Those autumnal scenes were so breathtakingly beautiful that I longed for my country, even though I was an urban creature.

Ottawa was to prove our testing ground. The culture shock experienced by the whole family defies description. As small a detail as the little flags waving in the used-car lots on Rideau Street brought home the distance we had travelled. Fifteen-year-old Christopher suddenly slumped over sobbing in the back seat of the car. "Look, Chris," I said in an effort to comfort him, "lots of London is ugly."

"Yes, but it's so interesting." For some time Brian and I would play a game where we would reconstruct for each other every building in King's Road between Smith Street and Peter Jones. It was harder on the boys than on Anne, who was only eight and who has always been very resilient. When Brian woke up in the mornings he missed his old school so much that he cried as though his heart would break. I took him in my arms and said, "Brian, you must be brave." He stopped, and I think he is one of the bravest people I know. All this may sound melodramatic, but one must remember the intensity – that precious hard gemlike flame – of our life during the previous four years.

At the age of forty I started out as a lecturer in the English department at Carleton at $7,000 a year. My classes began in the early evening so I hired a very nice woman to give the children their dinner. I was so appallingly nervous that I took to popping a Valium before facing the students. The most difficult was a large survey class covering English literature from Chaucer to D.H. Lawrence. I shall never forget mounting the stairs of the lecture theatre and seeing the legs stretching back into infinity like Satan's hordes. My impression is that I was absolutely awful, but I have since run into former students like the journalist Stevie Cameron who tell me I was a good teacher.

Then came a telephone call from someone at the Canada Council and the news that *John Addington Symonds* had won the Governor General's Award for non-fiction. The $1,000 that went with it meant that I had enough money to pay for the children's summer holiday. This too was an unexpected thrill, but the glow was diminished by a letter I had received from Dad before news of the award reached me. He had read my book and was appalled. I had disgraced the family, he wrote, and he was disgusted that I could squander all that scholarship on such a horrible subject. I was sitting on the edge of the bed when I read this letter; with tears streaming down my face, I tore it into shreds and dropped it in the wastebasket. Even after the Governor General's Award was announced publicly, my parents refused ever to mention the unspeakable thing I had done. They could not share my pride when in the *Observer* Philip Toynbee named *Symonds* as one of the three best books of the year, alongside Sartre's *Les Mots* and Hemingway's *A Moveable Feast*.

Dad wasn't alone in this attitude. Some universities wouldn't consider hiring me because of the subject matter of the book, and I received a number of disturbing anonymous letters. Nevertheless, as a result of the award numerous offers came my way. Professor Clifford Leech, the chairman of the English department at University College at the University of Toronto, offered me a position at $9,000 a year. I was so inexperienced in the ways of academe that I didn't realize I could have negotiated for a higher salary, more in line with the salaries offered to my male colleagues. The only reason I was even considered was that Professor Woodhouse, the college's previous chairman, who had refused ever to hire a woman, had recently died. But a teaching post at University College – for me it was a dream come true.

I wanted to return to Toronto, partly because the boys could then attend the sort of schools they had been familiar with in England, but also because I saw this as an opportunity to end my marriage. BG was still away at sea when I accepted the offer. He took the news calmly enough, then proceeded to wangle some kind of naval job in Toronto. Whenever I had suggested a separation to him in the past he had refused to consider the idea. I found a solid but unwelcoming house in Rosedale and settled tentatively into my new life. The only writing I managed to produce that year was a monograph on Leslie Stephen for the Writers and Their Works series published by the British Council. (It was anthologized by Scribner's, and each year I still receive a small royalty cheque.) To my surprise, I had discovered that I loved teaching. Again I found myself in a situation where my life was necessarily compartmentalized.

The atmosphere in Toronto in the late sixties was that of a continuous party. The Symonds biography gained me an immediate entrée into this unbridled social life. Cocktail parties were held every night of the week, screaming scenes were frequent, and everyone seemed to be having affairs. There were trysts on the roof of the Park Plaza Hotel. The publisher Jack McClelland hosted marvellous gatherings of writers. The *Telegram* columnist Dubarry Campeau and Serrell Hillman, the *Time* man in Canada, threw celebrated media parties. I was invited to the Sordsmen's Club, whose regulars included Pierre Berton, Jack McClelland, the architect John C. Parkin, and the painter Harold Town. Their wives were never present and the atmosphere was sexually charged. The invitation came only once because I am sure these playboys considered me too much of a prig. Jack once said to me, "Pat, are we ever going to have an affair?" "No, I don't think so, Jack." "I don't think so either," he shrugged.

Business was conducted in an alcoholic haze and two-martini luncheons at Le Provençal or the Courtyard Café were the norm. Dinner parties could be ruined when insults were exchanged. I had to ask McClelland to leave a party we were giving because he was so rude to Dubarry Campeau, declaring that she was a lousy reviewer. The poor woman rushed out of the house, wailing like a banshee.

Despite all this zaniness Toronto was still a deeply puritanical, deeply hypocritical city. My old friend Dorothy Cameron's gallery was visited by the police in 1966 for a show called *Eros*, laughably tame by today's standards. It was a devastating experience for her to be charged with exhibiting lewd material. There was a large photo of her in the papers, looking extremely elegant and scared as hell. She was convicted on seven counts of obscenity and fined $250.

The clothes at the time were gorgeous and provocative. A few years ago I went to an Yves St. Laurent exhibition at the Metropolitan Museum in New York, and was reminded of how pretty women looked in the late sixties in our boxy jackets, sleeveless shifts, and square-toed shoes. I had a stunning white dress in a Mondrian pattern. June Callwood arrived one evening at our house swathed in a long pink marabou boa. And those tight boots! I can remember a vinyl pair in vivid tangerine into which I used to struggle. I also had some black leather shorts. When I first appeared in this outfit, Anne howled in alarm, "You don't look like a mother!"

BG and I got caught up in this frenzy, but neither of us could handle it, particularly when our marriage was in such a precarious state. BG suggested that we have an open marriage, but this I could not bear. The tension of such an intolerable arrangement brought out the worst in both of us. BG refused to leave, and there was no way I could support the children on $9,000 a year. Equal division of family assets had not yet become the law, so a woman was in a very vulnerable position when a marriage broke up.

By now I was involved with Mavor Moore, whom I had long admired as something of a Renaissance man. We were drawn together by mutual admiration and mutual unhappiness. While he was only five years older than I, he seemed immeasurably wiser and more mature. A producer, actor, and playwright, he had been one of the leading figures in the formation of the CBC. At university I had met his wife, Dilly Faessler, shortly after their marriage, and I thought they were a golden couple, but things had gone sour. Mavor and I met at one of the Hillmans' parties when both partners were away. We began to talk, never imagining that it would lead to anything else. I spent our first real conversation chastising him for Dilly's unhappiness. We began to think that a new partnership would solve our difficulties. Such a decision could have been made only in a climate when sound judgment had little chance of prevailing.

Not many months after meeting we sat down with BG and tried to discuss a divorce in a civilized manner, but he refused to consider it.

By law there was no way I could initiate divorce proceedings. Adultery was still the only grounds for divorce in Canada. (Jack McClelland caused a sensation when he brought a gorgeous professional "co-respondent" to a party.)

I regarded Mavor in the same light as I had regarded Dad when he saved me from drowning by pulling me out of the water by my hair. At one point Mavor had argued that perhaps we should try to make the best of our marriages, unsatisfactory as they were. But I was so desperate for escape and survival that I persuaded him it was impossible for us to go on living in sham relationships.

Many a time I have reflected on the situation and wondered whether my actions were morally defensible. BG and I were no longer living as man and wife. I went to see a lawyer who assured me that if I left the marriage there was no judge in the land who wouldn't give me custody of the children. He advised me to take only those possessions that actually belonged to me. How few they were!

I finally made the terrible decision to leave, and probably did it in the clumsiest fashion possible. I took a room at the Women's Union at the university where the dean of women, Charity Grant, talked to me very frankly. She told me that I could not stay there indefinitely, and warned me of the possible legal consequences of my actions. As a result, I moved in with Mavor, in effect abandoning my beloved children. I could think of nothing else until I could gain custody of them. When one's world seems to be falling apart – and a marriage is a self-enclosed world – both parties are driven to the extremes of their personalities, and the children are usually used as pawns. I have witnessed many divorces, and it is hard to think of one where those involved have not become partially insane for a time. The custody battle was particularly painful, all the more so for the children. The centre of their lives was ripped apart and they were helpless onlookers at its dissolution. How heartbreaking it must have been to wake and discover that their mother was no longer there. Years later Chris said to me, "Mum, I just didn't understand at the time." And Brian unexpectedly gave vent to his suppressed hurt only in 1980.

Objects take on enormous symbolic value when a marriage ends. I lost all my books, the silver which my aunts had been giving me piece by piece every birthday, and Aunt Phyllis's pine furniture, which now graces a house in New Delhi. We had a complete set of stone-pink Russel Wright dinnerware. When I occasionally see a piece in a museum, I feel a real sense of loss. I have often said that possessions are simply *things* – but I only half mean it. These objects had a tactile connection to me; for years I had polished and cared for them lovingly. It was like losing a piece of one's past. I would automatically reach for a familiar kitchen utensil and, puzzled for a minute, wonder where it had disappeared. The other party has an unerring ability to hang on to something that has sentimental value for the former mate and usually only trophy value to the new possessor. In our case it was a pottery bowl that Brian and I had chosen together when we had gone on a wonderful long walk in London one spring day.

I introduced Mavor to my parents on the roof of the Park Plaza Hotel. After he had left, Mother berated me for my immoral conduct. "How does one meet people in these situations?" she asked wonderingly. I finally unleashed all my grievances and told her that I would not have rushed into marriage if I had not been so unhappy at home. I stormed out and we did not speak again for months. Once Anne and I were standing in the window of the house I was sharing with Mavor when my parents' car stopped outside at a traffic light. Mother had no idea where I was living. She was looking angry and miserable. I hated Anne to witness a scene in which she knew that Mother and I weren't speaking. I thought how terrible it would be if some division should come between Anne and me one day. My heart ached for my lost mother, despite our estrangement.

It was a difficult time in all our lives, but eventually the emotional turmoil settled. By 1969 BG was prepared to go to court. Mavor and I gave him the necessary grounds when a friend of Mavor's agreed to testify to seeing us together in an elevator of the Windsor Arms in Montreal. BG had already met his future wife in Sweden (while we were still living in England), and when I learned that an epistolary romance had been maintained, I was puzzled as to why he had put up such a fight to keep me. These things are inexplicable apart from the fact that no one wants to be abandoned, as I well know. Fortunately, we have always maintained a residual affection for each other.

"The past is never dead," Faulkner said, "it's not even past." Faulkner was an unredeemable romantic, and he often parodied himself with characters who constantly brood about the past. The present is what matters, and in order to live affirmatively it seems to me that one must absorb the past and even try to forgive oneself for one's mistakes. In the case of BG and me, this has been made easier by the magnanimity of our children and the satisfaction we experience in witnessing their strength and solidity. But, to be bluntly realistic, every divorce leaves ineradicable grievances in its wake.

4

A DIFFICULT WOMAN

If those early years as a naval wife were singularly lacking in Sturm und Drang, the ten years with Mavor more than made up for it. Not that this was Mavor's doing; it was simply the upheaval of a series of seismic disturbances in our lives.

We wanted to marry as quietly as possible. When I married BG I had worn a sort of antebellum gown with a flounced skirt. This time Anne (and my unconscious) helped me choose a simple red Cardin dress and white coat from Harridge's. Joan and Mavor's brother Peter were the witnesses at the brief ceremony at the Unitarian Church one Sunday afternoon. Nothing was planned to follow. Joan's husband, Hal, dropped by and took us all out to dinner. The whole occasion was marked by a kind of chilling sobriety.

Mavor and I bought a substantial house that would accommodate all my teenaged children on Macpherson Avenue in central Toronto. (By now BG had moved to Ottawa with his new wife.) Mavor, I felt, put every effort into being a good stepfather. Very shortly after the children were living with me again I overheard a conversation in the next room. "You're not my father," Anne growled. "No, I'm not," he replied, "and I never will be. But I'd very much like to be your friend." I wish I could say that I was a good stepmother to Mavor's daughters, who continued to live with their mother, but I was too nervous, too possessive, and too apprehensive. It was a great pity and my loss because they were all highly interesting girls and never cast me in the role of the Wicked Stepmother. Instead I became too preoccupied with Anne, whom I undoubtedly indulged, guilty for having disrupted her life. I was also extremely concerned about Brian, who had dropped out of University of Toronto Schools at the age of fifteen and was attending an alternative school, which proved a disaster. All he wanted to do in life, he declared, was paint. In this I supported him to the best of my abilities.

My teaching job at University College had started out happily enough. I was given a large office overlooking the grassy quad, and I thought that I had come home at last. Recently, while having a drink with a psychiatrist friend from New York at the rooftop bar of the Park Plaza Hotel, I pointed out the roof of Trinity, which I had attended as a student, and that of University College, where I had taught. "Well, you didn't have far to go," he remarked. "No, but it took me twenty years," I replied.

In 1966 there were still a number of faculty members who had been on staff when I was an undergraduate. My male colleagues seemed to regard me with benevolent puzzlement. I was given a section of "Nineteenth-Century Thought," which I would share with F.E.L. Priestley, whom I had greatly admired years before, and a warm friendship developed with this mordantly witty, kindly man. I learned to cope with a few insolent male students who couldn't accept me as a female professor, particularly as I didn't look like one. It never occurred to me that it would have been sensible not to wear a mini-skirt.

In those days each college at the University of Toronto had its own English department. The superstars were Marshall McLuhan at St. Michael's and Northrop Frye at Victoria. It was hard to feel close to either man. Frye assumed a self-effacing but totally false modesty while McLuhan was a reckless show-off. At my very first graduate oral examination the great man strode across the room and extended his hand: "McLuhan's the name." I had read *Understanding Media* on a brief holiday in Nassau with Mavor, who was an enormous fan and friend of McLuhan's. I was so excited by its abundance of exciting hypotheses that after reading a few pages I literally could not sit still and would pace the room, overstimulated by his provocative perceptions.

Most academics become irritated if they are forced to look at the world in a new way, whereas I love the unexpected and am attracted to intellectual oddballs. The venomous way his colleagues gossiped about McLuhan was shocking. He offended them by abandoning the traditional academic canon, but they were more distressed by his popular fame and by his conviction that he was absolutely right about everything. Nevertheless, I think he often felt cornered by the burden of celebrity. "How did I ever get into this?" he once asked a mutual friend in a tone of frightened candour.

He never disguised his contempt for most of his fellow academics, and he and Frye loathed each other. Graduate students were either ardently pro-McLuhan or deeply pro-Frye. Professor Norman Endicott was startled by a conversation he had with McLuhan as they waited for the lights to change opposite Trinity College. "Norman," he said, "something's got to be done about Norrie. He's ruining our discipline" – exactly what people were saying about McLuhan, who seemed to have abandoned literature for media studies.

Frye was venerated by the establishment, especially after the publication of his book on Blake, *Fearful Symmetry*. His learning was vast, he didn't appear on TV, and he subsumed everything under Aristotelian categories. McLuhan barely noticed my existence, but Frye made me feel that he respected me, and he was always immensely kind in a rather distant way. In later years, after the death of his wife, Helen, I used to lure him out of his reclusive Moore Park retreat to small dinner parties.

At University College I soon realized that a state of barely suppressed warfare existed between our chairman and the other senior English professors at the college. Woodhouse had brought Clifford Leech from Durham as his designated successor, and Leech's combination of arrogance and insecurity did not endear him to his colleagues. He was an odd little man of rather humble origins. He had strange glaucous eyes which he would direct towards a far corner of the ceiling when addressing meetings, but I understand that he was transformed when he was teaching Shakespeare. I realized he was an old-fashioned chauvinist when, at my job interview, he asked me questions like "Who is going to look after your children?" He clearly thought that I regarded my position as an aesthetic pastime.

During my first year he seemed to approve of me, but trouble erupted the year following. Aware that the British novelist David Garnett would be in America on a lecture tour, I suggested to Leech that we invite him to speak on the Bloomsbury group. (Garnett had once tried to seduce me on his houseboat at Chelsea Reach, an incident I didn't think it necessary to mention to my chairman.) Leech thought the idea of the lecture a splendid notion and left it in my hands to make all the arrangements. A day or so before David was due to arrive I learned that Leech was having an all-male dinner party for him at the Faculty Club. In disbelief I rang Peter Marinelli, the department's social secretary. "Peter, is this true?" I asked. "Yes," he replied wearily, "and oh, Pat, *please* don't make a fuss about it." Ignoring his advice, I immediately phoned Leech to register my indignation. "Mrs. Grosskurth," he said frostily, "this is the way things have always been done and this is the way they always will be done." "Professor Leech," I snapped, "this isn't 1066." "Well, will it satisfy you if you introduce his lecture?" To their credit, some of my colleagues also protested. Kathleen Coburn, the great Coleridge scholar, rang to commiserate with me and confided how she had been blocked from ever becoming principal of Victoria College. Leech finally had to capitulate, and when he rang to invite me to the Faculty Club, I accepted as though no previous conversation had taken place.

At the dinner I discovered that Leech had found another academic woman somewhere, supposedly to balance the sexes. He made an effort to be agreeable to me until Mavor – not yet my husband – appeared to pick me up, after which he lapsed into brooding silence. Was I flaunting an affair in front of his eyes? We walked off into the night, with David Garnett linking arms with us both as we took him back to Massey College. The next day David warned me, "Pat, you are in for the chop if you aren't careful. That man is determined to get rid of you."

Leech seemed relieved (and impressed) when I married Mavor, although I had quietly decided to retain the Grosskurth name. It was the name under which I had established myself professionally, and it was the name I shared with my children. One morning I arrived to find a sign reading "Mrs. Moore" on my office door. I insisted that it be changed back to "Mrs. Grosskurth." It was too much to expect to be known as "Professor." The men enjoyed that title, but I was always "Mrs." There were many similar indignities which I simply overlooked, otherwise I would have been constantly complaining about some sort of discrimination. Still these silent resentments accumulated.

I worked hard, very hard. Unlike colleagues who had been teaching for years, I was the new girl, and I sat up late night after night preparing for my classes the next day. I was also running a household and accompanying Mavor to innumerable social events, many of them connected with the construction of the St. Lawrence Centre, of which he was the artistic director. Its mandate was to be a focal point of Canadian plays as well as a town hall for discussions of timely issues.

As a naval wife I frequently had the feeling that life was taking place elsewhere. Now, however, I had been drawn into Canada's cultural life and I decided to throw myself headlong into it. I was appointed a governor of the National Film Board, where I soon learned how haphazardly public affairs are conducted. At my first meeting the members (some of them very distinguished figures like the Québécois actor Jean-Louis Roux) were sitting around mulling over an appropriate candidate as new head of the NFB. "Has anyone considered Hugo Macpherson?" I piped up naively. "Who is he?" they asked. "Well, he's an English professor who had an office across the hall from me, and he has now moved to the University of Western Ontario. He likes films." I was told to ring him and ask him if he would be interested. Astonished and delighted, Hugo replied that he would be. Judy LaMarsh, the secretary of state, thought he was a cool candidate because he wore jackets without lapels, and she appointed him commissioner of a vast organization for which he didn't have the slightest experience.

In Victoria I had listened eagerly to people like George Woodcock on the radio program *Critically Speaking* every Sunday afternoon. Now I myself was invited to review books on the CBC with well-known critics like Kildare Dobbs, Robert Weaver, and the encyclopedic Robert Fulford. William French, the book editor of the *Globe and Mail*, signed me on as a regular reviewer. Always short of cash, I wrote two small books to pay for the children's holidays. One was on Browning for Coles Notes, something I hid from my snobbish colleagues, although it was nothing of which to be ashamed. The other was a study of Gabrielle Roy for a short-lived series on Canadian writers initiated by Bob Weaver and Bill French, the first book in English devoted exclusively to her work. I don't think Roy was happy with my contention that she manipulated her characters like a puppeteer. During 1968-69 I turned out a weekly book column for the *Toronto Star;* later I was book editor for the *Canadian Forum*. How on earth did I fit all this in?

I loved the reviewing, but I squirm now if I read anything I produced in those days. Many of my reviews were arrogant and show-offish, liberally laced with words like "otiose." It is true that I lavished praise on Margaret Atwood's *Survival* and Alice Munro's *Lives of Girls and Women* – but woe betide anyone who criticized a sensitive Canadian author at that time. I am embarrassed by an intemperate review of Scott Symons's *Place d'Armes*. I still think it was a ridiculously pretentious book, but I needn't have taken a hammer to swat a fly. I also stand by what I had to say about Margaret Laurence's *A Jest of God* and Marian Engel's second novel, which I described as a disappointment after *Clouds of Glory*. Engel and I studiously avoided each other at parties, but one evening we ran into each other outside a cloakroom. I apologized for having hurt her and Marian burst into tears. "You are a very honest lady," she said. Later she produced the unexpected masterpiece *Bear*, which I praised to the skies; I cannot understand why it is not sufficiently recognized for the great novel it is.

I was so unenthusiastic about *A Jest of God* that I went to talk to Margaret Laurence about it – something I would never dream of doing now. Nothing she said in explanation of the book changed my view that it was pedestrian. I simply should have sent it back to Bill French. Jack McClelland disrupted a cocktail party by shouting that I had ruined sales, and apparently Margaret nursed a grievance against me for the rest of her life. (She and our mutual friend Adele Wiseman spent a lot of time brooding about their grievances.) In a letter written not long before her death she told me that the review had been "stupid." Gradually I stopped reviewing Canadian books altogether.

None of us realized that we were on the brink of a literary renaissance, one that was galvanized by Jack McClelland. I first met him when I received the Governor General's Award: he jumped up at the ceremony and made an impromptu speech, chastising the Canada Council for not doing more to celebrate our authors. Within a decade, thanks in large part to his encouragement, Canada was producing some of the finest writers anywhere.

I began to review regularly for the now defunct BBC journal the

Listener, and occasionally for the *New York Times*. I lost my chance to be a regular contributor to the *New York Review of Books*. On the advice of the British art historian Francis Haskell, who had written a laudatory review of my Symonds book for the recently founded *Review,* the editor, Robert Silvers, sent me Edmund Wilson's *O Canada,* an account of the impressions of Canadian culture he had picked up after spending a brief period here in order to avoid the IRS, whom he saw as hounding him to pay his back taxes. I thought the book simplistic and condescending, and said so. Silvers wrote back that I had not really understood (viz. "appreciated") Wilson, and enclosed a kill fee of $75. (Silvers was right: Wilson wrote perceptively about French-Canadian literature, an area ignored by Anglo-Canadian critics.) Mordecai Richler eventually reviewed the book. At that time, living in England, Mordecai was going through one of his I-hate-Canada phases and agreed with Wilson's contempt for our Calvinist attitudes. It was years before Silvers asked me to write for him again, and later when I was publishing frequently in the *Review,* we never alluded to the earlier incident.

This sort of occasional writing was manageable, although I stretched myself to the limit physically and was often ill. In 1968 I had a hysterectomy. With the demands of a heavy job and a family, another full-length book was out of the question. Mavor used to say that after the success of *Symonds* I was terrified of failure, but that had little to do with it. My university duties seemed to become ever more onerous. While I avoided administration, I took on so many graduate students that there was hardly enough time in the day to perform adequately. The universities had expanded in the prosperity of the late sixties, and young people were attracted to academic careers. October and April were particularly exhausting months when the graduate students had both oral and written exams, and these entailed the examiners' being more prepared than the students.

A few younger women such as Anne Lancashire were on the

staff, but as the senior woman in my college's English department I soon developed into the resident psychiatrist. The students seemed to feel relaxed enough with me to pour out their troubles. One incident put an end to this. A student persuaded a colleague across the hall from my office to interrupt a seminar I was giving with the whispered message that I was to see someone about an emergency. I discovered an agitated gay student who wanted me to listen to the account of his breakup with his boyfriend. From that moment I decided that I would listen to any problems concerning academic work, but personal crises were verboten.

I had been hired as an assistant professor, and three years later there were no indications that I would be promoted to associate. Each time I was passed over by men with lesser qualifications. I began to brood about my suspended status. At a meeting of the full professors (who were responsible for promotion and tenure decisions) my name had arisen, and one colleague remarked condescendingly, "Does the department really owe anything to Mrs. Grosskurth?" Michael Millgate reportedly replied that I was far better known internationally than anyone in that room, but still there was no action.

Finally I decided to confront Professor Leech myself. Throughout our conversation he never once looked at me directly. I began by asking if he could give me any explanation as to why I was not being promoted. Silence. I then raised the point that I was being passed over by men with far fewer publications, etc. Silence. "I would have thought, Professor Leech, that you at least would support me," I said craftily, hoping that this might elicit some response. At last he spoke: "I'll take your concerns to the committee." "And while you're speaking to them," I said firmly, "you might tell the committee that if I am not promoted within a week I intend to resign." What on earth had got into me? I had three teenage children for whom I was largely responsible financially. The shy young woman who had blushed if an admiral's wife spoke to her was no more. Within a week I received a brusque note from Leech announcing my promotion. I was not surprised that there was not a word of congratulation from my chairman.

Shortly after this incident Leech was forced to retire when he reached sixty-five. Professor Woodhouse had misled him with promises that he could stay on in the honorary position of University Professor beyond the mandatory retirement age. His wife returned to her home in Germany, and he lived alone and embittered in a book-lined apartment. I felt sorry for the old boy, whom I would sometimes visit. His kitchen was piled high with empty bottles of Bloody Mary mix. We became almost chummy, and he loved to gossip about people in the department.

It seems ironic that Dave Godfrey and I, who became friends on the Writers-in-Residence Committee, had to wage a battle to have Canadian books put on the curriculum, an effort that was greeted by sniping from our colleagues. Dave was a great nationalist, and a founder of Anansi Press. At a meeting that neither of us could attend, the committee voted to abolish the position of writer-in-residence at the university. I was stunned that Robertson Davies supported the cancellation of this program, confirmed subsequently by President John Evans, even though it was funded by the Canada Council. Dave and I made an appointment to see Evans, and our passionate arguments apparently convinced him to reinstate the position.

Rob Davies was then the first master of the newly founded Massey College, which he was intent on making into a replica of an Oxford college. While Davies had a considerable body of work behind him, he didn't enjoy real fame until the publication of the Deptford trilogy, beginning with *Fifth Business* in 1970. He was an extraordinary phenomenon in that his great creative period coincided with the last twenty years of his life, years in which people are supposed to fade away into senility.

Rob and Brenda Davies hosted splendid dinner parties at the college. Few academics were invited, and I was aware that I was invited primarily as Mavor's wife. I knew, too, that the students made fun of Davies as a pompous fop. I would glance down with embarrassment as a group of about twelve of us in evening dress made our way, crocodile fashion, across the Common Room before mounting the stairs to the private dining room. The students stared blatantly at this procession with vast amusement.

I liked the company of journalists, and my greatest pal was Nathan Cohen, the flamboyant drama critic of the *Toronto Star*, with whom I enjoyed many long lunches, usually at Sutton Place, during which we discussed literature, drama, everything under the sun. A Jewish boy from Cape Breton, he had created a colourful persona, replete with a silver-topped cane. He was the most brilliant conversationalist I have ever encountered. There was not a hint of romance between us, but one day I realized that he must be a bit in love with me because he said suddenly, "Mavor and I met you at about the same time – but I couldn't hurt my wife by leaving her." I changed the subject quickly. When he began to write critically of Mavor and the St. Lawrence Centre in his column, Mavor angrily and justifiably insisted that I stop seeing him. I missed those leisurely luncheons.

A DARK TIME

During those early years of my marriage to Mavor I saw little of my parents, who were constantly travelling. Then over eighty, Dad was working for the Grolier Company, and year after year he took the award as top salesman. Nevertheless, they lived very frugally while Dad put money away for Garry and Mother so that they could manage after his death. I was longing to show Mother my new home, but she never saw it. In 1969 she began to complain of extreme fatigue and was admitted to hospital in the late summer. Joan and Mother had not communicated in over twenty years, and Mother had never made any attempt to contact her, but apparently Virginia told Joan that her condition was serious, and some sort of ad hoc reconciliation seems to have taken place.

Dad was very vague about the nature of Mother's illness, so I telephoned the doctor myself. He was blunt. "Mrs. Moore, your mother is dying of lung cancer. Nothing can be done for her." Stunned, I replaced the receiver. Apparently she had had breast cancer some years before and had told none of us, and now it had spread to her lungs. She admired people who kept these things to themselves. Aunt Phyllis had died of breast cancer and she had talked openly about her illness before it claimed her. Her sisters abruptly changed the subject.

After class every day I would hurry to the Wellesley Hospital. Mother lay there, her eyes large with paranoid anxieties. As black orderlies passed down the corridor outside her door, she would whisper, "This place is full of sinister-looking people." Once she asked anxiously, "You do think I am going to get well, don't you?" "Of course," I reassured her. I longed to lean over and clutch her hand, and to smooth her hair back from her forehead. I wanted to be able to tell Mother how much I loved her, but I was frozen. I sat there bleakly, feeling absolutely nothing.

One afternoon in mid-September I was on my way to meet a new graduate class for the first time when Miss Stephenson, the departmental secretary, hurried out of her office to tell me that I was wanted at the hospital immediately. I decided that I had a responsibility to the students to give them a very quick summary of what we were going to do in the course. It was the wrong decision. By the time I reached the hospital Mother had lapsed into a coma. Joan and Virginia, who had kept vigil, went out to a nearby restaurant to get a bite to eat. Dad and I took over. Mother's breathing became very laboured and we heard a faint rattling in her throat. Finally the breathing ceased, and Dad felt her pulse. Gone. She began to stiffen immediately. In what seemed a blasphemous, horrible act Dad and I pulled and tugged until we managed to extricate her engagement ring from her little hand.

The nurses bustled in. They pushed us aside while they quickly covered her with a sheet. Dad paced up and down the room, muttering, "Oh dear. Oh dear!" My sisters, stunned, appeared at the door. I confess to a feeling of triumph, as though it had been my birthright, to be the one who was with her when she died. The next few days were a blur. Mother was so emaciated that I insisted the coffin be closed at the funeral. Her clothes were stored in our basement, and every time I saw her pathetic navy pillbox hat with its cluster of white flowers, I nearly collapsed.

I returned to my teaching duties. One morning I was hurrying through the cloister on my way to lecture, hoping to pop into the washroom first. A colleague stopped me, determined to commit me to writing a review for the *University of Toronto Quarterly*, a delay that meant there was not sufficient time to go to the washroom. After class I was unable to urinate – in fact, not for the entire day. About three o'clock the following morning I felt a dreadful burning sensation and rushed to the bathroom. The bowl was filled with blood. Mavor called an ambulance and I was taken to the Wellesley Hospital.

The diagnosis was nephritis, a serious kidney ailment. I was given antibiotics, but still the infection persisted. The chief internist was convinced that there was some connection between my illness and Mother's death. After persistent pleas he persuaded me to talk to a psychiatrist, Dr. H. I felt absolutely mortified when he moved me to the psychiatric wing. Heaven forbid that any of my colleagues should learn I was there.

One evening Mavor said to me gently, "I have something to tell you, and I want you to be absolutely calm. Joan and Hal are breaking up." In shock and disbelief I broke into uncontrollable weeping. Why should I react so extremely when I had never particularly liked my brother-in-law? The next night Dad visited. I kept choking back sobs. "My, my," remarked Dad, "we are emotional tonight." "Dad," I said, "something terrible has happened. Joan and Hal are separating." "High time," he replied dismissively; then, turning to an apparently greater concern, he asked, "What do you think of this Trudeau letting all these Biafrans into the country? Think of them walking up and down Yonge Street!" I began to laugh so hard at my bigoted father that I almost fell out of bed.

Undoubtedly Dr. H. did what he could to help me, but he never seemed to grasp that my overreaction to my sister's sorrow was displacement for my repressed grief over Mother's death. No matter how Mother had treated me, in my deepest heart I loved her passionately and knew she loved me too. But I needed a prolonged analysis years later to come to terms with my ambivalence towards her.

Dr. H.'s assistant once asked me what was probably a standard psychiatric question, but one that has lodged in my heart ever since: "What are your joys?" There were so many I couldn't begin to list them all: taking a different route home on my walk back from the university every day; making squash soup in the autumn; the dark skeletal branches of the trees on an overcast day in winter. It was a wonderful question, and even in the midst of illness and depression, I could find relief in contemplating the answer.

Mavor and particularly my children were my treasured supports during my hospitalization. Each day they would ring and say, "Be of good heart," advice we still offer comfortingly to one another. Once when Brian was visiting I mentioned that I had been born in the Wellesley. "And perhaps," this teenager with shoulder-length hair said gently, "you will be reborn here."

I had been thin before entering hospital; when I emerged almost three months later I was positively gaunt. An old friend with whom I had been to college didn't recognize me when we met for lunch. One would think that after this ordeal I would order things so that life would be relatively tranquil – but unfortunately it was not to be.

I continued to suffer periodic, sometimes debilitating depressions. I knew I was meant to be a happy person – as the gypsy at Epsom had told me some years before – but it was as though a glass wall separated me from the sustained joy to which I was holding out my hand. It is hard to recall now precisely what the experience was like except that I felt enveloped in a dark cloud of self-absorption. There were times when I believed that Mother had taken over my body, or that there was something evil inside me. It is easier to explain in negative terms. It is *never* waking in the morning eager to see what the day will bring. It is *not* feeling the joy of sunshine on one's face in early spring. It is *the absence* of a sense of giving pleasure and comfort to others. Occasionally I felt suicidal. One evening I climbed to Brian's room on the third floor to tell him what I was brooding about. I expected sympathy, but I received truth. "Mum," he exploded, "how can you be so selfish! Think of what it would do to us!"

Dad was extremely lonely after Mother's death and spent a lot of time at our house. He liked talking to Mavor. I cannot overstate the kindness and consideration Mavor showed him. Once Dad asked him if he believed in immortality, and Mavor pointed to his granddaughter Anne. Among us the silent, preoccupied man disappeared and Dad gradually regained the jolly, laughing self he had lost so many years before. He doted on Christopher, whom he saw as the son he would have liked to have had. I can still see him standing at the door after spending an evening with us, his hand on his cane, smiling: "Much obliged."

Nevertheless, we were concerned about him because he was sharing a house with Garry, whose behaviour was more bizarre than ever. One night Dad arrived at our door in a state of terror: he had to lock himself in the bathroom for fear Garry would harm him. We had a family conference, and it was decided that Garry would have to be put into the hands of the medical authorities. Apparently he was very docile when two attendants arrived at the house. He was placed in Whitby Sanitorium for a time. Dad died about a year later, distraught at the end because Garry was pressuring him for money.

For many years I had no idea of the intensity of my parents' misery, and certainly they never confided in their daughters. It was not until Dad's death that the full extent of their desperation was made palpable to us. When we entered Garry's room in the now-empty house we were horrified to discover an arsenal – swords, bows and arrows, knives, pistols, and a repeater rifle with a telescopic lens. My parents had lived with this situation for decades, often escaping to a motel when he became violent. All three sisters, after psychiatric advice, decided that we could get on with the lives of our families only by cutting off all ties with him. We felt it imperative to protect ourselves and our children from physical danger and emotional distress by distancing ourselves permanently from Garry, who refused to take his medication. Nevertheless, we were burdened with guilt for turning our backs on our brother. Dad had left him a small trust fund which lasted until his death in 1998. His ashes were mixed with those of our parents.

CONTROVERSY

I again threw myself into my work, but found little peace there either. In 1972 I was permitted to teach a course on biography and autobiography. I used certain basic texts like *The Odyssey,* the *Confessions* of Saint Augustine, Boswell's life of Dr. Johnson, and Rousseau's *Confessions,* replacing various other texts each year. I asked a specialist in each area to give the introductory lecture; one was Jack Robson, who generously gave his time to speak on John Stuart Mill. It was an exciting course, and the students invariably gave it a high evaluation. I was thrilled when the students' Anti-Calendar recommended it, describing me as one of the most charismatic teachers on the campus. However, a few of my colleagues felt that the course was a travesty of the basic canon, that biography wasn't a legitimate subject, and at least one of them set about trying to have it removed. As an undergraduate I had imagined that those who taught the humanities must belong to a superior species of being, but it didn't take me long to learn how petty and vindictive academics could be.

I continued to love my students and my classes and to maintain a passionate belief in the university. With my temperament and loyalty to learning, I was not a good choice as an appointment to the Committee on University Affairs, a buffer body established in 1973 by the Tory provincial government to make recommendations on how funding should be distributed among the fourteen Ontario universities. The free-spending days of support for higher education were over, and our central mandate seemed to be to identify areas where cuts could be made. Possibly someone had the mistaken idea that I could easily be manipulated.

The noted economist Sylvia Ostry and I were among the few non-political members of the committee. I was appalled by the animosity expressed towards the universities, encouraged by the chairman, Douglas Wright (later president of the University of Waterloo), who seemed to regard them as centres of elitism which needed to have their wings clipped. We visited most of the universities in the province. Over Christmas we were given a thick brief summarizing our findings. Tucked into the middle was a memo from the Privy Council enumerating areas where cuts would be made or fees raised, none of which had been discussed with the universities. It appeared obvious to me that the government had used the committee as a facade, a rubber stamp for decisions that had already been taken.

The document was marked "Highly Confidential," but I showed it to Mavor, who agreed with my interpretation. We decided to ask Claude Bissell, who had recently resigned as president of the University of Toronto, if he would look at it. (In my estimation, Claude was the best president we have had within living memory. As Norrie Frye said, "He never embarrassed us.") After Claude had studied it, he echoed my conviction that I had no alternative but to resign. Consequently, to the discomfort of the government, I resigned – very noisily – and began to make speeches about how the universities were being depleted. The whole situation was highly fraught, and naturally the government people encouraged rumours that I was hysterical. Nevertheless, I still have the letter from Sylvia in which she told me how much she admired my spunk.

But I was also angry with the students who staged sit-ins during this period. It was never clear why they were protesting. Canada was not involved in the Vietnam War but, as Bissell remarked, it was as though some virus had spread across the continent. One of the few times I lost my temper in class was in an exchange with a student who had led a demonstration at the Robarts Library. I raged at him that such tactics would lose what little public sympathy was left for the universities. The only good development in this period was the appearance in class of American draft dodgers, students far more mature than our own.

It is hard to recognize the edgy, agitated woman of those years. I seemed to be involved in one row after another. At the National Film Board I was a thorn in the flesh of Sydney Newman (who had succeeded Hugo Macpherson as film commissioner). I was egged on by John Grierson, the famous documentary filmmaker, who was also enraged by Newman's autocratic ways. Some years ago I came across Grierson's letters to me and inexplicably threw them out. How could a biographer be stupid enough to destroy such valuable historical documents?

ANOTHER ENDING

I longed to get back to what I fondly imagined would be the peace and quiet of the lecture hall, little knowing that the worst battle of all lay ahead of me. By now I had been promoted to full professor, but I was not destined to enjoy its gratifications. Sitting among my peers who made all the major departmental decisions, I felt as though as I had stumbled into a Boy Scout troop, and that I was a damper on all their fun.

It happened that my promotion coincided with a moment when an unusual number of candidates came up for tenure – fourteen in all. (The reason for the disproportionate number was the overhiring of Americans in the previous decade.) I listened in horror, thinking of mortgages and small children, as lives and careers were disposed of. I was not so sentimental as to believe that all of these people should be kept on, but there were certain colleagues for whom I argued strenuously. One was Peter Dyson, a Henry James scholar who had arrived from Princeton in 1968 and who had a reputation as a superb teacher. He and I had become friends when we got into a discussion about how I had tried to persuade a stubborn Leon Edel about Henry James's homosexuality. When Peter's name came up in the tenure debates, I caught a whiff of homophobia, but it was not something about which I could make any solid accusations.

The result of these deliberations was that twelve people were dismissed, Peter among them. I was sick at heart and during the summer did a lot of brooding. Peter hired a lawyer to fight his case. At a departmental meeting in the fall I made a sort of *"J'accuse"* speech, expressing my misgivings about the lack of consistent procedures in the tenure decisions. During the course of the year there was one stormy meeting after another. I had become *persona non grata* to my peers, living proof of the dangers of hiring a woman. A number of people who agreed with me kept their heads down out of the line of fire. In actual fact only a small group led the fight, but we were absolutely tenacious.

President John Evans reopened six of the cases, and three individuals, including Peter, were reinstated. Even more important, consistent tenure proceedings were instituted throughout the university. I felt as though we had been engaged in a holy war, and I was exhausted and disenchanted.

Although Mavor had been supportive in all these causes, my role as a self-appointed whistle-blower had not helped our relationship. Years later I met Daniel Ellsberg, who had leaked the Pentagon Papers to the *New York Times* during the Nixon administration. He seemed locked in that dramatic point in time, and I became reflective over the compulsions that drive such personalities. As Ellsberg said to me, whistle-blowers should never expect thanks.

In the early part of our marriage Mavor himself had been engaged in endless bickering with the politicians over the financing of the St. Lawrence Centre. I did not give him the moral support he needed. Leading parallel and overextended lives, we never had the time to establish real intimacy. We had both brought too much unresolved emotional baggage to the marriage.

At first we had done some travelling together. Sometimes I went with him to Prince Edward Island, where he had been a founding father of the Confederation Centre in Charlottetown. In 1968 I accompanied him to the World Theatre Festival in Budapest and Bucharest (also attended by Jean-Louis Roux), after which we went on to Turkey and Greece for a holiday. Mavor had always had a hankering to take a cruise. I pictured women preening themselves in fashionable wardrobes and had to be talked into it. It turned out to be one of the most wonderful trips of my life. In May 1973 we boarded a small Italian liner in Venice and sailed across the Mediterranean to Lebanon. Beirut, approached by sea, was a marvellous sight. At the ruins of Baalbek I bought a Coptic cross and a tiny Roman lachrymatory which marked the beginning of an obsessional quest for antiquities. We visited Rhodes, Cyprus, Syria, southern Turkey, Crete – all of which enriched Mavor's classical interests – and on our return stopped at Barcelona before disembarking at Genoa.

One evening shortly after our return, Brian, Anne, and I were walking along Queen Street, looking in the little shops. I pointed: "Look! Those are *Roman* bowls!" The next morning I hurried back to the shop. The young man received regular shipments of antiquities from his father in Lebanon. I bought the three little bowls, and each time there was a new shipment Sam would ring me at my office. I would rush down and return with some treasure. At first my taste was wildly eclectic – Sumerian, Egyptian, Greek, Roman. Gradually I became fixated on thirteenth-century Persian ceramics. These exquisite (and expensive) turquoise Kashan bowls and ewers became a passion. I sold my first editions, my mink cape, almost anything, in order to possess them. Apart from love affairs and biographical research, it is the only time in my life when I have been in the grip of a compulsive obsession. Not only were these things gorgeous, they were old, rooted, in ancient civilizations. In my new marriage I didn't feel rooted, and this passion may have been an unconscious projection of my longing for things that had survived.

Both Mavor and I, try as we might, could not overcome our guilt for having broken up our first families. I became particularly depressed every Christmas, feeling as though I were besmirching a sacred ritual. I felt doubly guilty for marrying the husband of a woman I loved and respected. She had told me that as far as she was concerned the marriage was over, but I felt – and still feel – that I had betrayed a friend. At the social events we attended, my status was predetermined: wife of a cultural icon. (Once we were separated, I discovered how fragile that position had been.) But I was no more suited to being the wife of a public figure than to trailing behind a naval officer, and I felt pulled between two poles: serious academic or reluctant socialite. What sort of life *did* I want?

I am not a great believer in astrology, but Mavor and I were both Pisceans – in other words, two driven people. More important than the stars was the fact that we each had internalized demanding mothers whom we couldn't do enough to satisfy. He was even more of a workaholic than I. Many people criticized him for becoming too quickly bored after starting some enterprise, but this desire for new challenges was attractive and I shared the same tendencies. (I have never been able to understand academics who spend their entire lives on a single subject.)

I recently reread Mavor's autobiography, *Reinventing Myself*, and was struck again at how much Mavor contributed to the cultural life of this country. It was very clear that public life was his element in those years, and consequently he felt restive with the demands of a prolonged relationship. My attempts to make a life where we would have more time together were met with resistance. Partly because of my pressure he took a position in the fine arts department at York University. There seemed little discernible change. We knew innumerable people but never seemed to form close mutual friendships. At parties I was constantly apprehensive that at least one of his old girlfriends would appear. He sometimes ordered alterations to the house without consulting me. I resented the fact that he assumed that he should have a study, whereas there was none for me. What I did seemed of secondary importance; certainly it was so in the eyes of my formidable mother-in-law, Dora Mavor Moore, the grande dame of the Canadian theatre, and a woman who absolutely terrified me. Every marriage has its irritations, and if Mavor were to write frankly about our marriage I am sure he would have a substantial list.

A temporary diversion absorbed some of my restlessness. The embargo on the Symonds memoirs was due to be lifted in 1976, and the London Library asked me to undertake the task of editing the manuscript. I was the logical choice, but someone like my English friend Timothy D'Arch Smith, who is a bibliographer by nature, would have been much happier at the onerous job of assembling footnotes. I accepted only because I was so eager to have some literary work, and I spent two summers at what for me was drudgery. One of my students, Cynthia Good (now president of Penguin Canada), assisted me. For reasons about which I am not altogether clear, the volume wasn't published until 1984, and of course by then I had lost any interest I ever had in it.

Mavor never enjoyed travelling as much as I did, so I began to go off on my own to places like Corsica and Madeira. Christopher had taken time off from university to backpack around the world, and I thought, If he can do it, so can I. On arriving back in Marseilles after a trip to Corsica, I had planned to visit Carcassonne (which I had once glimpsed from a train window) only to discover that France was in the grip of one of its innumerable rail strikes. I jumped on the last bus to leave the city and ended up in Grenoble, a real serendipity. After reading Wordsworth and Matthew Arnold I had always wanted to see the alpine monastery of the Grande Chartreuse. Its ethereal serenity, with cattle scattered about on the high plateaus, exceeded all my hopes. The monks, who had taken a vow of silence, lived in cells, and their meals were passed to them through a grating. Behind each cell their individual gardens were surrounded by high walls. Such peace was balm to my soul after the turbulence of the preceding years. At some point on one of these solitary trips, during a bout of homesickness, I remember thinking melodramatically, "I am preparing myself for a life of loneliness."

I did feel somewhat alone and isolated in my marriage. I am convinced that people who have rock-solid partnerships are not tempted to have affairs. That was not my situation. I became totally infatuated with the stunningly attractive Davidson Dunton, former president of the CBC, whom I had met when he was president of Carleton University in the sixties. A mutual attraction probably started then, but nothing developed until September of 1975, when I received a call from him in Ottawa saying that he was coming to Toronto and could I have lunch with him. That single encounter at Le Provençal was all it took. Our affair was exciting because it was furtive, but it was also soul-destroying because it inevitably involved deceit and guilt. Davy would have liked it to continue as a torrid romance, but that would have been impossible for me to handle. Like most women, I would have tried to domesticate the relationship.

Late one February night I was on the telephone to Davy when Mavor walked into the room. I imagine that he suspected something was going on. I confessed, and Mavor decided that the marriage was over. He was as adamant as I had been with BG. He had always admired Davy, particularly for the way he had steered the CBC through its early days, and I think it was particularly painful to him that I should be involved with someone in his own field. I do not think it was a matter of blame on either side. We now see that our marriage served as a transitional – and loving – bridge in each other's lives. Certainly we have remained very good friends.

Early the following morning, I was to leave for Mexico with my friend Sonya Sinclair. It was hard for poor Sonya to be faced with a travelling companion in a tremulous emotional condition. She promised that in Zihuatenejo I would find total tranquillity under a tree beside the sea. What I found was a group of couples who vacationed there together every year and partied every evening. The last thing I wanted to do was make small talk with total strangers. All I had brought to read were three novels by Joyce Carol Oates about murder and mayhem. I have never read a novel of hers since. Then I came down with a debilitating case of dysentery and lay day after day in a spartan room while lizards chased each other over the walls. It took me over twenty years to muster the courage to return to Mexico.

In 1976 Mavor and I were both due for a sabbatical. The original plan was that we were to go to England together, but Mavor had never been enthusiastic about the idea. I believe that like many celebrities in his own country, he would have felt lost in England, where he had no recognizable standing and no project to keep him occupied. When I returned to Toronto from the hellish Mexican trip, Mavor and I agreed that we would tell the children we had decided to separate, but no one else was to know. We continued to attend social events together, and most people assumed that I was simply going off to England for a year of academic research. We put the house up for sale, and I numbly packed the boxes of household possessions, some marked "Mavor" and others "Pat."

Women of my generation were supposed to make a marriage work. I told myself that I should have tried to find time to play bridge or badminton, hobbies we could have shared. But most of all I believed that I was being rightly punished because I had been unfaithful. Not long ago Mavor told me earnestly that I was too hard on myself about the failure of our marriage; that we should remember all the wonderful things we did for each other. It was an extremely generous thing for him to say. He is right, but I am still working on it.

I was determined to buy a small house in Toronto that would be waiting for me when I returned. Sheila, the real estate agent who had negotiated the purchase of the Macpherson Avenue house, now drove us around looking for a home for me. It was ludicrous. Mavor, who had made all the major decisions in our marriage, was determined to make this one too. My travels in Toronto had been confined generally to the university campus and to a few pleasant residential areas. Both the east and west ends of the city were terra incognita. Sheila drove us to a section east of Parliament Street known as Cabbagetown, after its original Irish settlers, which was now being gentrified. I spotted a "For Sale" sign on a house at the end of Spruce Street. "You wouldn't be interested in that," said Sheila, turning down a side street. While the car was moving I jumped out, then knocked on the door of the house. A nice Australian showed me around, and I knew immediately that this little 1870 cottage was meant for me.

Sheila protested because she didn't have the listing. Mavor protested for reasons of which I do not think he was altogether conscious. Did he want me to buy an old, broken-down place that would require extensive renovations, not a place where I would be undeservedly comfortable? It seemed ridiculous that a husband who was about to separate from his wife should have put up such spirited obstructions. I needed Anne's support, and as soon as she saw the house, she knew it was the right decision.

My worries about Brian dropping out of school had been resolved. He returned to do a makeup year for entrance into university and went at it with the determination of someone working on a Ph.D. As a result he graduated with the Governor General's Gold Medal and went on to win scholarships to the École des Grandes Études in Paris and to Oxford. Christopher's globetrotting adventures made me anxious. I used to tell him that he should have lived in the days of the Bengal Lancers. When he was in Australia I wrote an unsolicited letter of advice to the effect that I wished he would get a proper job. Little did I know that his wide knowledge of the world would eventually land him a position at the CBC as a documentary-maker. Many of our worries about our children, I think, reflect a failure to have sufficient faith in them.

Anne and Brian were both in university sharing an apartment at the time of the separation. Only a few days before I was to leave on my sabbatical, Christopher returned from his second backpacking trip around the world, accompanied by his girlfriend, Fiona MacLeod.

When he heard the news of the separation he looked bemused – as he has often done when confronted with unexpected situations within his eccentric family. The boys came into my train compartment to say goodbye as I left for Montreal, there to board the ship that would take me to England. I told them how much I loved them and how proud I was of them.

The train slipped out of the station. A former priest had comforted me: "You are going to find strengths you didn't know you had." A late starter in everything, I was on my way to face the first really great hurdles in growing up. "Je vais avoir cinquante ans," said Stendhal; "il serait bien temps de me connaître."

5

EXILE

When people speak of their "favourite cities," they are very often creating fantasies constructed from a few happy memories. Venice, Rio, Vienna – how many of their aficionados have actually lived and worked in these romanticized worlds? I would never name London as one of my favourite cities because we know each other too well. Depending on mood and circumstance, it has welcomed and rejected me, and I have loved and hated it in turn. What it does offer – even when I think I don't want it – is the reassurance of familiarity.

My arrival there in June of 1976 was entirely different from that of 1960. Sixteen years earlier I had the security of a family and the pleasure of a beautiful house. Now, raw from the separation from Mavor, I had no conception of the future. I felt like an exile, a transient who had no idea where she was going or what she might encounter. I had a vague notion that I might finally take up the long-deferred book on Matthew Arnold. On the way over, I had had a shipboard romance with a gratifyingly attentive Swiss, but once on land we were embarrassed and went our separate ways. I can't even remember Oscar's last name.

I had rented a flat from a colleague but couldn't gain possession of it until August. In the interim I moved into Crosby Hall, a university women's residence on the Embankment only a few blocks from the house in which all five of us had lived during the sixties. The weather was stiflingly hot, and I would lie in bed naked, covered with wet towels, and utterly bewildered about how I had come to find myself in

123

this situation. Finally, I phoned my friend Peter Dyson, who was taking a sabbatical in southern France with his partner, Marc Topham. Might I come and stay with them for a few days?

Peter and Marc drove to Marseilles to collect me. They were staying in the enchanting Provençal village of Roussillon, which was still a real village with a *boulangerie*, an *épicerie,* and a *boucherie*. I stayed for about a week, and one night I took them as a treat to a three-star restaurant, Oustaù de Beaumanière (I believe the bill came to slightly over $100), where we dined in the moonlight beside a pool. They gave me kindness and love without a hint of moral reproach.

I couldn't inflict myself on them for long as they were preparing to return to Canada, so I decided to travel around France, following the coast wherever possible. My Swiss friend had told me about a wonderful hotel in Giens, on a spit beyond Hyères, east of Marseilles. It was a Bonnard paradise: my room overlooked a pine forest that dropped steeply to the sea and a pool carved out of the rock. Beyond lay the rugged Île de Porquerolles, the setting for Conrad's novel *The Rover*. The setting could not have been more romantic, but it meant nothing in my solitary state.

An advantage of travelling alone is that one falls into conversation with total strangers in train compartments, and my comprehension improved immeasurably in the heated discussions over trivialities that the French love. In Provence the necessary contents for a genuine *bouillabaisse* can provide the source for endless discussion. There is general agreement that only in Marseilles can one taste the genuine article because there the essential ingredient, *rascasse,* will undoubtedly be fresh. True enough, someone adds, but the fish must have its head on when added to the stew. A third party interjects that it is also important to include *langouste* and mussels. General indignation. That may be how Parisians eat it, but that is only because the *rascasse* will not be fresh. A lively and agreeable conversation on this single topic can be maintained throughout the entire journey between Marseilles and Toulouse.

From Biarritz on the Atlantic coast I travelled north through Les Landes, the dense pine region I knew from the novels of François Mauriac. I had intended to avoid Paris, but in Bordeaux I was told that I would have to change trains in Paris in order to reach the Cherbourg peninsula.

In Paris, my overconfidence in my French would lead to trouble. On arrival I had an early meal off the Champs-Élysées, a touristy area I usually avoid. The man at the adjoining banquette and I started complaining about the service – and fell into conversation. I believe his name was Jacques. It transpired that we both liked jazz. Would I like to go to a jazz club with him? "*Bien sûr.*" That was my first mistake. I was a little puzzled by its name – the Garden Club. Was this some kind of horticultural society? Jacques drove us to a street not far from the Arc de Triomphe. I had been reading in the *Herald Tribune* that tourists were having their passports snatched, so I insisted on leaving mine in the trunk of the car. Mistake number two.

We entered a most luxurious club and descended a curving staircase to a dimly lit dance floor. As my eyes gradually became accustomed to the gloom I discerned a couple – sometimes a threesome – in noisy and intimate embrace only feet away from us. I pointed, incredulous, but my companion looked totally unconcerned. I told Jacques I wanted to leave. He shrugged his shoulders: we had only just arrived. With my passport in his trunk, I was obliged to stay.

A man approached and asked me to dance. Every time I passed Jacques I gave him a sharp kick. I found that if I kept changing partners, I was left relatively unscathed. Actually when I turned down invitations – or suggestions – the men were very polite and didn't take offence. In the background were moans and screams which I pretended to ignore. I asked one very attractive man what he was doing in a place like this. "This is a very nice place," he assured me, "and the people are *très gentils*." Another man – married less than a year – told me that he and his wife looked forward to coming every week. Regulars, like at a pub.

Finally people began to drift away, but not in the drunken, boisterous way they do at pubs. Jacques, who hadn't danced all evening, reluctantly rose to pay the bill. I sat dejected and exhausted from the effort not to succumb to the atmosphere, with perhaps a tear coursing down my cheeks. "*La pauvre*," lamented the married man with genuine sympathy, "*elle est triste.*" At last my passport was returned to me – I had given up all hope of ever seeing it again – but Jacques didn't move the car. *Qu'est-ce qui se passe?* "He [the married man] likes you and wants the four of us to spend the night together." *Comment??* The other car pulled up beside us, and from his window the married man apologized effusively. He was *désolé, absolument*, but his wife was totally *épuisée* (I wasn't surprised considering the activities in which she had been engaged), and since she had to get up early in the morning, he feared our arrangement wasn't possible.

Driving down the Champs-Élysées I harangued Jacques for having misled me. Didn't he realize that people could pick up diseases from such indiscriminate sex? "*Tout est possible*," he shrugged. It was dawn when I slunk into the hotel, flushed with embarrassment. No one paid the slightest attention to me.

When I awoke, I thought it best to spend the day in spiritual pursuits to cleanse my priggish Canadian soul. I prayed in Notre-Dame. I spent hours wandering up and down in Père-Lachaise. Unfortunately I tripped on a *pavé* and my ankle swelled alarmingly so that I could hardly drag myself up the steps of the Gare Saint-Lazare the following day. I changed my plans and decided to return to England after staying a day or so in Rouen. There the people seemed immeasurably kind. A doctor looked amazed when I thanked him effusively for bandaging my ankle, as though I were thanking him for saving my life.

The Bayswater flat was by then available and at first I rather liked it – a place all my own. The weather was milder; I began to make half-hearted trips to the British Museum. But Matthew Arnold held no excitement for me. Then as I grew accustomed to the Bayswater section, my dislike of it started to grow. I hated the bleak square, I hated Westbourne Grove, and, above all, I hated the brassy vulgarity of Queensway. The flat was small, cramped, and dreary. My sense of disconnection was so extreme that it verged on dread. The only things I had brought of my own were a little bronze Persian horse and a tiny Greek head of a woman. Every time I climbed the stairs – covered in a sickening shade of brown – and put my key in the lock I was assailed by a terrible homesickness.

My self-esteem wasn't helped by the number of men who seemed eager to assuage my loneliness. A woman in my position, I discovered, attracts the sharks. Melvin Lasky, the editor of *Encounter*, and Martin Esslin, the head of drama in the BBC, were interesting men, but not particularly nice people. Others took advantage of my vulnerability when I first stumbled into the London literary world. There was the editor who wouldn't give me any books to review when I rebuffed his sexual advances. Another stopped sending me books when I told him as tactfully as possible that I couldn't come to grips with his own novel, which he had given me to review. Yet another flew into a fury because I had done a review for a rival editor whose wife was having an affair with him. I would pass the bag ladies who seemed to congregate in Bayswater, and think, horrified: God, am I going to end up like that?

I suspect I was more than slightly crazy for several months, although I attempted to live as normally as I could. A few years before, in one of the numerous French courses I had taken, the instructor asked a student to give an example of how one would use the verb *"se débrouiller"* – to cope, manage. She sketched a dramatic scenario: one arrives in Paris to find one's luggage missing, one's money stolen, no hotel room available. *"On se débrouille."* With my propensity for disasters, I

127

perked up and *"se débrouiller"* immediately became my favourite French verb. One mislays a husband, one screws up one's life; like a muddled Robinson Crusoe, *"on se débrouille."*

I had to create some kind of viable social life. Invitations would come only if I myself made an effort. I had dinner parties in that grungy flat to which I invited grand people like Gaby and Noël Annan (Lord Annan, soon to be vice-chancellor of the University of London, has always been one of my greatest professional supporters.) I renewed the acquaintance of Ian Scott-Kilvert, a former neighbour in St. Leonard's Terrace. Ian, head of the literature section of the British Council, took me under his wing. A product of Harrow and Caius College, Cambridge, he spoke with the clipped accent of a pre-war BBC announcer. He had been a great hero during the war, parachuting into Greece and working with the partisans.

Ian, who was divorced by then, would cook me a wonderful meal every week and take me to meetings of the Byron Society, of which he was then president. The Byron Society is a literary fan club whose members include many distinguished figures. They hold annual events and excursions celebrating the poet's life. Ian took me on the trip to Byron's school, Harrow, where he excitedly pointed out places that had meant much to him. He was one of the truly good people I have been privileged to know, and I believe there are more of them in this wicked world than we tend to acknowledge. He knew I despised his ardent Toryism, and he simply tolerated my ravings about Margaret Thatcher as part of my zaniness. Ours was an example of the possibility of a friendship when one doesn't share an ideological congruity. It would have been impossible in a marriage.

Another long-time friend, the supremely sophisticated but kindly novelist Francis King, attended meetings of PEN with me. Sometimes I would spend weekends in Tenterden with the veteran writer Harford Montgomery-Hyde and his wife, Robbie, in their beautiful Queen

Anne house. One afternoon Robbie and I were walking in the garden. "Pat," she said sharply, "you've got to stop being Peter Pan." I was taken aback by this rebuke. Harford had recently dedicated *The Cleveland Street Scandal* to me, and I knew Robbie suspected that he fancied me. Now she was suggesting that men were attracted to me because of my seeming helplessness. Angry I might have been, but I needed a jolt like that to stop feeling sorry for myself.

As my byline began to appear regularly in the papers, my professional life became more disciplined and the sharks moved off to other waters. Through various contacts I was asked to review for the *Observer,* the *Daily Telegraph,* and, best of all, on a regular basis for the *Times Literary Supplement* by John Gross, who had abolished the practice of anonymous reviews when he became editor. There was a startling improvement in my writing in comparison with the work I had done for the *Globe and Mail* and it was a relief not to know any of the authors whose books were sent to me. I love reviewing because it demands such close reading to identify what one likes or dislikes in a work. It's necessary to give the reader an incisive summary of the contents, but also an informed judgment. There is always the temptation to be overly self-referential but this is an indulgence that should be resisted. At its best, reviewing is another means of self-education, shared with others.

One of the first long review-articles I did was a piece on Gail Sheehy's *Passages.* The book struck me as a popularized, watered-down version of Erik Erikson's theory of the particular challenges people have to face at each stage of their lives. I was too obtuse to recognize that it contained a message for me: that in living alone far from those I loved I had to find my own emotional strength. In a way I had relied too much on the closeness of my children. I was at one of those critical turning points in what Erikson calls the life cycle when there is an opportunity for real growth.

Intellectual arrogance occasionally became one of my aggressive defences against insecurity. I think this probably explains my negative reaction to a small book on Byron by the doyenne of English biographers, Elizabeth Longford, which Gross sent me to review. I still consider it not up to the standard of her great biographies of Queen Victoria and Wellington. Ian was greatly distressed by the review even though it was only mildly critical: Lady Longford was an honoured member of the Byron Society and thereafter I was forbidden to attend any more meetings.

HAVELOCK ELLIS AND FRIENDS

Some years earlier I had considered writing a biography of the sexologist Havelock Ellis. It was a natural choice since Ellis had collaborated with Symonds on *Sexual Inversion,* a study of homosexuality. I had written to his widowed mistress, Françoise Lafitte, who made it bluntly clear that she would take no part in such an undertaking. Now, late in 1976, I received a letter from her son, Professor François Lafitte, informing me that his mother had died, and that if I would like to visit him in Birmingham, he would be very happy to see me.

With my mind still half focused on Arnold, I made the journey to Birmingham. Lafitte was a small irascible man of febrile temperament but great integrity. He obviously venerated Ellis, whom he called his "adoptive father," although he was the son of another man. He had become executor of the Ellis estate. During lunch we argued rather heatedly about Freud, who I insisted was a far greater figure than Ellis. In the sitting room, over coffee, to my amazement in view of our intense discussion, he announced mildly, "If you would like to write a biography of Havelock, I will give you every assistance." "May I have a few days to think it over?" "Of course."

I returned to London and for days lay sleepless, mulling over this invitation. Of course I must do it. Without consulting the University of Toronto or considering where the funds were to come from, I phoned Lafitte with my answer. "I'm delighted," he replied. I then had to write to the president of the university to request a year's leave of absence without pay. But how was I to live during that year? I drew up a list of all the grant-giving bodies and began the long, slow process of acquiring recommendations and letters of support. With the able assistance of David Sorenson, a gifted former student who was doing graduate work in England, I compiled a list of the libraries holding Ellis material. It also occurred to me that it was time to get a literary agent. If I had a publisher, my chances of obtaining a grant were much enhanced. I actually had no problem persuading my former editor Peter Carson of Allen Lane (formerly Longman) to contract the book, but I still interviewed a number of agents – none of whom seemed right – until a letter came from Jacqueline Korn of David Higham Associates. She suggested that we have lunch. I liked her immediately. Her combination of warmth and toughness appealed to me and while publishers often quake when they have to do business with her, I am still a happy client more than twenty years later. What I have particularly appreciated is the fact that she treats me with the same consideration that she gives to her high-earning authors.

With Noël Annan as one of my referees, I was awarded a Guggenheim grant. Of course there were many moments of panic still ahead. At times of discouragement I would repeat words that a friend had taught me: "*Courage, mon coeur!*" It was fourteen years since I had written the Symonds book, and now I had to absorb the seven volumes of Ellis's *Studies in the Psychology of Sex*, as well as his many other writings. In addition I had to learn all about his life and a good deal about the state of sexual investigation at the time Ellis produced his epochmaking work. Most of Ellis's letters, I discovered, were dispersed among American libraries.

I was befriended by Michael Holroyd, whose biography of Lytton Strachey I had greatly admired. He had by then embarked on his biography of Shaw and had spent a good deal of time in America doing research. He offered some excellent practical advice about resources and contacts there. While the Strachey book had been a great critical success, Michael was in a constant state of anxiety about money in those days, and I remember him as usually tired and dishevelled, far different from the confident figure of today who, I read recently, considers £70,000 a year a fair living. He deserves every penny of it; without any academic safety net, he had undertaken a courageous and hazardous enterprise with the huge Shaw biography.

I began to look after myself more carefully and went regularly to an exercise class at Knightsbridge, coyly named "Granny's" but filled with attractive young "Sloane Rangers"; still I loathed cooking for myself and mainly existed on delicatessen food. Anne scolded me when she came over for Christmas. "Mum, you should really start cooking proper meals for yourself. It would give you creative satisfaction." No, it wouldn't − not in that awful flat. But I have always admired those disciplined people who set a pretty table for themselves and prepare nourishing meals. It is a fine exercise in self-nurturing.

The Victorian scholar Barbara Hardy and I used to fantasize that we were like the women who sit on the windowsill at the beginning of Doris Lessing's *The Golden Notebook* and congratulate themselves on their freedom. Barbara, however, became disenchanted with me. "The trouble with you," she said, "is that you like being married." I was still hoping against hope that Mavor and I could reconcile. He rang me one night in tears. An affair he had been having had broken up, and perhaps, he suggested, there was a faint chance we could get together again.

He decided to come over and visit me in March. When I opened the door to him and he saw the delight on my face, he made it clear that he had no interest in a reconciliation. He denied ever hinting at such a possibility. We went to talk to a Jungian therapist; after some hours she leaned forward and shouted at me, "Pat, you have to face the fact that your marriage is over!" Until that moment I hadn't completely believed it, but it was the kind of shock I needed to realize that I was without any emotional props. Peter Pan had to acquire a shadow.

A month later I was walking down Berkeley Street and, passing a Cook's travel office, thought, "I am completely without ties – there is no reason why I can't just pack up and go." I knew that a man who lived in Geneva had some Ellis papers, so I walked in and they booked me a flight and accommodation at the Hôtel des Bergues. It was an absolutely crazy thing to do without first checking with the owner of the papers. Not surprisingly, when I arrived in Geneva I discovered that he was in New York on a visit. Because of the time difference, I had all day to sightsee; at night, I would try to reach the owner of the letters by telephone.

On my first morning I decided to take a launch around the lake. The boat was about to pull away from the dock just as I was buying my ticket, and I ran to catch it. A man leaped on behind me, just clearing the gap between dock and deck. As we passed the French border "La Marseillaise" suddenly blared out, and the jumper (who was sitting behind me) and I laughed heartily.

It was a blustery day so I was driven to find warmth in the inner cabin below. There I joined two actors from the Berliner Ensemble, which was playing in Geneva at the time. We entered into a lively conversation. Suddenly the man who had jumped on so dangerously appeared on the steps, smiling inquiringly at us. He later told me that he had followed me because he liked my laugh. The four of us had a wonderful time chattering, never giving a glance at the scenery. When we reluctantly parted, the Germans extended a warm invitation to attend a performance as their guests.

I set off for the tourist office, my new companion in tow, to inquire how to reach Voltaire's house at Ferney. (I have returned to Geneva many times, but I have yet to visit Ferney.) The tourist office was closed, and as I climbed to the Old Town I began to wonder why this young man was attaching himself to me. He asked all sorts of direct questions, which I evaded. "How are we going to become friends if you don't tell me something about yourself?" he asked.

We sat down for lunch and I looked at him directly for the first time. He had intelligent brown eyes behind large horn-rimmed glasses, a slightly receding hairline, and a delightfully boyish smile. It emerged he was in his thirties, almost young enough to be my son. There was no danger in relaxing and having a pleasant time. Jorge was an Argentinian whose two brothers were among the *desaparecidos*, and he had left his country for the usual political reasons. He was a translator at the United Nations, in the middle of a divorce, tired of New York, and visiting Geneva to see whether he would like to settle there. Lunch stretched into late afternoon, we laughed a lot, and we arranged to meet again that evening when I had to resume my telephone search for the owner of the Ellis papers.

When I finally made contact with this elusive prey, I learned that he had deposited his letters with Yale. In the meantime a passionate love affair ignited with lightning speed. Jorge was highly amused by an anxious remark I made: "I haven't a very nice body." I had my hair done – when was there time? – and out of the blue the stylist said: "It's amazing how falling in love can make a woman look so young." How did he *know*?

Eventually we turned up at the Berliner Ensemble. Our friends took us off to a beer garden, remarking on how radiant we looked. The next day I was to return to London. I kept waiting for Jorge to say, Please stay. Instead we talked about meeting in the fall when I would go to America to do my Ellis research. He also knew that the following week I was booked for a Swan's tour of Sicily while he was planning to travel on to Spain. A few days after my return to London I rang New York, and he picked up the phone immediately. He had been so miserable in Madrid that he had cut short his visit and had literally just walked in the door. "Why didn't you stay in Geneva?" he asked. "Why didn't you ask me?" "Come over – please – as soon as you can. I love you and I'm sure we can work things out."

I wished that I had never committed myself to the trip to Sicily, but in the end it brought an unexpected gift. At the airport in Rome, just as our group was boarding the plane, I met a woman who was to become one of my most cherished mentors. This was the distinguished psychologist Dr. Marie Jahoda, known as Mitzi, who had just published *Freud and the Dilemmas of Psychology*. Twenty years older than myself, she had had vast experience of life. After being imprisoned by a right-wing government in Vienna, she and her former husband, the sociologist Paul Lazarsfeld, moved to New York where they taught at New York University and Columbia respectively. Some years later, she moved to England where she married Austen Albu, who had been a minister in Harold Wilson's cabinet. A tiny person, she had one of the most formidable intellects I have ever encountered. We were Goethe's "elective affinities," and our conversations in Sicily and burgeoning friendship allowed me to retain some sort of emotional balance during those ten days. We agreed that once I started writing I should send her chapters of the Ellis book at regular intervals.

The tour leader, Peter Kidson of the Courtauld Institute, was a superb lecturer, but I felt as though culture was being rammed down our throats. At Syracuse I wanted to sit among the poppies and gaze out at the sea and think about what I was going to do about Jorge. Nevertheless, I was fortunate to be included in a little clique comprising Peter, the Albus, and some nice Americans (who have also remained friends) who met for drinks every night before dinner. It was in the amphitheatre at Taormina that I suddenly decided that I wouldn't wait until fall but would leave for New York as soon as I could wind up my affairs in London.

With a dismal year in London behind me, the summer of 1977 became one of the most joyous I can remember. Jorge greeted me ecstatically and took me to his apartment on Forty-second Street near the UN. At first we played like children, roaming New York, attending Mostly Mozart concerts, the opera, the ballet, the theatre. One weekend we took the train out to Montauk and walked on the sand dunes. New York is wonderful in the summer. I had been starved for lighthearted fun like this.

There were Ellis papers at Columbia, and every day I would take the 104 bus up Broadway. When I had worked my way through this material I set off on research forays to Los Angeles, Austin (Texas), and finally Boston, returning to New York and Jorge between trips. New York was my post office, my base; it was like being on a liner in mid-ocean when the past has receded and the future is not yet contemplated.

I also made a trip to Toronto to see the children. When I returned to New York I received a frantic call from my agent, Jacqueline, who was in town. She and her American associate had been trying everywhere to find me. The renowned Robert Gottlieb, editor-in-chief of Alfred A. Knopf, wanted to bring out the American edition of the book and was very keen to meet me. I went to see this boyish figure in his kitsch-lined office. I could never figure out his compulsion to fill a room in the venerable firm with plastic monkeys and Minnie Mouse dolls. It was well known that he had a large collection of vinyl handbags in his home, yet he had a genuine passion for literature. He had been crazy about the Symonds book, he said. Why had it taken me so long to write another? I explained that I had three children and that it had been necessary to have a full-time job, one which made it impossible until now to do the sort of book that required a great deal of research. Gottlieb offered a small advance but what mattered was that I would have the Knopf imprint.

Jorge discouraged me from seeing old friends in New York lest they disapprove of our age difference. I was much more conscious of it than he was — that is, when I thought about it at all. (Vivienne Westwood is very gutsy to be married to a man twenty-five years younger than she.) Jorge was so mature for his years that it was never an issue when we were together. How silly it all was! What if our genders had been reversed? Even so, I was careful to divulge the relationship to very few people, and only Anne and Brian actually met Jorge.

The one thing that occasionally troubled me was Jorge's possessiveness and his jealousy of any other man whom I might meet in my travels. By now he had definitely decided to move to Geneva. The plan was that I was to pack all my London files into a car and we would drive to Switzerland to start a new life together. We were intoxicated, we were totally infatuated. But our dreams for the future belonged to Nephelococcygia, the imaginary city built in the air by the birds in Aristophanes' comedy.

My last American research trip was to the Mugar Library at Boston University. It was late August and unbearably hot, but freezing inside the archives where I had to wear a heavy sweater. The unpleasant archivist put me in a glass cage where my every movement could be observed. It was here that I found the most important cache of all: the complete correspondence between Ellis and Françoise Lafitte, the closest relationship in his life and the one that I believed provided the key to a real understanding of the man. I worked feverishly sorting and transcribing their letters. I was permitted to photocopy only a small number of them. By the time Jorge arrived in Boston to take me up to Cape Ann for the Labour Day weekend I had shed pounds. In hindsight I can see that my priorities were becoming clear. Writing my book was now my main concern. ——

A couple of weeks later I returned to New York. It was lovely to sit in our favourite restaurant, One Fifth Avenue, and curious that we chose an establishment which was decorated like an ocean liner, perhaps an unconscious reflection of our relationship. Still, I felt restless: the book would never be finished unless I adhered to a rigorous routine. I remembered how impressed I had been at Tenterden, looking out at Harford in the garden as he worked away with total concentration on his biography of Stanley Baldwin. I persuaded Jorge that I had to return to England, and he agreed reluctantly, on condition that he come over at Christmas and that we leave for Geneva in the spring. I shall never forget him waving and waving as I departed from Kennedy.

Back in London there were stacks of photocopies from the Library of Congress and other institutions to sort through. I have always believed that it is important to create a skeletal frame for a book as early as possible. My autumn was spent in working through the days and in the late afternoons returning to the exercise classes at Granny's. I resumed seeing my old friend Ian Scott-Kilvert. He, of course, had no idea of Jorge's existence, and had convinced himself that he was in love with me. In the meantime masses of flowers would arrive regularly, wired from New York. Only David Sorenson and I were there to admire them as they filled up the tiny flat.

Unbidden doubts started to surface. Could I really bear to spend my life in Geneva? Would Jorge allow me to write or would he resent it if I weren't free to play with him whenever he wasn't working? I also fretted seriously about the age difference. I consulted Mitzi one weekend while staying with her in Sussex, as we were washing up after dinner. "It will work if you aren't a jealous person," she remarked. While I had not yet experienced the kind of jealousy Jorge felt about me, I knew it was entirely possible: I had an explosively jealous temperament. My marriage with BG had unravelled over an indiscretion on his part, and I had been miserable when Mavor confessed his colourful past to me. Jorge used to laugh at my fears about our future but my anxieties were more realistic than his reassurances. As the Beatles used to sing, "Will you still need me, will you still feed me, when I'm sixty-four?"

My Nautical Home

Jorge announced the date that he would be arriving in England for his Christmas break and the unexpected length of his stay – six weeks! Six weeks of the two of us in that cramped flat. Six weeks in which I would be unable to work. And London, unlike New York, is the dreariest, most funereal place in the world at Christmas.

I could see no gentle or civilized way of breaking off the affair. Jorge had always said that he would never let me leave him. In retrospect I realize that I should at least have tried to write a letter, outlining why I had become convinced that we couldn't have a long-lasting relationship. Always too quick off the mark, I impulsively rang him with a fabricated excuse: I told him that I had met someone my own age. He was incredulous. From time to time batches of my summer clothes would arrive from New York, and I was filled with sadness and remorse. On my birthday, March 16, a telegram arrived from New York: "Leaving for Geneva Saturday 18th It was all very very real Will cherish Memory of it Happy Birthday Much Love." Years later Jorge remarked that I had broken off the relationship not because of the age difference but because instinctively I knew that our temperaments would clash.

I hardened my heart and submerged myself in Ellis. Some weeks of the winter I spent in Birmingham with François Lafitte and his wife, Eileen. François had inherited a large chest in which he and I found masses of letters. I had to sort these out – backbreaking work – but the pieces began to fit together with other sets of Ellis correspondence that had turned up in the States.

I still had some interviews to conduct with people who had known Ellis. Only one of his girlfriends, Faith Powys, was still alive. She had been deeply enamoured of Ellis, once following him to Cornwall where he spent his winters, and clearly still was. She may have been obsessed with him, but she was also reticent and idealistic.

Ellis's particular fetish was urolagnia, a fascination with women peeing. Faith was the single person in the world who could tell me how this perversion was enacted, but on the three visits I made to Folkestone, I could not bring myself to ask the crucial question. Nor did I tell her that I had in my possession copies of two extraordinary letters – one from her to Ellis, protesting that she could not participate in his sexual ritual, and another from Ellis to Françoise, complaining that he was finding Faith an awful bore and hoping that he could discourage her from following him to Cornwall again. There was no way that I could hurt her by quoting those letters.

The biographer Ronald Clark once said to me, "When you write a biography, you always hurt someone." It is true that people can be offended by an interpretation of the subject if it doesn't accord with their image or by an account that somehow affronts their self-esteem. These don't trouble me. But I will omit a piece of information that is not absolutely necessary if I believe it will cause real pain to a living person.

That second year in England was a great improvement over the previous one. Ian Scott-Kilvert was temporarily upset when I told him that I could not marry him, but he later realized that we could never be more than good friends. He was too conventional for me; I was too unpredictable for him. By now I was seeing a businessman named Jim, whom I had met through our mutual enthusiasm for jazz. What particularly impressed me about him was that he knew all the words to "The Glow Worm." We went on some nice trips together – Florence in the winter, Spain in the early spring – but the relationship started to deteriorate just before the Nice Jazz Festival in the summer of 1978. I could not afford the trip and didn't want to interrupt my work. He threw a tantrum, saying I had promised months before and he would be bitterly disappointed if I let him down. I allowed myself to be persuaded, but felt resentful. Immediately we arrived in Nice I hated the noise and the pervasive smell of barbecue, and he agreed that we should leave and make a leisurely trip through France, visiting places like Clermont-Ferrand and Vichy which had always intrigued me.

He remained annoyed with me, however, and lectured me that I didn't really know anything about jazz, I simply enjoyed "pleasurable sounds." Mostly he was angry because he knew I was still pining after Jorge. He sometimes spent evenings with his old Oxford crony Kingsley Amis, who really understood jazz – so much so that they would drink quantities of whisky and talk knowledgeably about Kingsley's huge record collection late into the night. Kingsley used to say that the words to "The Glow Worm" ("Shine, little glow worm, glimmer...") were technically among the most perfect lyrics in the English language. After one of these musical evenings, Jim's licence was suspended for a year for drunken driving, and I had to master London driving whenever we went anywhere.

While I was making good headway with the book, it was clear that the writing would take more than a year. I obtained another year's leave of absence from the university and a Killam fellowship. It barely sustained me since it was far less than my university salary would have been. I was determined to move to a quiet cottage somewhere outside London, but nothing I saw suited me. One day I read an ad in the *Times* for a houseboat at Chiswick Mall, on the outskirts of greater London, but the rent was far more than I could afford so I threw the paper away. After a series of discouragements, I decided to go and look for the boat.

At the bottom of the curving street leading from Hogarth

Roundabout, three houseboats were moored. I knocked at the first door and asked if it was to let. No, try the one farthest out in the river. An aggressive-looking man opened the door and showed me around. It was a *coup de foudre* – with the boat, not the man. The owner, an actor who had had to leave America during the McCarthy era, had gutted a large coal barge and created the most exquisite living arrangements.

On the top level he had built a delightful sitting room with windows on three sides. A wrought-iron winding staircase led down to the living quarters. There was nothing primitive about it: radiant heating, a dishwasher, a washing machine, and garbage disposal. The only difficulty was that the rent of the *Mayflower* was well beyond my means. By arguing that if we dealt directly with each other, we would avoid an agent's fee, I persuaded him to reduce it slightly. The rent was still imprudently high, but I had to have it.

Never in my life did I feel so close to nature. I sat at a table in the superstructure and wrote easily and happily, often with Cleo Laine and Scott Hamilton tapes in the background. At noon I would take my lunch out to the deck. It was usually low tide then and the peace was beyond description. In the afternoons I walked along Chiswick Mall, basking in the lush water gardens that extended to the edge of the river. The rise and fall of the tides twice a day never lost their fascination for me and I would regularly check the height of the tide. The Thames often flooded; when it did, large silent crowds would gather to watch the metallic water creep slowly across the road towards the houses, all of which had barrier gates.

Late in October I had an appointment for a routine mammogram in Pentonville Road, on the other side of London. I did not want to take time away from the book, but I reluctantly made the long trek to the clinic. I should have suspected something when the technician told me that she wanted to do another set of tests. The following day my doctor rang. A suspicious lump had appeared on my left breast, and he was going to send me to an eminent Harley Street surgeon.

Mr. S. (surgeons are known as "Mister" in England; this one shall be known as S. for reasons that will become apparent) was handsome in a silvery way and extremely arrogant. He had not yet seen the results of the mammogram, but after examining me digitally, he rather dismissed the possible seriousness of two lumps he felt. "You don't want an operation, do you?" he asked. At our next meeting, in mid-December, he confessed that he had left the mammograms in his car, but now that he had examined them he realized why there had been so much concern. Nevertheless, he went on to say: "If you were on the other side of the Atlantic, they would operate immediately, but that's not the way we do things here. I'll have a look at you in a month and we'll see what develops." If surgery were required, he strongly advised that I have it done privately because if I was on the National Health I would be seeing a different doctor each time. I told him that I had very little money, but somehow it would be found.

Clouds began to appear above my floating paradise. One day I was quietly typing away when the curtains burst into flames. Fortunately my irascible landlord was staying temporarily in a small flat at the other end of the barge and was able to douse the fire – caused by his own faulty wiring. Then he discovered that there was water in the bilges. (I was never entirely clear what the bilges were.) He would have to anchor the boat out in the middle of the river, he told me, and I would then row back and forth to land. Fortunately this didn't come to pass.

Cold foggy weather blanketed the river, and I was driven down to the bowels of the boat to work. When Brian and Anne came for Christmas, they accompanied me on my scheduled visit to Westminster Hospital, where the surgeon again declared that he was going to wait a while longer before deciding whether to operate. He seemed far more interested in my old white fox coat than in me. He had just bought his wife a wolf coat, he said. I replied that if she were in Canada, she would be lynched.

The delay allowed time to finish the book if I worked around the clock, but Mr. S. was being overly reticent in view of the family history of breast cancer, which had been fully outlined to him. I remember the exhausted way I trailed along the dreary streets, worn out from the constant state of suspense. Jim's reaction to the news of suspected cancer was to fade from the picture. One night when I was raging against him, Brian remarked philosophically: "Well, Mum, remember the Alberta Hunter song: you reap what you sow. You always made it abundantly clear that you weren't really interested in him."

Nevertheless, the kids and I had a happy holiday together. One evening the river police drew up beside the barge and asked us if we wanted to be evacuated because the flood tide was rising to a dangerous level. No, no, it was exciting and we wanted to stay. "Well then," they lectured us sternly, "you'll have to pull out a link in the anchor chain or the boat will be swept away out to the North Sea." We went ahead with a great party on New Year's Eve, but around midnight I told everyone that they would have to leave early or they wouldn't be able to get across the flooded water garden. I've never seen guests scurry away so fast.

At the beginning of February 1979 the whimsical Mr. S. suddenly decided that he would operate as soon as a bed became available. The Ellis manuscript had just been completed, and Peter Carson and I sat up most of one night editing the book. François had already read it. This was the only occasion on which I permitted a subject's executor to read the manuscript. It was, after all, an "authorized" biography, and I have always assumed that "authorized" means that one writes exactly what the family wants made public. François and I met in the Charing Cross Hotel. His hands were trembling: this was not the Havelock he had worshipped. Nevertheless, this decent man asked only that I remove a single sentence in which I described his mother as anti-Semitic.

In mid-March I went into a ward at the Westminster Hospital with seven other women. My bed was close to the door, and in the anteroom I could hear the surgeon and his flunkies sitting around gossiping. Eventually, with a weary sigh of impatience, he rose and his retinue followed him from patient to patient.

Just before the operation the registrar assured me in an offhand way, "You know, of course, that the lump is benign." How on earth could he be so confident even before a biopsy had been performed? Prior to the operation they gave me a drug, possibly pethidine, producing the most ecstatic psychedelic experience. The tulips on my table were the quiddity of redness, the yellow daffodils were distilled sunshine. The nurses later told me that they suspected some women returned to the hospital simply for another dose of the drug.

After the operation I was informed casually by a junior doctor that the lump was only a bit of fatty tissue and I could go home. Home. What did that mean? In the immediate future it meant packing up to resume my teaching duties at Toronto in the fall. With the completion of the Ellis biography my writing career seemed to be on hold once more.

I was very tired after the strain of the previous months. Ian suggested that I recuperate at a small hotel in Cornwall at Lamorna Cove, just west of Penzance. Here I could climb the cliff nearby and walk for miles among fields of daffodils to Land's End. Amazingly enough, the hotel had once been a converted chapel in which Havelock Ellis had lived for years early in the century.

In June 1979 I returned to Toronto and finally moved into the Cabbagetown house purchased three years before. Mavor and I had had an odd arrangement in which he had bought the house from me the previous year with the understanding that I would buy it back on my return. Mavor's taste and mine were very different, and he had made some changes, none of which I liked, without consulting me. I resented being charged for them, even though some were necessary repairs. I had to raise a mortgage, and we went together to see my bank manager. Mavor was accustomed to taking charge. "Now, Mr. Lopez," he said, "if you would just take some notes." Mr. Lopez slowly lit a cigarette and leaned back in his chair, watching him narrowly. After Mavor had left, Mr. Lopez turned to me: "When are you going to stop letting people push you around?"

Mavor was not at all happy to have me back in Toronto. As I was settling in I needed a screw for which I could not find a duplicate in the hardware store. Remembering that he had a tin of screws of all shapes, I rang and asked him if I might borrow it to look for the one I needed. "Pat, you are not to bother me about anything. You are completely on your own now." I replied that I had no intention of bothering him, that all I was requesting was a single screw. Later I laughed ruefully at the double-entendre, which neither of us appreciated at the time. He relented, and I still have the entire tin of screws.

By the time I left England I had built up an interesting circle of friends and spent wonderful weekends at the theatre and art galleries. Now I had to forge some kind of new single life for myself in Toronto. Good friends like the journalist Martin Knelman and the editor Bernadette Sulgit were clearly worried about my state of mind. I felt violated at a party when Mavor's former girlfriend maliciously described every detail of my house for me. Was this what life was going to be like? Yet my cottage was very precious to me, and when I got up in the morning I would sit at the top of the stairs and gaze happily at the soft light flooding in from the north and east windows. I started to create a garden, and would go out while the dew was still on the leaves to spray the roses.

Strangely I could not imagine myself back in the classroom again. In mid-August I woke one morning to discover a large lump on the breast which had been operated on in England. I made an appointment to see a surgeon at St. Michael's Hospital. Fortunately I still possessed my English mammogram. Dr. Nick Colapinto examined me, and after dressing I went into his office. "Sit down," he said. "I have something terrible to tell you. In England they left in the carcinoma. The cancer appears to have spread."

I entered hospital again, by now highly skeptical of the medical profession. Was I to have a radical mastectomy, a modified mastectomy, or a lumpectomy? Even the surgeons disagreed among themselves. My children gathered around my bed and we had a family discussion about it. Christopher, who had just started to work for the CBC and was now married to his girlfriend, Fiona, had very little money but he paid the difference for a private room. I was moved beyond words, especially when he said, "Mum, we love you so much."

I still had a year to run on my Killam grant. That would give me time to start another book. I knew that the radiation would completely debilitate me, and my only hope for my own salvation was to get back to writing. Therefore I opted for the lumpectomy, the least invasive procedure (advocated by Dr. Leo Mahoney), if it would give me a year's grace. Dr. Colapinto sat on my bed and argued that I was committing suicide. How strange all this was given my primordial anxiety about my breasts. When the surgeons saw that my mind was set and that I intended to return to England, they urged me to initiate a malpractice suit against Mr. S.

The return to England was predicated on the fact that I was now focused on another target. I had long been interested in Princess Marie Bonaparte, a descendant of Napoleon's older brother Lucien. She was the founder of the French psychoanalytic movement and the woman who paid the Nazis the ransom to bring Freud out of Vienna. From my hospital bed I negotiated a contract with Jack McClelland. (Faced with medical expenses after the operation, I had told Jacqueline

Korn that I couldn't afford an agent, and this resulted in our only separation.) A friend rang to tell me that the husband of a mutual friend in London had died, and that she planned to turn her drawing room into a large bedsitter. I decided that it would save me a lot of energy to have accommodation waiting for me when I landed in London.

I rented my house to a group of students. Six months after returning to Canada, I was on my way back to England.

6

Annus Horribilis

This latest uprooting was a complicated affair. I left for England from New York, where there were various matters to which I had to attend. First, Bob Gottlieb insisted that Knopf do the copy-editing of the Ellis book, a unilateral decision that was to anger the British publishers. Gottlieb was highly critical of British editing, and while he didn't need to be so openly tactless about his contempt, I have found then and since that American editing in general is far more meticulous. I also had to negotiate a contract with him for the Marie Bonaparte book. I had no problem persuading Gottlieb to publish the book, but he wouldn't go farther than an advance of $15,000, and none of my arguments would budge him. Little did I know that eventually I would have to do two books for the price of one.

I was also to have a meeting with Dr. Kurt Eissler, head of the Freud Archives, who had been collecting material connected with psychoanalytic history for years. It was a worthy project; masses of letters to and from Freud would have been lost forever without the Archives' efforts. At this point I did not realize that Eissler was depositing the documents at intervals in the Library of Congress with arbitrary (and often incomprehensible) dates assigned for when they would be accessible to scholars. In several telephone conversations he had been very encouraging about the Bonaparte book. He invited me to lunch at his apartment on Central Park West, and his secretary telephoned in advance to inquire solicitously about my tastes in food.

I was ushered in to meet a tall, attenuated Viennese gentleman, remote, yet with impeccable manners. He sat down on one side of his desk, I on the other. A uniformed maid brought in my lunch on a tray. "Dr. Eissler," I asked, "aren't you having lunch?" "No," he replied, "I never eat." It was a very disconcerting experience munching away as he sat opposite, expressionless and in total control of the situation. The historian Peter Gay later told me that he had had exactly the same experience with him. I once asked the *New Yorker* writer Janet Malcolm if she had ever seen Eissler eat, and she looked startled. Then she recalled that every time she had interviewed him for her book *In the Freud Archives,* he had placed a single tumbler and an enormous bottle of whisky on the table in front of her.

I had brought along my copy of Eissler's book on Leonardo da Vinci, but he refused to sign it without giving any explanation. He very helpfully gave me the names of people to contact in London and Paris, acquaintances and colleagues of Marie Bonaparte, then saw me to the elevator with grave courtesy.

I crossed to Central Park after our meeting and sat down, feeling strangely and disturbingly mournful. Brian was in New York at the time, but I had no idea where he was on that particular day. He has always been reassuring at dark periods, and I tried to envisage what gallery he would be visiting in that vast city. My low spirits might have been triggered by an encounter the previous night. I had visited old friends, and the husband, a doctor, had scolded me for my recklessness in choosing a lumpectomy and urged me to return to Toronto to have a radical mastectomy. Perhaps, though, my depression was also a premonition that all was not well with the Bonaparte project.

But the die was cast. After arriving in London it would have been sensible to find a place of my own but, feeling frail, I found it much easier simply to take the room in the home of my acquaintance. At first the arrangement didn't seem too bad. Avice had a pretty maisonette on three floors above a butcher shop near Marble Arch. My large bedsitter, the former drawing room, was on the first floor. But there were no comfortable chairs or adequate lighting by which to read. Worse still, I had to share the kitchen with Avice. She said warningly that she *knew* if anyone had ever crossed the threshold of her kitchen when she wasn't there. She was extremely fussy that everything had to be in its allotted place, and the longer I stayed the more irritating this became. I was constantly apprehensive about not emptying the kettle properly or failing to fold the towels just as she insisted they must be hung.

I began to eat out more than I could afford. I took friends to a neighbourhood restaurant, Le Chef, in order to repay their hospitality. Avice knew all about these arrangements since she could overhear my telephone conversations. Recently widowed, she was lonely, and she began to take it for granted that she should be included in these invitations. Gradually she insinuated her way into my life. For this I must bear much of the responsibility. I felt sorry for her, introduced her to my friends, realizing only later that I was letting myself fall into a subservient role. Probably in her mid-seventies or more (she was very coy about her age), Avice and I shared no interests. She had no children, had never worked, and had been totally spoiled by her husband. I was now expected to fill his role of fetch and carry, and I particularly resented her assumption that I would walk her dachshund every night. She often remarked that she envied no one because she had "done everything." We all mean something different by "everything," but in Avice's case, it seemed to consist of pre-war London nightclubs and Riviera resorts. Since this had been the "real" part of her life, the handsome, regal-looking woman simply sat in her upstairs drawing room, always impeccably groomed, waiting for – what?

It was clear that I brought a certain drama into her life. Indeed I had plenty in my own at the time. It must have given Avice just a bit of a frisson to tell her friends that Anna Freud had been ringing me.

Then there were all the discussions with a lawyer about a malpractice suit against Mr. S. I was encouraged in this by Dr. Helena Wright, who had been a great pioneer in the birth control movement in England. Helena was ninety at the time, crusty but full of energy and sharp intelligence. We had met when I interviewed her for the Ellis book. She was very indignant about what she saw as a clear case of medical negligence and grew fond of me, treating me as though I were the daughter she had never had. Her son, Dr. Beric Wright, made no bones about his resentment. One evening he entered her flat to find us drinking martinis. He walked through the room without addressing a word to us. Helena leaned over and whispered to me: "I'm supposed to be an old lady in a rocking chair with a cat at my feet." Nevertheless, she bullied Beric, who was head of the British United Provident Association, to arrange for a woman doctor, Dr. Patricia Last, to accompany me to most of the meetings with the solicitors.

I also had to get on with the Bonaparte book. I went to Maresfield Gardens to meet Anna Freud, the daughter of the founder of psychoanalysis. Freud's "Antigone" (as he called her) was the assiduous keeper of the flame. She had been a great friend of the princess so it was imperative to talk to her.

Her reply to my first note had been puzzling. She mentioned that Havelock Ellis had accompanied Freud to America on his voyage in 1909. Ellis had never met Freud, nor had he ever visited America. Was it possible that Freud's daughter didn't know a great deal about psychoanalytic history?

I was still very much in awe of her father, whom I regarded as one of the great liberators of mankind. I could hardly believe it when I found myself in his sitting room, the famous couch still there and the bas-relief of Gradiva on the wall. I tried to absorb as much as possible before Miss Freud — no one ever thought of speaking of her simply as Anna Freud — entered.

I was greeted by a small, thin woman in dowdy handmade clothes and cropped hair that looked as though she occasionally attacked parts of it with her sewing scissors. Despite her stoop, there was nothing self-effacing in Anna Freud's sense of her own importance. She served me tea, but the atmosphere was that of an audience with royalty, something I didn't question at that stage of my life. Miss Freud interrogated me closely about my reasons for wanting to write the book. I told her that I had been intrigued by Marie Bonaparte's account of her unusual childhood in her autobiography. "There is a second part to that autobiography," she told me, "which covers the years of her analysis with my father." She paused. I waited expectantly. "It is totally unavailable." She volunteered no information as to its whereabouts. All she would say was, "Biographies cannot be written unless people want them written." This was disconcerting to say the least, but like Scarlett O'Hara, I would think about it tomorrow. I could not afford to be alarmed and instead comforted myself with the thought that Professor Tillotson had been discouraging about finding Symonds's memoir. Somehow, this one would turn up too.

I made an unlikely friend during this period, a psychoanalyst who at one time had been the archivist of the British Psycho-Analytical Society. This was Masud Khan – or, as he preferred to be known, Prince or Rajah Masud Khan. He was undoubtedly the most flamboyant character I have ever encountered. "Why do you want to write about that tiresome woman?" he asked when I first rang to make an appointment. When he opened the door of his elegant flat in Palace Gate I was startled by the sight of a very tall, striking Pakistani, his long dark hair flecked with grey, wearing a red velvet caftan embroidered in gold. It was clear that I wasn't what he was anticipating either. (That white fox coat was indispensable.) He had had one cancerous lung removed – his voice was very hoarse – and he became interested in my brush with the disease. Notorious as an *enfant terrible*, he had been divorced from the famous ballerina Svetlana Beriosova and had been expelled from the society for having a sexual relationship with a student.

At our first meeting he apologized profusely for not entertaining me adequately. Perhaps he had expected someone whom he would not have felt like entertaining. Masud, I soon realized, was remarkably well read and wrote like an angel. (His books were mostly on perversions.) We got into the habit of sitting up late night after night drinking whisky while he regaled me with psychoanalytic gossip and prepared me for the minefield I would encounter in Paris. Masud would sit in an impressive studded leather chair, which he said (in an offhand way) had been a gift from the Spanish ambassador. An awful snob, he remarked that these days his patients were confined to duchesses. It was difficult to detect when Masud was telling the truth and when he had launched into fantasy. Certainly he counted many famous people among his friends; his father, however, was not a rajah, but a veterinarian who had made a fortune from a chain of cinemas in Pakistan.

At the time I was an honorary research fellow at University College, London, and I used to regale colleagues there with stories about "the prince" when we met for lunch. They became very skeptical when I told them that he had come down from Oxford with a first, and they rushed to the library to check this assertion in the Oxford yearbook. Apparently he had achieved a low second. I found all this highly amusing, still far from suspecting how dangerous Masud could be.

I developed a regular routine of working at the library of the British Institute of Psycho-Analysis (headquarters of the Psycho-Analytical Society) where I systematically read through all Bonaparte's articles in the *Revue française de psychoanalyse*. The princess seemed to have had a peculiar fascination with murderesses, whom she would visit in prison. Also, despite Freud's disapproval, she had undergone a surgical procedure in which her clitoris was moved so that she could experience greater sexual satisfaction. The woman was becoming even more interesting than I had imagined. It was clearly time to go to Paris to interview people who had known her.

Since returning to London, I had resumed regular reviewing for the *Times Literary Supplement*. One book I admired greatly was Mavis Gallant's *From the Seventeenth District*. I had read her stories for years in the *New Yorker* and had friends who had known her well in Montreal and who talked about her courageous move to Paris many years before. Perhaps these particular stories appealed to me so much because they were about dislocated people, the sort of person with whom I had begun to identify. This sense of dislocation was exacerbated by British Immigration and Inland Revenue, who were hounding me about my status in the U.K. I made regular visits to Lunar House in Croydon to assure them that I was not an illegal alien. I always took a large book because it was sometimes hours before my name was called.

I was determined to meet Gallant and arranged with the CBC to interview her at her apartment during my initial research trip to Paris. But first I had to meet Dr. Serge Lebovici, the man who Dr. Eissler had told me would be my most important contact – "an affable fellow," he described him. We arranged a rendezvous late one evening after a meeting of the Paris Psychoanalytic Society. Dr. Lebovici quickly drew up a list of people who could give me information about the princess. My memory is that he, like Eissler, was very encouraging about my project.

I made a trip to Saint-Cloud, on the outskirts of Paris, to meet Bonaparte's daughter, Princess Eugénie, whose father had been Prince George of Greece. She seemed a rather scatty woman, but she possessed some very interesting memorabilia, including a dolls' house which had belonged to the czar's daughters and a diary kept by the young czarevitch. In the course of our conversation she mentioned casually that a Franco-American woman, Celia Bertin, was at that minute working on a biography of her mother. This woman too had been recommended by Dr. Lebovici! Apparently Bertin's project was also known to Anna Freud and Kurt Eissler, but they hadn't felt it necessary to mention it to me. I began to feel as though I were involved in some bizarre intrigue.

Masud had suggested that I meet Dr. Victor Smirnoff, who was to become a close friend over the years. He had spent a good deal of time in America on a Rockefeller grant and spoke perfect English with a slight drawl. He had a perpetual air of weariness which made his company relaxing. At one time a close colleague (and an analysand) of the most famous of all French analysts, Jacques Lacan, he had broken with Lacan over his autocratic ways. Worldly and sophisticated in comparison with my rather ingenuous friend Ian Scott-Kilvert, Victor nonetheless shared with Ian an innate decency. These are the companions one cherishes.

Another was to be Mavis Gallant. She and I finally had our interview in her tasteful apartment. At first she seemed surprised that I was a Canadian but intrigued that I was writing on Marie Bonaparte, because the subject had once been suggested to her by a publisher. She began to pull down volumes she had collected, and I still have them tucked into my large psychoanalytic collection. She was intrigued by Dr. Lebovici's list and scanned the page of names and addresses in his large rounded script. As a writer she was interested in learning the areas of Paris in which the psychoanalysts lived.

I had never operated a tape recorder before, but I started out without undue nervousness. Mavis spoke spontaneously and the interview was superb. When we had finished, I discovered to my horror that I had neglected to push the "record" button. Mavis was absolutely charming about it but insisted that we do it professionally in a studio on my next visit.

Back in London, I was sitting with Avice one evening tinkering with my tape recorder in an effort to retrieve some of my conversation with Mavis. Suddenly I heard Mavis's voice. "Tell me about this woman – Avice – your landlady."

Horrified, I realized that *after* the interview I had turned on the record button and forgotten to switch it off. Now I couldn't suddenly push the stop button since Avice had sat up intently after hearing her name. In frozen embarrassment we listened to the rest of the conversation.

"Well," I reply to Mavis's question, "there are certain subjects one avoids."

"Such as?"

"The class system, for one."

"You mean she's a snob?"

"To put it mildly. But let's talk about someone interesting like Helena Wright."

I have no recollection of how I stumbled out of the room that night. The following morning I awoke to find Avice standing beside my bed in her dressing gown, something she had never done before. "Darling," she said, "wasn't that amusing last night?" I was overcome with admiration. Could anyone have handled the situation with more grace? I imagine the poor woman had had a sleepless night, but had decided that if we were to continue living together in the same house, she had to clear the air. In retrospect I have tended to demonize her at times, but in fact she was simply a rather superficial, self-indulgent woman who found it difficult to share her house.

Masud expected a full report of my Paris visit. I showed him Lebovici's list. Opposite those I should trust he put a tick, and a cross beside the others. Opposite Lebovici's name was an enormous X. When I subsequently showed the list to Victor Smirnoff, he agreed entirely with Masud's judgments. In other words, Masud had a strong streak of intelligent perception which was unfortunately flawed by his paranoia and grandiosity.

Late in February 1980, I returned to Toronto for three weeks as there were plans, developed by Vincent Tovell, then a producer with the CBC, to turn my book on Ellis into a documentary. I stayed with Marc and Peter, and the poor souls were taxed beyond endurance. I came down with some awful virus. I remember Peter saying that he feared I would not be strong enough to resume teaching. Mavor rang me one morning to mention casually that we had been officially divorced the previous day. He was going to be away for a time so he offered me his lovely apartment on Bernard Avenue. Aware that I was a burden to my friends, I moved into it for the remainder of my visit. Such was the strange relationship between my former husband and myself.

I stopped in New York on my way back to England and met with Bob Silvers at the cluttered office of the *New York Review of Books*. I had just written a piece for him, one of many I was to write through the years. We had lunch and talked for hours about every subject under the sun. He is one of the journalistic figures for whom I have the greatest respect, and he is undoubtedly the best editor I have ever encountered. Nothing escapes his questioning eye, and he pushes one to do better work than one dreamed oneself capable of.

In London I resumed a compartmentalized life. I continued to work on the book as though no serious obstacles had arisen. The slow process of the lawsuit ground on (although the lawyer was not slow in sending me bills), but Mr. S. made it clear that he was going to oppose me, and of course he was supported by the Medical Defence Union. In addition the immigration officials were making life increasingly difficult. The only way I could stay in the country, it would appear, was to marry someone. I left a crazy proposal on Michael Holroyd's answering machine. I was laughing so hard I don't know how he could grasp what I was saying, but understand it he did – and with great embarrassment explained that his accountant wouldn't permit him to marry me.

I next approached Francis King. We were having drinks before going off to a PEN meeting. He thought it was a hilarious idea, and envisaged the marvellous literary reception we would have. His partner, David, entered the room. "There seems to be a lot of laughing in here." We broke the news. "Let us be the first to tell you. We are going to be married." All the way to the meeting David, who was driving us, warned Francis sternly of the consequences of his rash acceptance, and that the Home Office was investigating such marriages of convenience. We soon dropped the harebrained scheme, but David was always very nervous of me.

All the pressures were getting to me and my sometimes bizarre behaviour was evident even to myself. I felt as though I were tied together with loose string. Or like a Jean Rhys woman hanging on to a ledge by her fingertips – only to discover that it was covered with the shards of broken glass that are embedded in many British walls. I was extremely gratified when Gaby Annan reported to me that John Gross had said that no matter what I was going through, he could always count on me as the complete professional in my work.

My elderly mentors provided me with an anchor. I got into the habit of having tea with Helena Wright every Thursday afternoon, after which I would meet Kitty West (J.A. Symonds's granddaughter) at Costa's, a Greek restaurant in Notting Hill. Kitty, an editor at John Murray, was an extremely worldly figure, still wearing a flapper's shingle in her seventies. All my life I have been drawn to strong older women of great intelligence. One could say that I was seeking a mother figure, but I am inclined to think these were re-creations of my grandmothers, women who combined the warmth of Nana Owen with the intellectualism of Nana Langstaff. They were, after all, the reliable pillars of my childhood. I was rich indeed with my trio of wise women – Mitzi, Helena, and Kitty.

Nor did a week pass without my seeing Ian Scott-Kilvert. We did many things together, including trips to visit the Montgomery-Hydes at Tenterden, where I loved to sit in their serene yellow drawing room with its beautifully carved mantel and high windows. One time Robbie exclaimed spontaneously, "Oh Pat, what memories you are going to have when you are an old woman!" Yes, but would I ever achieve wisdom along with age?

One evening in early April, Ian and I had a lovely relaxed dinner in Covent Garden. About three in the morning I awoke with the most terrifying intense pain I have ever experienced. Groping for consciousness, I realized it was in my left breast, the one that had been operated on. The telephone was in the sitting room one floor above me. Avice was asleep on the top floor. On all fours I dragged myself up the stairs, one agonizing step at a time. I finally reached the telephone and rang the senior partner at the medical clinic I attended. "It sounds as though you are having a heart attack," he said coolly, "but there is no point in going to a hospital on a Friday night. Swallow a bottle of aspirin and come and see us tomorrow." I did exactly that and slept like a baby.

A BLESSING IN DISGUISE

In the morning the pain was gone. I saw my own doctor as soon as I could get to the clinic, and he told me that on Monday he was sending me to see a specialist at the famed cancer hospital the Royal Marsden. The weather that weekend was glorious, one of those rare periods that sometimes break into England's sombre climate. And – strangely – I felt positively ecstatic about the beauty of life. On Saturday evening I attended a glorious performance of *Hamlet* at the Royal Court with Jonathan Pryce in the lead role. The visitation of the ghost was depicted as an internal persecutor, and Pryce writhed and struggled with his superego. I was absolutely transfixed, having forgotten for the moment the terrors of the previous night. On the Sunday I had lunch with friends in Chelsea, and again drifted through the day as though it was bliss simply to be alive.

All this changed on Monday. As soon as I entered the surgeon's office I said, "Mr. B., I think I ought to tell you that I'm involved in a malpractice suit." "Yes, I've heard," he replied warily. "Well, I just want to assure you that you and I are starting from square one." "I'm very relieved to hear it." After examining me, he was blunt with the truth. "I can tell you immediately that it's cancer. But we'll confirm it by a mammogram." He made no reference to the earlier lack of treatment, nor ever raised it subsequently.

Up until this point I had held myself together, but once the technicians got to work, I started to weep hysterically. With the tears still streaming down my face I stumbled across Fulham Road to Tatters, an elegant vintage clothing shop. Here I ordered three exquisite, very feminine outfits. They were in silk and satin with ruffles and flounces. (They did not prove completely impractical because I wore one to the *Ellis* publication party.) I suppose I had just emerged from an encounter with mortality, and in order to reassure myself that I was still very much in this world I had to buy something to wear in the future – and incur a debt that I would have to pay off.

Still teary, I hailed a taxi. "What are you blubbering about?" the driver asked me. "I have cancer." "What makes you think you're so special?" I didn't think I was special – anyone could develop cancer – but I was in a state of shock from the sequence of events. He continued to harangue me, with references to his "old woman," who had died while I had the affrontery to be alive. I threw some money at him and demanded to be let out. Still shouting insults, he drove along slowly beside me. People sitting outdoors at a nearby pub viewed this bizarre scene curiously. With all the nice cab drivers in London, why should I have encountered this madman?

The cancer, which had spread to the lymph glands, was confirmed. A few days later Claudia de Lotbiniere, a wonderful friend I'd met when I first lived in London, drove me to a clinic in Holland Park where a mastectomy was performed. Everything connected with this episode is rather blurry. I know that I recited the Twenty-third Psalm as I have done before every operation. BG happened to be passing through London at the time and paid me an affectionate visit. A few days after I returned to Connaught Street, Brian arrived on his way to Paris to study at the Sorbonne. He was appalled to learn that Avice hadn't made me so much as a cup of tea. But, after all, why should she take on an ailing woman?

For some time after I left hospital the world seemed filled with wonders and miracles. I was in that joyous delusional state that many people experience after surgery. Coleridge once remarked that the convalescent sees the world in its true colours, and perhaps it is the case that only then are we filled with all the wonderment of the universe. I asked the surgeon if I might visit Brian in Paris. He agreed grudgingly, only on condition that I take very gentle care of myself. Little did he know how many flights I would have to climb to reach Brian's apartment in the Marais, or that my son would insist on walking incredible distances to find a restaurant that served *cervelles*. But oh, what a good time we had! Brian had booked me into the Hôtel de Brésil on the rue Le Goff, where Freud had stayed in 1889. On my arrival Brian asked, "How would you like to go to one of Lacan's seminars?" Would I! It was held in the Institut Océanographique in the rue Saint-Jacques. (Lacan was so paranoid that he kept changing the locale.) His daughter-in-law, Madame Miller, adjusted his earphones reverently and the audience fell into a state of religious trance. At the end Lacan suddenly announced that this would be his last public appearance. He raised his hand slightly: "Adieu."

Brian came over to London for the publication party for *Havelock*

Ellis given by Peter Carson. The book, dedicated to Mitzi, was a handsome edition with a Man Ray photograph on the cover. I wore the prettiest of my Tatters dresses. The book received good reviews on both sides of the Atlantic and was nominated in the creative non-fiction category for the U.K. National Book Award. In Canada it did not make the short list for the Governor General's, which infuriated Jack McClelland.

Some months later Anne accompanied me to the U.K. awards ceremony. *Ellis* hadn't won, and Anne kept telling me how proud she was that I was such a good sport. When she was eleven years old I taught a summer course, and she would often come and sit at the back of the room, later advising me on how to improve my delivery. "Don't say 'uh' so much." As an adult she has frequently sat in the front row of lectures in various cities, beaming at me with pride, occasionally glaring at a hostile questioner. It was a comfort to have her with me at the awards event.

Despite her moral support, though, I was in fact miserable not to have won the prize. I desperately needed the money. (The research alone, I once calculated, had cost me well over $125,000.) Ellis was not the sort of subject that sets the world on fire; yet, despite all the interruptions in the writing, it had set me on a firm course as a biographer. Not one, however, that was ever going to make any money.

In this book I believe I found my particular voice, a voice I like to think is sometimes slightly ironic. A great reader of novels, I incorporated into my works many techniques associated with novel-writing: allowing suspense to build up through a series of peaks, followed by a quiescent stage as details leading to a dramatic climax again gradually accumulate.

When Masud first saw me after my hospitalization he was very upset by the weight I had lost. My appearance seemed to reawaken anxieties about his own health. I took Brian over to meet him one night. He was in one of his manic moods, pacing around the room.

"Your mother," he announced, "has tertiary cancer, but I have only secondary cancer." (When I later repeated this to Victor, he remarked dryly, "Masud doesn't know his ass from his elbow. He's confusing it with syphilis.") At one point – as though he were a magician – he suddenly flashed a silver dagger which he held at Brian's throat. Brian sat there unflinchingly, but in the taxi he said, "I'm not meeting any more of your crazy friends. I refuse to meet this psychic tomorrow." He was referring to Helena and her belief in spirituality. He relented, however, and they got on splendidly. The last thing she said to me as she lay dying in the Royal Free Hospital a couple of years later was, "How's Brian?"

My appearance gradually improved, especially as I followed my gay hairdresser's advice to drink Guinness and raw egg. (My doctor was puzzled by the unexpected rise in my cholesterol level.) I dropped by Masud's flat to leave a copy of the Ellis biography with him. He later sent me a note telling me how wonderful I looked, and went on at rapturous length about how he and I were among the superior people, "cocks of the walk," who could beat cancer. More of that later.

My health problems continued over the summer. I saw the surgeon every week or so, and one night he dropped by to visit me. I hadn't meant to say anything about the ongoing malpractice suit, but I suddenly blurted out, "You know a terrible wrong has been done to me, yet you refuse to do anything to help me." To my surprise, he replied, rather wearily, "I'll testify for you." Eureka! Unlike Diogenes the Cynic, it seemed I had actually found an honest man.

I shouldn't have been so quick to idealize Mr. B. Without consulting me, while I was under the anaesthetic he had inserted a silicone bag for a restructured breast, now a hard rock that protruded unnaturally from my body. My system rejected it, and that summer I spent a small fortune on antibiotics. One night the silicone bag burst, and again I had to go into hospital. I felt utterly forlorn coming back to an empty house and had the strong impression that Avice had deliberately gone away that weekend. Relations between us were now strained to the breaking point. I had a telephone installed in my room, but it was simply an extension of hers. She had established a custom where I was to leave my door open when I was out. I now signalled my independence by keeping it closed all the time.

Late in July Mr. B. scheduled an appointment for the end of the day. When I sat down he offered me a glass of ouzo, a gift, he explained, from one of his Greek patients. From his grave manner, I fearfully awaited some terrible revelation about my health. What he had to tell me was that he couldn't testify for me after all. His specious reasoning was this: Mr. S.'s father had been the registrar when he was in training; hence this made Mr. S. his "brother." And, according to the Hippocratic oath, one brother could not testify against another.

Masud had always urged me to drop the malpractice suit because he was convinced that they would defeat me on a technicality. Sound common sense, but I was beginning to see that some of the things he had said to me were not only fantastical but downright nonsense and had to be addressed. One evening I arrived at his flat in a very sober mood. "Masud," I said earnestly, "you have been giving me misguided advice. You seem to believe that we are superior beings who can beat cancer. In the eyes of God we are all equal. We have no better chance than anyone else." His face darkened with anger as he sat there silently brooding. I got up and went out the door, never to return. One never contradicted Masud. The ending of any friendship is always a painful experience, and I still blame myself for the way I have handled difficulties with various people. Nevertheless, through the years I have come to realize that the dazzlement of some early attraction is a gossamer thing, and that real friendships have a comforting solidity about them.

The summer of 1980 I reached an insurmountable obstacle in my work on the Bonaparte biography. I had become friendly with

Ronald Clark, whose biography of Freud I had reviewed warmly in the *TLS*. He told me that there were a lot of Freud papers in the Library of Congress. I wrote asking if the library had anything of Marie Bonaparte's. They replied that they possessed *everything*, including the manuscript of the second part of the autobiography, the key to my research. This material had been deposited there by Kurt Eissler and Anna Freud, embargoed until some far distant year like 2024. Neither of these eminent figures had informed me of this fact, and I was not to learn the reason for their silence until Celia Bertin's book came out in 1982. I wrote an article for the *New York Review of Books* at that time, recounting my ill-fated year and the fact that someone had given Bertin photocopies of all the restricted material. In 1980 there was no way I could proceed with my book.

The only bright spot that summer was the birth of my first grandson, Evan. He had been expected on August 8 – Dad's birthday – but on July 30 Christopher rang me in tears to say that being present at the birth of his son was the most moving experience he had ever had.

Nevertheless, it is not surprising that I was close to despair about the prospects ahead. The Bonaparte affair and the uncertainty about my health made the future look bleak. The following weekend I sat for hours in a deck chair in Hyde Park. Lost in thought, I underwent what I would describe as a dark night of the soul. Surely, I said to myself, I could extract some wisdom from what I had been through. All I could do was live life as responsibly as possible. Where could I now take some control? For some months I had been having a sporadic affair with an attractive married man. This had to stop. It was sleaze dressed as romanticism, and I would tell David that our relationship was at an end. It was a small but very important first step. I now regard my cancer as a gift that enabled me to gain partial access to my real – and, one hopes, better – self.

7

THE GIFT

Coincidence, fate, or destiny? Some weeks before I made that small but crucial decision in the park I had received a letter from my old flame at Trinity, Bob McMullan. His sister, Betsy Roche from Toronto, had sent him a subscription to *Saturday Night*. In the second issue he received he read a review of *Havelock Ellis*, bought it, and sent a fan letter from England to *Saturday Night*, assuming that I was still living in Toronto. It was directed back to England by my old friend Bernadette Sulgit, who was then managing editor of the magazine.

I had seen Bob briefly in England in 1964 just before BG and I returned to Canada. Bob and his first wife had recently returned from a period in South Africa, he had somehow contacted me, and we invited them to dinner at St. Leonard's Terrace. In turn we had been invited to their home in Beaconsfield. As couples we didn't seem to have anything in common, and if we had continued living in England, we would have slipped quietly out of their orbit as people do. Then, a few years later – just before I married Mavor – Bob (by now divorced) dropped in to see me while visiting his sister in Toronto. On neither occasion did I feel a glimmer of romantic feeling for him. Readiness is all.

I can remember clearly that August 8 morning (Dad's birthday again) – the day after my weekend in Hyde Park. The deep depression still lingered but the morning began early with an interview with a journalist from the gay magazine *Spare Rib*. I had taken my time to reply to Bob's letter, and we had finally arranged to have lunch that day. The bell rang. I opened the door. I hadn't remembered his nice smile, but I was even more startled by his warm and empathetic expression. Nothing in my previous experience of him had prepared me for this transformation.

We went off to a pub, the Victoria, for lunch. He told me that he passed my door every day on his motorbike en route to work at his insurance company. Incredible. His life in recent years had been even more dramatic than mine. He, too, had married twice. After the war he had returned to China, where he had successfully rebuilt his father's business. Then the Communists came to power and for years he was under virtual house arrest. Eventually he was the last European to get out of Tsingtao (now Qingdao), a port located about halfway between Shanghai and Beijing. He then set up in business in Hong Kong.

His professional life had been a roller-coaster, involving numerous ventures in South Africa and England, and the loss of several near-fortunes through forces beyond his control. What impressed me was that he had always risen, like a phoenix, full of humour and wisdom. Where once I had been painfully shy with him, I now felt completely relaxed. This pleasant man bore no resemblance to the arrogant youth who had treated a nineteen-year-old so cruelly at the dance in Hoggs Hollow. I thought I would love to have him as a friend.

He suggested that I hop on his motorbike and we ride up to Queen Mary's Rose Garden in Regent's Park. It had never been a favourite place of mine and the weather had turned overcast, but we strolled around, holding hands in the most natural way possible. When I returned Avice remarked on my glowing, happy face.

But romance still did not occur to me. Here were two people in their late fifties who had made many mistakes, who had been battered by life and had acquired a certain humility. Then small details began to coalesce in my mind. Bob pointed out the beauty of the cloud formations as we were driving up Gloucester Road, an observation so unexpected that I turned and looked at him with new appreciation. Another afternoon my friend Elsie Smith was visiting, and it was clear that Bob was genuinely interested in her pottery-making, and eagerly questioned her about the double-cube room at Wilton House near Salisbury, which she had recently visited. I had told Bob about David and he was shrewdly understanding. One day he took me to my appointment at the surgeon's. (Mr. B. and his nurse came to the door of the waiting room to peer curiously at him.) As we drove back along King's Road Bob started singing "I'll Be Around," that old Mills Brothers song from our era. What he was telling me was that he intended to outlast David. And he did. David took the news graciously.

And so we embarked on an old-fashioned courtship. Before I went to sleep I would slip a note partway through the letter box, and when he passed early in the morning he would replace it with one of his own. I rode around London on the back of his motorbike. "Fine behaviour for a middle-aged woman," sniffed Kitty. Still, she couldn't help being enormously charmed by him when he dropped me off at Costa's for our weekly dinner. "You're going to marry him," she predicted.

In early September Anne arrived in London. She had graduated in law from Osgoode Hall in Toronto and had won a post-graduate fellowship to the Bartlett School of Architecture to pursue urban studies. After walking in and finding Bob and me sitting on the floor having a picnic, she remarked, "He seems to be around here a lot."

Mavor also arrived – ostensibly to see how I was faring physically. Avice was out, and when he made us a pot of tea, I warned him to memorize exactly where he had picked up everything. Later at Le Chef he told me that he was going to marry Sandra Browning, an opera singer. I think he had feared that I might burst into floods of tears, but

I calmly congratulated him, and after a minute mentioned, almost casually, that I was planning to get married myself.

He looked dumbfounded. We returned to my room to wait for Bob. He was late, and Mavor grew restless, eager to get back to his hotel. Then the door opened, and Bob came in with a smile that said, I know we will like each other. The next day Mavor rang and said that he thought I had found the perfect partner, a man of integrity who was in no doubt about his identity. He was genuinely enthusiastic and I know that he felt happy for me – and undoubtedly relieved as well.

Within a month of meeting again, Bob and I decided to find a place in which to live together. (How thankful Avice and I were to see the last of each other!) We took a flat in Park West on the corner of Edgware Road and Kendal Street. Surprisingly enough, the landlord turned out to be the father of the Freud scholar Jeffrey Masson. Masson had been a Sanskrit professor at the University of Toronto. I had never met him there, although he once attended one of my seminars. At that point he was undergoing psychoanalytic training, and even the frosty Eissler was soon to be captivated by his vivacity, eventually appointing him as his assistant and second-in-command at the Freud Archives.

We later learned that Masson *père*, a gem dealer, had bought the flat for his son. Apparently Jeff had plans to become curator of a Freud museum in Anna Freud's house in Maresfield Gardens. He visited us only once, accompanied by a German girlfriend. It was the first time he had seen the flat, and he inspected it approvingly. Bob found him delightful, but I remarked that there was something oddly disturbing about him. Shortly thereafter he made his notorious self-destructive speech about Freud's dishonesty in abandoning the seduction theory, a charge which caused an uproar in psychoanalytic circles. It became the subject of Janet Malcolm's book *In the Freud Archives*, first published in instalments in the *New Yorker* in 1983. Masson was in fact biting the hand that fed him. He was later to publish his apostasy in book form, *The Assault on Truth*, which I reviewed critically in the *Globe and Mail* in 1984.

It was around this time that Ian Scott-Kilvert finally lifted his ban on my attendance at the Byron Society, which he had imposed three years earlier when I had published the unfavourable review of Elizabeth Longford's study of Byron. As Bob and I entered Brown's Hotel, someone stopped us at the foot of the stairs. "Lady Longford is looking for you." Trembling, I mounted the stairs feeling very much as though I was about to have a confrontation with the headmistress. A friend, William St. Clair, hurried up to me with the same message: "Lady Longford is looking for you." We entered the crowded room, and suddenly an enchantingly pretty white-haired woman appeared before me. "Are you Phyllis Grosskurth?" she asked. "I know you hated my book on Byron, but I have been longing to meet you." I fell in love with her on the spot, and she has told me since that she had an overpowering instinct that we were meant to be friends.

When I had tea with her the next week I burst into tears. How could I possibly have hurt this lovely woman with my supercilious review? I have seldom met a more generous, kindly, unpretentious woman. There was no sense of the imperiousness of being a countess; in fact, at an early age she had been a Labour candidate. After having ten children, in her fifties she began to write her distinguished biographies. I found that I could open my heart to her about anything and her response would be one of total honesty.

THE VIRGINIA WOOLF AFFAIR

I was very busy that fall of 1980 becoming domesticated again — buying groceries, cooking, doing all the things I hadn't done for years. In addition I became embroiled for the first time in a heated literary controversy. I think it was the middle of August when John Gross phoned from the *TLS* to say that he had two books in which I might be interested: I could review both, he suggested, or one, if I preferred. The first was Mordecai Richler's new novel. No; after my experiences at the *Globe and Mail* I wouldn't touch anything by a Canadian. Then what about the final volume of Virginia Woolf's letters?

"Have a heart, John. There has been so much written about the previous volumes that there is nothing left to say." "Oh, come on, Pat. You always like a challenge."

I rue the day that I let John talk me into it. As usual, I did a great deal of background research, some of it suggested by Michael Holroyd. I was startled to discover in the appendix to the *Letters* that there had been three suicide notes, not two as had always been assumed. I was also struck by the similarity of the wording in all the notes, and by the fact that they read as though they had been dictated.

Playing detective, I took the train to Lewes, where I examined the police reports and the local newspaper coverage of the suicide. I became convinced that there had been some sort of cover-up. Leonard Woolf's statements to the police were contradictory, none of the family attended the inquest, he had a mistress, etc., etc. Accordingly, I wrote a long piece for the *TLS* in which I implied that the marriage had not been as perfect as the Bloomsburyites would have us believe, and raised the possibility that Leonard had somehow colluded in Virginia's death.

John was intrigued by the piece but clearly regarded it as too hot to be personally involved with, so he handed it over to someone else who did a heavy edit. It was perhaps the first time any review I had ever written for the *TLS* hadn't been printed exactly as I wrote it. It appeared as a review-article on October 31, 1980.

For some time my old friend Noël Annan, by then vice-chancellor of the University of London, had promised to take me out to lunch to celebrate a laudatory review he had written of the Ellis book for the *New York Review of Books*. For one reason or another we had post-poned our meeting until late fall, and it so happened that we met at Tante Claire only days after the appearance of the Woolf article. Instead of the pleasant lunch we had both envisaged, Noël spent the entire time lecturing me on how wrong I had been, what a splendid man Leonard was, how he had gently pointed out the flowers in his garden to Nöel's wife, Gaby, and so on. Ironically enough, in his *New York Review of Books* review, Noël had remarked upon the special quality of truthfulness that marked my writing.

Abusive letters poured into the TLS office, and every morning Bob would go to the door to pick up what he described as "the slings and arrows." Many of the letters were actually very supportive, but some academics asked me nervously not to tell anyone that they agreed with me. One man – who had publicly hinted at what I had said boldly – claimed that he could not, as a result, get a job in London or at his old college, King's, in Cambridge.

A particularly curious incident involved the eccentric Shake-spearean scholar A.L. Rowse, probably most famous for his theory that the "dark lady" of the sonnets was Emilia Lanier, a lady-in-waiting at court. I had met him some years before when I was doing work on the nineteenth-century historian J.A. Froude. A friend in Toronto, the Macmillan publisher Rache Lovat-Dickson, had written in advance asking if I might meet him, and he had warned Rache not to send him "a New York Jewess." Eventually Rowse relented and agreed to see me. I was staying with some Oxford friends, Larissa and Francis Haskell, who were fascinated by our encounter at All Souls College and wanted to know every detail of the meeting with the notorious curmudgeon. The surprise on Rowse's face when he saw me was manifest, and we had a very lively conversation laced with his usual invective against "third-rate minds."

Some years later he published an egregious book on the history of homosexuality, and I wrote a mischievous review for the *Observer*, poking sly fun at him. Although Rowse was known to dislike Bloomsbury and all it stood for, he saw my TLS piece as a chance to vent his spleen at my *lèse-majesté*. This is the letter that fell through our letter box.

> Dear Mrs. Grosskurth,
>
> I see that you have been described by two people who knew the Woolfs well, as 1) very silly, 2) pestilential.
>
> Of course, you are a very silly and conceited woman. And the first step you should take to improve is to realise this and make a new beginning.
>
> Perhaps this is too much to hope for, and I doubt whether you have it in you to make a new start.
>
> In my opinion – with twice your age and experience – you have intelligence enough to do better with your faculties; if only you have the sense and humility to take telling from those who know better than you. If you do not recognise this, it is a sign of stupidity, and that is incorrigible.

How was I to reply? Bob conceived the idea of photocopying the harangue and sending it to him, with a covering letter that someone using his name had sent this unpleasant missive to me. He broached the subject to an academic friend who had joined us for dinner one evening. "I'll write it!" cried my friend. He felt that I had gone too far in my review, but he got into the spirit of the prank. After dinner he settled himself in a corner of the room and rapidly composed the following letter.

Dear Dr. Rowse,

I am sorry to bother you about a trivial and somewhat embarrassing matter, but I remember so well meeting you in Oxford some years ago and the great encouragement (and dedicated copies of your books) that you then gave me, that I feel that you can now give me some helpful advice.

I have just received (and send you a photocopy of) an illiterate, ill-mannered, hysterical and complacent letter from someone who has signed it with your name. I realise how deeply embarrassed you will be when you see this, and that is the reason that I am showing it to you before making it public. You will probably want to take legal action against someone who is abusing your reputation because it will obviously arouse such ridicule when it becomes known.

Thank you again so much for all your advice (how long ago was it?) − I learnt so much from you that I know you will help me now.

With thanks and good wishes.

My friend had overdone it a little bit with this florid ending and Rowse might have been suspicious. However, a few days after I sent the letter off, Rowse replied:

Dear Mrs. Grosskurth,

I am glad to have your address and to be told of the "great" encouragement at our meeting at All Souls, which I have not forgotten. I don't know about "great", but I was full of good will and anxious to do my best for you. I thought I had made a friend. The next thing I remember from you was a thoroughly supercilious and dismissive review of my book, *Homosexuals in History*, an unfriendly act. That, from a young writer to a much older one, gave me the idea that you were pretty conceited. No harm in that – plenty of people think I am conceited. I don't mind: I am all in favour of people having a good conceit of themselves, if justified by the work they do. No doubt you will justify it by your work long before you reach my advanced age, for I regard you as both intelligent and ambitious.

I don't know about your latest work, not having seen a copy of your Havelock Ellis. But I should like to receive one, in exchange for a book of mine, since I know something of the Cornish side down here.

Perhaps we should start the New Year on a better footing and justify the hope I had of finding a friend in the young woman from Canada, whom I thought I had helped. Thank you for writing and saying so.

Best wishes for good luck in 1981.

Yours ever

A. L. Rowse

For weeks books from Rowse poured in with flowery inscriptions. Then they abruptly stopped. Rowse may have been genuinely nervous that I planned to make the matter public. Until this moment, I have not.

A few months later I was invited to a luncheon given by a delightful London hostess, Lady Mander. As soon as I stepped through the door I saw Rowse standing in the drawing room. My hands were clammy, so I went into the bathroom to wash them. They were still clammy, and when we shook hands I noticed that Rowse's hands were clammy too. During lunch he carefully directed all his remarks to me. Lady Mander had actually invited us together in all innocence and had inadvertently ended the feud.

The Woolf review had become something of a *cause célèbre*, and one man told Bob that people thought the cancer had affected my mind. If I were writing it now, I should phrase my suspicions far more moderately. Indeed, I regret that I wrote it at all. I don't think it did anything to enhance my reputation, and although I defended my position vigorously, who knows what aggression my unconscious might have been unleashing? It would have been preferable if I had reviewed Mordecai's novel. Better still, I should have turned down both books.

THE INTERVIEWS

Late in 1980 I began to take stock of my situation. I had been so caught up with the new relationship with Bob that I had pushed my predicament over the Bonaparte book to the back of my mind. But hard financial facts stared me in the face. I had spent all my publishers' advances for the Bonaparte book, I could not afford to pay them back, and I had no alternative project.

At this point Brian arrived for Christmas. I had long been in the habit of discussing my work with him, and I turned to him for advice. "I've always thought you were working on the wrong subject," he said, "You should be doing Melanie Klein." Klein was the leading figure in the British psychoanalytic movement, yet I knew nothing about her and had never read a single book she had written. I had met some Kleinians at dinner parties; I had also met people who spoke of her disciples with horror.

"But they'll never give me access to the papers," I protested. "Try," Brian replied. And so I did. I made an appointment with Dr.

Hanna Segal, the leading Kleinian psychoanalyst and Klein's designated successor. She was an impressive woman, stocky, with a mannish haircut, smoking a cigar. I laid my cards on the table. I told her about the Marie Bonaparte fiasco and confessed that I was totally unfamiliar with Klein's work. She emphasized that unlike the Freudians, the Kleinians believed in open access. She would discuss my proposal with other members of the Klein Trust. The answer, which came surprisingly quickly, was that I could have total access to Klein's papers, which were stacked up in a room in Dr. Segal's house in Hampstead.

My reaction was mixed: relief, apprehension, panic at the immensity of the task I had taken on. It amazed me that no biography of Klein had yet appeared, apart from a short monograph by Dr. Segal in the Fontana Modern Masters series. My various publishers agreed to the change of subject – but naturally I would receive no more money. All I had to live on was my Killam grant. (I understand that nowadays the university supplements these grants to bring them up to the level of one's professorial salary.)

In the spring of 1981 we moved to Kynance Mews in South Kensington. The house had potential charm, but only a few sticks of furniture. Fortunately Bob and I shared the same taste. We bought a few essentials and decorated it in turquoise and white, transforming it into a charming nest.

I made another vital decision: I would drop the malpractice suit, which was bleeding me dry. This resolve followed a meeting with a barrister who gravely told me to think very carefully about what I was getting into. As we were about to embark on a court case, he warned that I must do so with my whole heart and soul. Dr. Patricia Last had accompanied me to the meeting, and as we walked away I asked her what she would do if she were in my place. "I really don't know," she replied with a worried frown. Only I could decide. Apart from the strain on my finances, the lawsuit was not life-enhancing, and I needed all my energy for the ambitious project to which I was now committed.

Compared with Melanie Klein, the work required for the Havelock Ellis biography had been child's play. I had to master Klein's theories, which were notoriously difficult to understand. I set about reading her papers in chronological order. Many was the morning I awoke puzzling over psychoanalytic terms I thought I had understood the previous night. The concept of "projective identification" was particularly troublesome. At the same time I began to interview members of the British Psycho-Analytical Society, who proved extraordinarily helpful. I have often said that these professionals educated me. Different people had varying perceptions, for example, about what the death instinct meant, but through the articulation of these differences, I acquired a wonderful theoretical training.

Most psychoanalytic societies form splinter groups. The British created a kind of compromise in the early forties when a split was threatened by the arrival of Anna Freud on the scene after the Freuds fled Vienna. Anna Freud claimed that Klein's brand of psychoanalysis, which emphasized the importance of the complicated inner life of the infant, was heresy, whereas Klein insisted that she represented a logical development of Freud's ideas. As a result, the society was divided into two sections. Students could study under Klein (the "A Group") or with adherents of Anna Freud (the "B Group").

I talked to people representing both groups. There were three women who refused to discuss Klein with me: her implacable enemy Anna Freud; Paula Heimann, once one of Klein's most fervent supporters before they had parted bitterly; and Klein's daughter, Melitta Schmideberg, who had not spoken to her mother for twenty-five years before Klein's death in 1960. Their failure to cooperate was a great pity because I would have given their views a fair presentation. One great source of help, however, was Klein's son Eric Clyne,[1] a dear man who truly wanted an honest biography to be written and seemed pleased that his mother would receive adequate recognition. Eric, a successful businessman, had an incredible memory, and provided me with names of people, such as his mother's housekeeper, who would be helpful.

From the beginning I tried to make it clear to everyone that I was not writing a partisan biography. Some of the Kleinians felt that I could not really understand Klein's theories without having had a Kleinian analysis. I replied that this would endanger my independence. Nevertheless, Klein's theories had an extraordinarily personal resonance for me. Freud had virtually ignored women, but Klein's main preoccupation was the development of the girl child, beginning with that vital relationship with the breast. How remarkable that I, who had always had such an obsession about breasts, should end up writing about a woman whose theories were based on the infant's perception of the good and the bad breast. Klein also wrote about different kinds of depression – manic and mournful – and for someone like me who had suffered periodic depressions all my life, her work struck a deep chord. She also wrote frankly about the prevalence of envy and its manifestations in aggression. I was especially drawn to her theory of reparation, in which we try to atone for past harms we have caused.

The final passage in her 1937 paper "Love, Guilt and Reparation" left me profoundly moved.

> A good relation to ourselves is a condition for love, tolerance, and wisdom towards others. This good relation to ourselves has developed in part from a friendly,

---

1 Like many others, he changed the spelling of his name during the war.

loving and understanding attitude towards other people, namely, those who have meant much to us in the past, and our relationship to whom has become part of our minds and personalities. If we have become able, deep in our unconscious minds, to clear our feelings to some extent towards our parents of grievances, and have forgiven them for the frustrations we had to bear, then we can be at peace with ourselves and are able to love others in the true sense of the word.

Those words lodged deep in my heart, and in a sense I think they marked the real beginning of my reconciliation with my mother, who still, even in death, was part of my inner life. In short, Melanie Klein changed the way I looked at myself and at the world. Marie Bonaparte would have been tame stuff in comparison.

There were striking similarities between Klein's life and my own, although I had to be extremely careful not to identify with her too closely. We were, in some ways, mirror images of each other. She was the youngest of four children, whereas I was the eldest. She, too, had had three children, except that her daughter was the first born. She had been through a difficult divorce. Born in Vienna, she had flowered late in Britain. Like me, she had lived in many houses. Her professional life, like mine, was dogged by controversy and male chauvinism. The Kleinians were alert to my growing enthusiasm, and in my longing for acceptance, I was delighted when an ardent Kleinian analyst, Betty Joseph, declared me "an honorary Kleinian." The Kleinians and I continued for some time in this state of collusive fantasy.

I soon discovered that I could not have stumbled upon a more controversial figure. Many of the British analysts resented Klein, a central European, taking over their society. "What has happened to our

British society?" Claire Winnicott asked me.[2] There was no one who didn't have strong views about Klein. It was hard for many people to accept her account of the complicated, turbulent mind of the infant. Totally autocratic, she forced one to agree with her completely; if not, you were her enemy. She had no compunction about expelling her own followers into outer darkness if they disputed her ideas or promulgated theories of their own. This could mean real financial hardship if they no longer received patient referrals. I am certainly glad that I never met her; I doubt that I would have liked her particularly. Nevertheless, she struck me as an immensely intriguing figure – and that is the major demand I make of anyone about whom I write.

It is not easy to find an appropriate biographical subject, but I believe that Melanie Klein and I were meant for each other. Mystical as it may sound, I also believe that the subject comes to the writer clamouring to be brought to life, a view shared by many biographers. During the first year of work on the book I experienced moments of terror at my recklessness in taking on a task of this magnitude, but I had to bed my fears and often repeated the familiar mantra "*Courage, mon coeur.*" In this Klein served as a role model. She endured obloquy from the psychoanalytic community for her theories on the vivid phantasy life of infants, but she soldiered on. I never forgot the fact that despite a lifelong struggle with depression, she emerged triumphant, so that her last years were the most sanguine of her life.

The preparatory work for the book involved far more than a mastery of the theoretical concepts. Klein was born in Vienna in 1882 and had moved to Budapest after her marriage. I had to learn much about the political climate in central Europe in the first part of

---

2 She was the widow of the famous child analyst D.W. Winnicott, who had been a colleague of Klein's but laid greater stress on the role of the mother than on the phantasy life of the infant. (In Kleinian theory, phantasy spelled with "ph" refers to unconscious processes.)

the century, the situation of the Jewish population, and the possibilities open to a woman of that generation. I could not afford a research assistant, and in any case, I do not think anyone else can extract the information that the writer finds significant.

The most important part of biography-writing is the task of getting into the skin of the subject. I would compare it to an actor who studies his role intensely, both his character's view of the world and others' view of his character. Naturally different biographers will regard a subject differently, just as actors are continually reinterpreting Hamlet. My methodology is based on the pithy description of character given by Henry James. "What is character," he asked, "but the determination of incident? What is incident but the illustration of character?" How the subject behaves, how others react in certain situations, illuminates the inner person.

Part of the fascination of the research was the unusual encounters it afforded. Bob was longing to meet Masud Khan, whom I had not seen since our charged conversation about cancer. Masud accepted an invitation to dinner, only to have his secretary send us a telegram on the appointed day to say that he had suddenly been summoned to Buckingham Palace. It was well known that Klein had strongly opposed Masud's candidacy as a qualified psychoanalyst. Not only had I alienated him by accusing him of arrogance in his attitude to cancer, but now I was writing about a woman whom he loathed. One day he rang and suggested a questionable deal. If I would make available to him all the relevant manuscript material I turned up ("Not just gossip, Pat"), he would give me access to his private archive (which included papers he had filched from the society's archives). "That's very generous of you, Masud," I replied coolly, "I'll think it over." I never got back to him.

Around this time Charles Rycroft, the eminent analyst, was having dinner with us. I asked him if he had ever received a silver salver from an anonymous donor. Charles looked perplexed. No, he had not.

Masud had told me that he had gone to Asprey's and ordered a salver to be sent to Charles without any card attached. This was his way, he told me, of thanking Charles for resigning from the society in sympathy for the way he had been treated. God knows how many other such fabrications he had uttered. After Masud threatened to blow up the institute, it was locked up like a fortress. There was another story that he had taken out a contract on an analyst whom he considered an enemy. I saw him only once again, about three years later, when I was addressing a psychoanalytic group called the 1952 Club. He was drunk and accused me of outrageously erroneous things, but in those surroundings – and in his state – there was no point in engaging him in debate. Possibly he had a contract on me as well.

Then there was R.D. Laing, who had become something of a pop figure after the publication of *The Divided Self,* with his controversial views on schizophrenia. He gave one of the frankest and most interesting of the interviews I was accumulating in his account of his experience as a student when Klein was the reigning monarch. To my surprise, he subsequently rang and invited me out to dinner. He picked me up at the institute and we walked to Odin's, a lovely old London restaurant. I found his abstracted, weary face very attractive and we could have had a fascinating exchange, but my nervous aggressiveness ruined the evening. I lectured him about everything under the sun. I brought up his stagey appearance when he had appeared in Caxton Hall in black. ("Actually it was brown," he recalled with the hint of a self-satisfied smile.) I went on to harangue him about his neglect of his former analyst, Charles Rycroft, and, warming to the attack under the effects of alcohol, I waxed indignant about how he was responsible for mental patients wandering the streets. (He strenuously denied that he had ever advocated the closing of mental hospitals.) He was in a sad mood, in any case, because of the breakup of his marriage to his German wife. "I feel sorry for her," I said. "So do I," he agreed mournfully. At the end of the evening we were both drunk, and he did not have enough money to pay the bill. I had to lend him the cash, but he never repaid me. Who could blame him? I returned home in such a giggly state that Bob was furiously jealous and spent the night on the sofa.

Probably the most unexpected encounter occurred in Edinburgh where I travelled to interview Dr. Jock Sutherland, one of the best known of the object-relations theorists.[3] While there I was taken under the wing of a hospitable American, Susan Shatto, who gave a small dinner party for me. One of the guests, a doctor, remarked casually that he had a friend who had been analyzed by Melanie Klein as a child in Scotland. Bells rang. Klein had written a much-discussed book, *Narrative of a Child Analysis*, recounting the most lengthy case study of a child on record. But that analysis was described as taking place in Wales during the war. "Do you think he would see me?" I asked eagerly. The doctor became evasive: his friend had gone to the country with his family for the weekend.

The following morning Susan pushed a note under my door at the hotel where I was staying. The man who had been analyzed by Klein wanted to see me. Could I be at a drinks party at twelve? When I arrived at a beautiful house in the New Town, the mysterious gentleman was waiting for me with an eagerly expectant expression. After we were introduced, I said rashly, "I take it that you are Richard." He looked puzzled. "No, I'm David." "But you're Richard also." He was completely bewildered. Had I made a terrible mistake? Then I had an inspiration. I asked him about an episode that had especially irked "Richard" in those years. "Do you remember the bus conductress?" "Do I remember the bus conductress!" he cried, and imitating her

---

3 Object-relations theory can be summarized superficially as the view that no one exists as a solitary being. In all our relationships we enact some form of our earliest significant encounters.

broad Scots accent he shouted, "Half-fares stand up!"

David had no idea that he had been the subject of a famous book. I spent the afternoon at his flat with my tape recorder while he recalled everything he could from that experience when he was nine. He had an excellent memory and was delightfully open. The analysis had taken place in a Girl Guide hut in Pitlochry during the Blitz. (A plaque now marks the spot.) At one point he picked up my copy of the *Narrative* and kissed Klein's photo on the cover: "Good old Melanie." The encounter with "Richard" was probably my greatest coup. Much of the preparatory reading and research required for a biography never sees the light of day; a thrilling revelation like this makes it all worthwhile.

There were other discoveries. Through Eric and other sources I learned that Melanie Klein had analyzed her own children, a practice that would be considered by the psychoanalytic community an outrageous abuse of parental power. The first time I had accompanied Hanna Segal into that cluttered Hampstead room where she stored Klein's papers, I picked up two large bundles marked "Hans" and "Melitta" – the names of Klein's older children. "What are these?" I asked. "They look like case notes," Segal replied. By my next visit they had disappeared. When I had incontrovertible proof about Klein's analysis of her own children (most of which I had gained from Eric), I visited the leading Kleinians to tell them frankly what I had discovered. I didn't want them to be able to accuse me of springing startling information on them when the book appeared. There was general consternation. One man exclaimed, "My God, I'll have to go back to the drawing board. No wonder she emphasized the life of phantasy!" Hanna Segal remarked warily that she would have to check with Betty Joseph, who had analyzed Eric. But surely she must have known – and repressed that knowledge from herself – when we both saw those bundles of case notes.

Perhaps it was at this point that the Kleinians began to be alarmed about the revelations my book might contain. They were put on guard too when, at the insistence of my agent, Jacqueline, I requested written permission to quote from interviews and documents, something I should have asked for right at the outset of the project. Years later I learned that a series of nervous strategy meetings took place. One of the most decent men I interviewed was an Independent,[4] John Bowlby, the progenitor of attachment theory, a man loathed by the Kleinians. After our last meeting, he came to the door of his office and warned ominously, "They will tear you apart the way they did me."

That very night I accompanied Betty Joseph to the annual Ernest Jones Lecture (given by Frank Kermode that year). I repeated to her what Bowlby had said. Was this true? Would her group turn on me? "No, of course not," she reassured me.

MELANIE KLEIN AND AFTER

Happily not all my time in London was spent in work. Bob and I were building a life and a wonderful group of friends together. Helena had died, but Elizabeth Longford and I had become very close, meeting for tea and long conversations in her Chelsea flat. Her whole family is an amazing collection of literary talent, of whom the oldest daughter, Antonia Fraser, is perhaps the best known. Elizabeth's husband, Lord Longford, is regarded as the greatest of British eccentrics, but Bob always says that he is a shrewd old bird. He has the wonderful ability to devote total attention to the person to whom he is talking, absolutely oblivious to whether the individual is a celebrity or an unknown. Now

---

4 The Independents refused to be sharply identified with either the "A Group" or the "B Group." Winnicott and Rycroft were also Independents.

in his nineties, he visits prisoners regularly, although he was widely criticized for persistently advocating the release of Myra Hindley, the infamous Moors murderess.

We saw a lot of Anne and her English boyfriend, Julian Snowdon, whom she married early in 1982. At weekends we explored every variety of pub, attended art galleries, loved the National Film Theatre. From time to time I thought vaguely of becoming a permanent London resident, but the financial obstacles were too horrendous. Bob made very little in the insurance business, and I knew that I could not support myself on literary journalism or royalties from the sort of books I wrote. By now I was running out of grants. Since taking leave in 1976 I had existed on two Guggenheims, two Killams, and a Laidlaw fellowship. In the spring of 1982 I was awarded a second Laidlaw grant as well as a Rockefeller fellowship. Neither was sufficient to live on for a year, but I persuaded both agencies to split the grants into six-month periods. This anxious anticipation of renewed funding every spring could not continue indefinitely, and I was beginning to tire of being an expatriate. I used to gaze longingly at pictures of my Cabbagetown cottage, which Bob had nicknamed "Sprucey Baby."

The hardest part of returning to Canada would be leaving Anne behind. I was almost distraught at the thought of parting from my only daughter, who had now settled in England permanently. Anne seemed as upset as I at our impending departure. "Couldn't you wait a few more months?" she asked.

The mother-daughter relationship is mysteriously deep, and Klein had illuminated it for me in many ways. Sometimes when walking I feel as though I am moving the way Anne does. When she has suffered, I have wondered if I was suffering more in order to lighten her pain. Melanie Klein would call this projective identification, and if it is carried too far, it can become a form of unconscious pathological power. With time I have accepted that my daughter is a mature adult, not the little girl whose hand I used to hold on her way home from school. Spunky and resilient, she is perfectly capable of solving her own problems. The irony of Klein's view of reparation and identification is that with her own daughter she could not separate theory from practice. She viewed Melitta as an extension of herself and, unable to accept her as an adult, forced them into a permanent estrangement. This is what Mother did with Joan, and almost succeeded in doing with me.

Understandably, the University of Toronto could not hold my job open indefinitely. (Bob often joked that I thought a sabbatical meant being away for seven years!) But one of our major problems was Bob's future. Would he be allowed into Canada, and how could he make a living? In September 1981 we had returned to Toronto on a visit mainly to see my new grandson, but also to inquire about Bob's prospects. He spoke Mandarin fluently; an old friend in the insurance business suggested that he would hire him to train Chinese recruits. So far, so good. Nevertheless, he was permitted into the country only on a six-month visa despite the fact that his sister was a Canadian citizen and that he had enlisted in the Canadian army in 1943.

We arrived back at the end of May 1982. When we drove up to the house the grass was waist-high. My heart sank. A series of students had occupied the house during my long absence. When we entered we found everything spotless. On the dining table a note was propped: "The house has been good to us, and we think we have been good to it." After a life of constant moving I wanted to stay in this place for the rest of my life.

I still had one year free in which to work on the book, and I began writing within ten days of our return. Bob was very brave about starting again – as he had done so many times in the past – but we were extremely anxious lest he be deported. Finally, through the combined intervention of the writer Christina McCall and Lorna Marsden, a former student of mine and at that time head of the feminist National Action Committee on the Status of Women, he was given landed immigrant status, but he did not dare leave the country for three years until he could apply for citizenship.

Those first months of anxiety were a severe strain. I would wake in the mornings with acute panic attacks and decided that I must seek professional help. In England, shortly after my cancer operation, I had gone to Masud for advice in finding someone who would charge me a fee within my means. He immediately complied, telling me that it was essential to get therapeutic help when one has cancer, and that in his case he had had another analysis with Miss Freud. He then rang one of his former analysands, an American, who was already making a name for himself. Dr. Y. lived in north London in an area very difficult to reach. After a few visits I abandoned seeing him. However, when Bob and I moved into Kynance Mews, I could have the use of Bob's car to make a weekly visit. By then I had embarked on the Klein book, and in retrospect I think Dr. Y. was almost more interested in what I was uncovering about Melanie Klein than he was in my problems.

Nevertheless, in our last session he gave me the name of an excellent analyst in Toronto, and when I phoned Dr. C. he took me on immediately. For a number of years I went to him for what he described as psychoanalytic therapy once a week (which increased to twice during my struggle with the Kleinians). I am not sure how he accomplished it – apart from helping me to face myself and my fears honestly through constant dialogue. I am of the firm belief that skilful clinicians are born and are not the products of rigorous training. Empathy is the essential quality required, and certainly the ability to administer tough love. Dr. C. was a decent and straightforward human being. But even a "good analyst" isn't the solution for everyone. I was fortunate that we seemed to be the right fit. Few people go into serious analysis in later life, but with me it worked – because I desperately wanted to be calm and consistently contented.

My apprehensiveness, he explained, was rooted in the uncertainty of my relationship with my mother, and he made me see that it was in my power to surmount these anxieties. He described my condition as "reactive depression," and he refused to treat it with antidepressants. I have seen Prozac help troubled friends, but in a way it is a kind of Band-Aid which does not deal with deeper problems. Analysis gave me more than the "common unhappiness" which was all that Freud would promise. It made me realize that my expectations for myself were too high, and that there was great pleasure to be found in small satisfactions. After all, long before I encountered Dr. C., my favourite adage was Voltaire's "Cultivate your garden" – even though Voltaire didn't exactly match practice with precept. When Dr. C. and I finally parted we both knew that I had not developed into a perfect human being by any means, but at least I was one who had greater control over her anxieties.

I used to be a world-class worrier. Bob conceived of a technique to address the problem. He kept a notepad in his bedside table and would occasionally pull it out and date a page. Then I had to tell him my top three or four worries in descending order. For a long time the first one was "Will I pay off the mortgage?" We would pull the pad out at intervals of three or four months, and find that previous worries had evaporated entirely, to be replaced by others. We finally ceased consulting the list altogether.

Before my return to England in 1979 I had left the papers connected with *Havelock Ellis* – the various versions of the manuscript and all my files – with McClelland & Stewart for safekeeping in the expectation of donating them to the Thomas Fisher Rare Book Library at the University of Toronto. There they would be appraised, and I would receive a tax certificate. In 1982 I rang Jack McClelland and asked if he would return them to me. Yes, of course.

Time passed, and I rang Jack again. He was evasive. After that I was always passed on to his secretary, Marge Hodgeman, who was maddeningly unhelpful. Eventually Jack invited me to lunch in the Prince Arthur Room at the Park Plaza. During the meal he behaved in an oddly distracted way, his handsome raddled face even more tense than usual. Finally, over coffee, he turned to me.

"Pat, we've had our differences in the past."

"What are you talking about, Jack? We haven't had a cross word in years."

"Well," one of his enormous sighs, "the fact of the matter is that we seem to have lost your papers. The insurance company says that you will have to sue us."

At first aghast, I then broke into laughter. I could not believe that I had another lawsuit on my hands. A lawyer was hired and for months some kind of negotiations ground on. Then the biographer Elspeth Cameron came to interview me about Jack for a profile she was writing for *Saturday Night*. I told her the story of the missing papers. When her article appeared, someone at the Fisher read it and said to her colleagues, "Surely we have those papers?" They checked – and there they all were, beautifully catalogued and in the stacks. Someone at McClelland & Stewart had prematurely shipped them off, leaving no record of their whereabouts.

Despite these stresses, we settled happily into our first real home. There was much work to be done, and with a monumental effort to live within a very tight budget, the mortgage was paid off before I retired. As for the Klein project, I have never written a book which afforded me so much intellectual enrichment. Every morning I would rush to my desk, not knowing how the story would unfold that day. I was my own Scheherazade. I can remember thinking how wonderful it was to be carrying that whole world around in my head. Bob read and commented on every chapter as I finished it, something he has continued to do to this day.

The manuscript still in progress, I returned to the University of Toronto in the fall of 1983, determined to stay clear of academic politics and to concentrate entirely on my teaching. The wounds from the bitter tenure battle had not healed, so I moved out of my beautiful office in University College to a smaller one in New College, two doors away from Peter Dyson. I once again felt very much the new girl, especially during the first week when my colleagues were walking around with glazed expressions. I thought they were cutting me, but they were in fact totally preoccupied with their classes. Those years at New College, where I stayed until my retirement, were the happiest teaching days of my life, although sometimes even now if I happen to be walking through the halls of University College I gaze nostalgically into the rooms that were once so familiar to me.

Much had changed in my absence. Two years before I left for London the English departments in the separate colleges were merged into one super-department on the model of the University of California. While we might have had our differences within the colleges, at least there was some sense of esprit de corps. Now the chairman presided in the old library building, which we called "the Kremlin." The university had grown so large and impersonal that there were many of my colleagues whom I never met during the years remaining before my retirement.

Humanists were replaced by scientists and lawyers in the university president's chair. It is remarkable how many physicists occupy high administrative positions. One of them once told me, "If you don't keep up with new developments, you soon fall behind," and administration provided a safe haven for those lacking creativity. There was constant anxiety about funding; the shrewdest among the faculty took administrative positions in order to secure higher salaries. Faculty were urged to take early retirement, only to be replaced by young people on contractual jobs with no sense of real commitment and in a constant state of worry about their futures. Classes became over-crowded. I continued to invite students to my home and many reported feelings of total alienation, seeing different people in every class. A few began to negotiate over their marks, and one angry woman almost assaulted me because I wouldn't raise her B+ to an A.

In this tense atmosphere and with the anxiety over Bob's status in the country, I was suddenly hit with a tax audit. This is a frighten-ing experience, especially as one feels singled out for having done something wrong. I felt aggrieved because I had been careful to keep proper records, including all the receipts of my research expenses. A pattern, however, began to emerge. Toni Onley, the West Coast artist, was audited first. He made a highly public protest by burning a great pile of his paintings on the beach. Next to be targeted were the musi-cians of the Toronto Symphony Orchestra, who were suddenly not permitted to deduct their instruments as a business expense. At this point I went public, supported by the Canadian Association of University Teachers. We now had targeted individuals representing various fields in the arts. More and more people then came forward. Many artists would have been absolutely destitute if they had had to pay the sums Revenue Canada was demanding. With a large group making a united and vociferous protest, a group who had access to the media, Revenue Canada backed down. In the end I had to pay a frac-tion (albeit considerable) of the sum originally demanded, and I found myself an excellent accountant.

Overall, I was more mature and confident than I had been before the period in England, and this was reflected in my teaching. At New College I was allowed to offer a course on the history of British psychoanalysis as part of the women's studies program. The English department (including my female colleagues) were scathing about the validity of studying women's issues. I can remember the expression of astonishment on one woman's face when I argued that the program was filled with eminent faculty, including the Miltonian scholar Mary Nyquist, who was director of women's studies at that time.

My course was mainly concerned with a study of Klein's theories. Since, unlike Freud's, her emphasis was on the development of the woman, it was a logical part of the curriculum. I did not trumpet my feminist views; after all, I had lived them. I heard that Paula Caplan (who was known for her work on female masochism) had complained that I was not a real feminist and that I should be replaced. Her proposed substitute was Jeffrey Masson!

The course attracted wonderful students, and that first year I ran excitedly across the quad to our meeting every Tuesday. The women ranged in age from their early twenties to over seventy. Highly intelligent, impressively articulate, they included social workers and therapists. The course also attracted auditors, including Elizabeth Smart, the author of *By Grand Central Station I Sat Down and Wept*, who was living in Toronto that year. Elizabeth became very vocal, interrupting people when they were speaking, arguing vociferously. Finally, at the beginning of a class, I made a short statement to the effect that the course belonged to the students enrolled in it, and the auditors were there (I put it politely) as a courtesy. Elizabeth was never seen again.

By the end of the year the class was so reluctant to part that I suggested we form a women's discussion group. We met every month for three years, supportive, informative, and enthusiastic. As I began to travel on lecture tours, the group slowly dissolved, as such groups eventually do. Nevertheless, I believe those three years enhanced all our lives. With one of its participants in particular, Marion Walker, a member of the fine arts department, I formed one of the closest friendships of my life. I must add that in the first couple of years I taught the course I was still very much under Klein's spell, and I am afraid that I tended to proselytize. When a student told me later that she had been afraid to say anything critical of Klein, I was horrified that I had been behaving like Klein herself. The young woman's frankness was appreciated, and after that I tried to ensure that no one felt restricted in disagreeing with either Klein or me.

I also taught first-year survey courses. Some professors believe they are too grand for this, although Northrop Frye never did. First-year students deserve the very best instruction available, and it is a thrill to encounter young minds still open and unjaded. There had been a big change in the classes during my absence in this regard: older, retired people were now part of the group, and this mingling of maturity with the freshness of youth made the experience in the classroom particularly enriching.

In my graduate class in biography and autobiography, I gave the students an assignment to describe an incident as if written in a diary, autobiography, or biography. Since almost all of them gravitated to the highly personal confessional mode I soon abandoned the practice. A salutary lesson to memoir-writers! I renewed the old custom of inviting specialists to address my undergraduate course. Some were more memorable than others: I think of a priest from St. Michael's who talked on Saint Augustine. He had great confidence but was not particularly inspiring. I took him to lunch at the Faculty Club, hoping to have an interesting theological discussion with him, but he was intent on boasting about how he had survived the 1987 stock market crash by his wise investment decisions.

I still had to return to England several times for further research. Eric Clyne had told me that he had a lot of family papers in his loft. From the beginning I pleaded with him to let me see them, but he always had an excuse: the paper was too fragile, the ink was too faint, the German was too archaic. Finally I persuaded him to release them, and I found a translator. Melanie Klein had left a brief autobiography which always struck me as suspect, a sanitized version of her life, although Hanna Segal believed in it implicitly. By the summer of 1984 I had written a major portion of the book. Now I had to rewrite almost half of it in view of what I was learning from those family letters.

Klein had depicted her family as cultivated and civilized, but the letters revealed a dysfunctional family with an ineffectual father and an overbearing mother on whom Klein was neurotically dependent. It was strong stuff, and certainly far more interesting than the mythologized pablum the Kleinians had been fed. Yet these revelations did nothing to undermine my admiration for Klein's theoretical contribution.

As I have said, Eric Clyne was extremely cooperative through-out my research. After a consultation with his children, he gave me the letter Melitta had written to her mother announcing her decision to be an independent woman, no longer an appendage to her mother. At the same time he gave me Klein's last pocket diary, which I still cherish. But even he became a bit nervous about what those unpublished letters might contain. "Tell me," he asked, "is there anything in those letters that might embarrass my family?" "Well, Eric," I replied, "it is difficult to know what might embarrass people." The following morning he rang me at my hotel. "I've been thinking. You must tell the truth exactly as you see it."

In the summer of 1985 I went to England for the unveiling of a plaque on Melanie Klein's Regency house in St. John's Wood. It was a wonderfully happy occasion for me, and I felt honoured to be invited for lunch in the house. I remember walking away afterwards with Betty Joseph and Hanna Segal. Betty remarked that on an occasion like this she wished that she believed in an afterlife. "I wish you did too, Betty," I remarked. Dr. Segal looked at me sharply. "Do you really mean that?" I tried to explain that the sight of Klein's granddaughter, also called Melanie, a beautiful young lady who bore a startling resemblance to her famous grandmother, was a form of immortality. But she seemed disturbed. I believe that she had always assumed I was Jewish because of my name, and now she realized that I was a Christian.

The following day I visited Dr. Segal. She had always been extremely pleasant with me, and I had shared meals with her family. For the first time I detected a distinct chill. By this time she too had read the translated letters and, without consulting me, had phoned the translator (whom I was paying), instructing her not to translate any more of Klein's poetry. (Dr. Segal's husband thought it might harm Klein's reputation.) "What do you think of Libussa [Klein's domineering mother]?" I asked. She shook her head sorrowfully. "When I think of the way she used to talk to me about her saintly mother!" Then – as if to forestall further discussion – she turned her attention to the cricket she was watching on TV with her son.

I had made it clear that no one outside of the publishing world was to see the manuscript before publication. As the release date approached in the spring of 1986 I was very edgy about the Kleinians' reaction. When *Publishers Weekly* gave it a wonderful advance review I rang Betty Joseph in England to tell her. I suppose I hoped she would soften if she thought the general reaction would be favourable. I believed (and still believe) that I had written a celebratory book with a strong predilection for Klein's theories, as well as admiration for the way she had triumphed over her own depression. Nevertheless, I had shown her as a human being – vain, autocratic, domineering. The Kleinians were always talking about the ability to tolerate ambivalence. Did they have the ability to accept both the good and the bad in their own idol?

One of Klein's books was entitled *Envy and Gratitude*; I dedicated my book to Brian, "with love and gratitude." Without him the work would never have been written.

Melanie Klein: Her World and Her Work first appeared in the United States, heralded by a splendid review by Sherry Turkle in the *New York*

Times Book Review. I was highly curious as to who would review it in the *Globe and Mail* in Canada. Bob and I went downtown late the night before it appeared to pick up a copy. When I saw whom Jack Kapica, the book editor, had chosen – Jeffrey Masson – I broke into hysterical laughter, but by the time we arrived home I was in despair. Knowing full well that I had given Masson's book on Freud's apostasy over the seduction theory, *The Assault on Truth*, a highly critical review two years before, and also that Klein was a *bête noire* with Masson, it seemed mischievous beyond words for Kapica to choose such a partisan critic. I swore that I would never again review for the *Globe and Mail* as long as Kapica was book editor.

Apparently many people wrote to the paper to protest, but by then I was in England for the British publication. On arrival I rang a woman I considered a friend, Irma Brenman-Pick, one of the leading Kleinians. Bob and I had often been entertained in their house. Irma now proceeded to slash the book with a harshness I had never detected in her before. Finally I asked, "Irma, was there *anything* about the book you liked?" A long pause. "No, I don't think so."

Bob took me off to Brittany for a few days so that I could pull myself together. It poured during almost the whole trip and inside the car I wept buckets. There were rumours that the Kleinians intended to boycott the publication party at Canada House. There was no sign of them until the speeches began, at which point a large phalanx of familiar figures advanced from the back of the room. When the high commissioner proposed a toast to the success of the book, they refrained from raising their glasses.

The next few weeks were a nightmare. Hanna Segal attacked me violently in the *Sunday Times,* particularly for unwittingly confusing two suicides, both former patients of Klein's. That I had taken the Kleinians seriously on their own self-evaluation struck me suddenly when, after my moaning on about Hanna Segal, Elizabeth Longford asked me,

"Who is this Hanna Segal? I've heard of Clancy Segal, other Segals, but never Hanna Segal."

The Kleinians proved to be feral and formidable when on the offensive. They planted reviews, prevented the publication of favourable reviews, and attempted to halt the sale of foreign rights. Betty Joseph did her best to turn Eric against me, and the poor man was caught in a tug-of-war. When perceiving themselves as threatened, the Kleinians behaved just as their critics had warned. Indeed, there were enough ominous signs before the book came out. Melanie Klein had spent her entire life being attacked and she passed on to her followers a siege mentality, a sense of the necessity of constantly being alert for blows from unexpected quarters. Now I, whom they once had flattered and praised, was demonized.

Some weeks before I left Canada the Institute of Contemporary Arts had rung proposing a "debate" with Juliet Mitchell, the author of *Psychoanalysis and Feminism*. "A debate on what?" I asked naively. Since Juliet was widely regarded as an apologist for Freud, I had insisted that a Kleinian such as Hanna Segal or Irma Brenman-Pick should also appear on the platform.

After I experienced the first shock of the Kleinian reaction I couldn't decide what to do about the debate. At a luncheon at the House of Lords the Longfords advised me against participating because they feared I couldn't tough it out. In a telephone conversation the eminent Jungian Anthony Storr advised differently. "If you don't appear, they'll call you a coward." That settled it.

Juliet Mitchell and Irma sat collaboratively at one end of the platform, I at the other. Charles Rycroft had asked if I would like him to come along. In the ensuing bloodbath in the packed hall Charles stood up and made an impassioned, eloquent speech in my defence. I have always been grateful to that decent man.

The day following the debate – odd as it may seem – Bob and

I were married in Marylebone Registry Office, with Brian, Anne, and Elizabeth Longford as witnesses. In the afternoon we were given the blessing in the Anglican church we had attended while living in London, but our rector refused to marry us because we had been divorced. It seemed to me the height of hypocrisy considering that he had no compunction about being an active gay member of the clergy.

The events surrounding the publication of *Melanie Klein* were among the worst experiences I can recall, yet the book was to lead to ten of the most interesting years of my life. Although the Kleinians tried to destroy the work, it was translated into several languages (despite its length) and is now used extensively as a textbook of Kleinian theory, the concepts explained in language that a layman can understand. Klein had been relatively unknown in America until the publication of my biography. Now I was bombarded with invitations to speak all over the United States, Europe, and South America. It provided Bob and me with a wonderful way to travel, a focus in which we met interesting people and made many fast friends. But I was a good deal less starry-eyed about the psychoanalytic profession.

I have often thought of Milton's words in *Areopagitica*: "Books are not absolutely dead things, but do contain a potency of life in them to be as active as that soul was whose progeny they are."

8

HOBBIES: NONE

"What are your hobbies?"

The question was put to me by a woman who was to introduce me as a speaker at an event. I was stunned. Hobbies? I hated the word. Weren't hobbies things like stamp collecting? The evening arrived, and as I sat waiting on the platform she told the audience that I was a workaholic because I didn't have "hobbies." What I consider part and parcel of my life – music, gardening, travel – are apparently hobbies. What about friendship? A hobby? She might have asked about "interests," but even that word is inadequate. What gives me most sustained satisfaction, what is an absolute necessity, is writing. But how can one separate writing from the rest of one's life? Since I started to write seriously, almost everything in life seems somehow related to it. Opera, novels, jazz, gardening, even watching mindless television make one more than just a writing machine.

The two works that most affected my life were the biographies of John Addington Symonds and Melanie Klein. (Perhaps I should add *Havelock Ellis* since it inspired Bob to contact me again.) *Symonds* was my springboard to a professional life; *Klein* opened up an exciting and sometimes disturbing wider world.

Here's one illustration of what I mean by the interlinking of different aspects of a writing life. In the early summer of 1988 I made one of my periodic visits to England. When I arrived, Anne told me that a good friend of mine, the psychoanalyst John Padel, had recently telephoned her with the news that the National Theatre was mounting a production of a play called *Mrs. Klein*, and he thought I should be alerted. Puzzled, I made a beeline for the National Theatre; sure enough, a play by that title was opening in about three weeks. I then proceeded to the British Institute of Psycho-Analysis, where the librarian reported that a man named Nicholas Wright, apparently the literary officer of the National Theatre, had made a few visits to the library and had sat there reading what she described as "old books."

I contacted John Rush, at that time the agent for film rights at David Higham Associates, who managed to obtain a copy of the script. As I read through it I saw that Wright had based his three characters on a chapter of my book, "Mothers and Daughters," using my interpretation of the relationship between Melanie Klein, her daughter Melitta Schmideberg, and Paula Heimann (who becomes the surrogate daughter) as the basis for his plot. John learned that Wright had gone to a solicitor and was told that it would be advisable to do some original research of his own. I couldn't find a single example of "original research" in his play, but we could demonstrate that there were enough similarities between the book and the play to prove that he could not have secured the details from any other source. As a result, an acknowledgment to me was inserted in the program and I received a tiny royalty. If I had pushed for more, John warned me that we would have had to go to court, and he seemed very reluctant to do that.

I had tickets to attend the opening night at the Cottesloe with Anne, but I was so distressed by what I regarded as Wright's cannibalism and his failure to contact me that I couldn't face the experience. I gave my ticket to William St. Clair and flew home to Toronto. Since then the play has been produced internationally, and eventually I was able to see productions in Washington, Toronto, and New York. It became another vehicle through which Klein became known to a larger public.

A memorable incident occurred one evening after the performance in Washington when I was participating in a panel with the producer and a Kleinian analyst, Elliott Jacques. A man in the audience suddenly collapsed. Someone screamed, "Is there a doctor in the house?" Half the audience stood up. Those of us on the stage became the audience for the real-life drama happening below us, with paramedics and a stretcher-bearer rushing through the seats. Then, as though nothing had happened, it was back to a discussion of the legitimacy of using real people in a literary context.

Uta Hagen was so compelling as Klein in the New York production that she made me almost glad the play had been written – and in Uta I made a vibrant new friend who is unfazed by age. I might have the ability to write biography, but not the special talent needed to dramatize my insights. Uta and I talked about the issue of fictionalizing the lives of real people. It is a practice that makes me distinctly uncomfortable; Uta had no such qualms. But then, she didn't have the stake in Klein that I had. I was particularly disturbed when Wright depicted Klein throwing a glass of wine in Melitta's face and forcing paper into her mouth, incidents which he had invented. I hope I never meet Mr. Wright.

Everything about Melanie Klein continued to attract controversy. Her reputation as someone with dangerous ideas was promulgated by the European émigré analysts who had been adherents of Anna Freud's ego theory, which treated the unconscious as something too fragile to explore. Yet in some centres, such as Los Angeles, there were Kleinian splinter groups that had parted company with mainstream classical analysis.

One lecture led to another. At the Austen Riggs clinic in Stockbridge, Massachusetts, I ran into the man with whom I had started analysis in England. A few days later I discovered that he had given a lecture which seemed to be based on historical material he had learned from me in our sessions while I was researching Klein. I rang him and asked for clarification. He began to shout at me, accusing me of paranoia, litigiousness, and so on. The following week I saw him at a reception in New York, where he walked past me without a sign of recognition.

This latter encounter occurred in April 1987, when I was invited to be the luncheon speaker at the annual meeting of the American Psychological Association. Just before the event started I joined the usual lengthy queue in the women's washroom. Two women standing ahead of me were talking. "Are you going to the luncheon?" one asked. "Yes," the other replied, "I might as well since I'll never read the book." I repeated this conversation in my opening remarks, and it brought down the house. "I don't know where you're sitting," I said, "but I'll do my best to summarize more than five hundred pages in the short time I have."

One of the people in that New York audience was Carole Morgan, an analyst from Los Angeles, who was subsequently responsible for my receiving a whole series of invitations to that city. Carole thought it would be interesting if I spoke on the history of women pioneers in the psychoanalytic movement to a group of female analysts in the Los Angeles area. However, by now the book had created wide interest among the broader psychoanalytic and scholarly community, and the audience was much larger than Carole and her committee had anticipated.

I bought a ribbed grey Armani jacket and a silk Ungaro top with a pattern of grey and black roses. This became my standard uniform for innumerable lectures. On this first visit I stayed in a private house in Beverly Hills, where each morning a butler (who had previously worked at Buckingham Palace) brought my breakfast with the New York and Los Angeles papers tucked into the pockets on either side of the tray. The odd thing was that my hostess hadn't read my book, hadn't even opened a copy of it, but she saw my name as a drawing card. *Melanie Klein* was the hot item of the moment. There are stars like the Paris analyst Joyce MacDougall in the psychoanalytic firmament; I was a passing meteor.

Astroturf was spread over the lawn of my hostess's garden, where the audience sat while I spoke from the patio. As I left the podium I noticed a couple of burly cops walking through the house. When I asked why they were there, I was told that an intruder had been seen in the neighbourhood. A year or so later Carole revealed that while I had been lecturing, there had been several death threats against me, phoned in to the police station, and that one had been traced to the house where I was staying.

Los Angeles was to be the site of several bizarre happenings during my visits. It was an intriguing mixture: laid-back people in hot tubs and an analyst who returns to find her cat killed and its blood smeared over the walls, a crime for which she suspects another analyst. Nevertheless, I loved to stay with Carole and her husband, Jud, in their beautiful house high in the Santa Monica Mountains above Topanga Canyon. Standing in their pool and looking around at that serene and beautiful landscape was my idea of Shangri-La. The talks and lectures on Klein allowed such unexpected experiences. For a time I was absolutely seduced by the exoticism of this world, expecting to be boarding planes to California, to Chicago, even to Topeka, Kansas, into the indefinite future.

Since I had got into hot water by writing about one controversial woman, I followed it with another, a small book on Margaret Mead, part of a series on modern women that Emma Tennant was editing for Penguin. At one time I had considered writing a major book on Mead but was firmly discouraged by her executor. Thank God, because I found the woman totally unsympathetic. Unfortunately my book appeared at the end of the series and it sank without trace, since the first titles to be published were hammered. A pity, because while it is brief, it gives a succinct account of Mead as a woman and as an anthropologist. As a result of my independent study of Mead I subsequently became a great supporter of Derek Freeman, whose *Margaret Mead and Samoa: The Making and Unmaking of an Anthropological Myth* had caused an uproar when it was published in 1983. Freeman made a cogent and persuasive case that Mead's research in Samoa had been superficial, if not downright dishonest. I also appeared in a documentary film on the controversy made by the Australian filmmaker Frank Heimans.

One summer day in 1988 I received a call from my American agent, Claire Smith (she has since died). Had I ever heard of a group of people around Freud who had received rings from him? Of course, these were the members of his "secret committee." Claire had been having lunch with a well-known editor, Jane Isay, then at Addison-Wesley, who wondered if I would be interested in writing a book on the committee. After the pain of the Klein book, I had sworn that I would not write on another psychoanalytic subject, but this one intrigued me. It was amazing that no one had ever tackled it before; indeed no one had known of the existence of the committee until Ernest Jones published his biography of Freud in 1953. Jones had emphasized the importance of the committee in the crucial decision-making period in the early history of psychoanalysis, but he was clearly so prejudiced against Freud's favourite, Sandor Ferenczi, that it was tempting to pursue the true story of the inception and dynamics of the committee. There were two aspects to the subject that particularly appealed to me. In the first place, I knew that there were masses of unpublished papers to be examined, and I also liked the idea of tackling the technical challenge of a group biography. After my experience with the Kleinians, I felt that I understood something of the dynamics of group behaviour, how people who share the same ideological beliefs can indulge in punitive actions collectively while assuming no responsibility for their actions individually. I was sorry to leave Knopf, my long-time American publisher, but the subject was irresistible.

This book entailed a great deal of travel, as the papers were widely dispersed. I spent much time at Columbia, which holds the Otto Rank correspondence with Freud as well as the *Rundbriefe*, the round-robin letters exchanged by the six members of the committee who made all the major decisions about the organization of the psychoanalytic movement. Janet Malcolm describes the biographer as "a professional burglar" and talks about "the voyeurism and busybodyism that impel writers and readers of biography alike." While there is some truth in what she says, the main fascination of biography for me is in fitting all the pieces of the vast jigsaw puzzle together, and this was a puzzle of extraordinary complexity.

In England there was a large collection of papers in an agency called the Freud Copyrights, housed in the most unlikely place, Wivenhoe, a tiny port southeast of Colchester, Essex. How was I going to be able to work regularly in such an out-of-the-way spot? An angel came to my rescue in the person of the mystery writer Ruth Rendell.

My first real acquaintance with Ruth occurred when someone alerted me to the fact that she had placed a copy of *Havelock Ellis* in the murderer's bookcase in *An Unkindness of Ravens*. Then we actually met when we were both speaking at a bookstore, A Different Drummer, in Burlington, Ontario, in 1986. I introduced myself to her in the washroom. She was travelling with her husband, Don, who was highly amused by the way I talked casually about penis and breast envy, oblivious to the fact that the largely older audience was sitting there in a state of shock. To my surprise Ruth later turned up at the British publication party for *Melanie Klein*. That fall she and Don came to the International Festival of Authors in Toronto, and this occasion was the beginning of a close friendship between the two couples.

When I was at my wits' end about the logistics of Wivenhoe, Ruth generously offered me a cottage on the grounds of Nussteads, their wonderful sixteenth-century house in Suffolk, and also the loan of a car to make the hour's drive back and forth every day. My difficulties were not over. As Ronald Clark once remarked, "There are always difficulties with every biography. But with each one the problems are different." While I was permitted to examine some material at Wivenhoe, I was denied access to the Freud-Ferenczi correspondence – probably the most important piece in the puzzle.

At this point Ruth invited for dinner some country neighbours whom she thought I would find interesting. The couple were Arno Pomerans, the translator, and his wife, Frieda. As I was bewailing my predicament about the Ferenczi letters, Arno asked mildly, "Are you prepared to do something illegal?" "No, of course not," I replied primly. "That's a pity," remarked the genial Arno, "because I have a set of the correspondence in my study. At one point I was supposed to translate it but we couldn't reach an arrangement." My scruples instantly vanished in the excitement of this unexpected bonanza.

Something should be said here about Ruth Rendell, who then and since has been enormously generous to me. The visit to Nussteads was my first real opportunity to get to know Ruth. While Elizabeth Longford and I had immediately experienced a *coup de foudre*, I believe that most true friendships need time in which to develop. My early impression of Ruth was of a formidably disciplined woman who early every morning exercised in her small but impressively equipped gym for an hour. She would then sit down at her computer and pound away until noon. I was astounded by the facility with which she could write. In the afternoons she would go for long walks and then spend the rest of the day reading. (Her retentive memory is filled with the most arcane information.) A fine cook, she also prepares dinner every night.

I learned that she is deeply religious, a regular churchgoer like Bob. She loves clothes, and even though she has made a fortune from her books she seems to remember that she wasn't always rich. She still buys basic items from Marks & Spencer which she mixes with Donna Karan. One of the most enjoyable things we ever did together was to prowl through the Harvey Nichols January sale. When I pointed out a red dress in which she would look stunning, her immediate response was, "I wouldn't get enough wear out of it."

Ruth loves good restaurants and, totally unembarrassed, gives vent to great bellows of laughter, especially at bawdy jokes. She can be moody and easily bored, and at times I make myself scarce. The huge disparity in our incomes sometimes makes me uncomfortable, but it says much that we have not let it interfere with our friendship. Her loyalty to her friends is touching and I was thrilled when she dedicated one of her Barbara Vine novels, *No Night Is Too Long*, to me. It didn't take long to realize that this was a profoundly complicated woman who maintains a centre of total privacy. There are certain areas of her life into which I would not dream of prying. I am fascinated by her fertile mind, which is unlike any I have ever encountered.

To introduce me to Arno was a kindness typical of Ruth. In addition to the Ferenczi correspondence, which he sent off to me in batches, the correspondence between the members of Freud's secret committee was so extensive that I had to assemble a whole team of people to translate them from the German. Nowadays their communications would be relayed by e-mail – extremely efficient, but likely lost forever to historians.

The major figure in my team, Matthias Nowack, concentrated on the *Rundbriefe*. He lived in Speyer, south of Frankfurt, and in the summer of 1989 I went over to work with him. How nice it was that he happened to live in that lovely old town with its heavenly Romanesque cathedral, to me a much more attractive place than the touristy Heidelberg. Bob and I then went on to make an extensive tour of Germany. We spent some time in Goslar, in the middle of the Harz Mountains, an enchanting town more often associated with the travels of Goethe and Wordsworth than with a rendezvous of Freud's secret committee, which was my principal reason for exploring the area. The Brocken, the mythical site of Walpurgisnacht, is nearby, at that time just over the border with East Germany; here curious crowds with field glasses would gaze up at the East German fortifications on the mountain.

While we were there we picked up a copy of the *Times* and read that Harford Montgomery-Hyde was dead. Earlier that year Kitty West had died, followed by my dear friend Ian Scott-Kilvert.

I had reached an age when every year brought the loss of people who had played an important part in my life. Two years earlier, Virginia had died prematurely. Her death left something unfinished in my life because we had long been separated by physical distance and ancient rivalries. A great sadness followed because I felt that I had never truly known or fully appreciated my brilliant sister.

This particular cluster of deaths left a great emptiness, dulling my anticipation of returning to England. When I expressed this to Ruth, she replied, "Well, then, come over now to see us." As one grows older I think one should be ready to make new friends, and at this stage of my life, most of mine seem to be about twenty years younger than I.

Bob and I travelled by train to Berlin from Hildesheim, where we left the car. Before the war Hildesheim had been one of the most picturesque towns in Germany but it had been left in ruins by Allied bombing, and only gradually are the marvellous old medieval sections being restored. The problem with a lot of German renovation, unlike that in France, is that rebuilt towns tend to look like something out of Disney. In the coach armed soldiers patrolled the aisles, and the frightened people in our compartment became nearly hysterical when I

Saying goodbye to Anne after my visit to Toronto in 1979.

The luxurious but damp Thames barge *Mayflower*, Chiswick Mall, London,
at low tide. *Havelock Ellis* was written here during 1978-79.

Dr. Helena Wright, birth control pioneer,
advised me on my malpractice suit in 1980.

My Canadian publisher and friend Jack McClelland on a business visit in 1981.

Marriage number three to Bob, June 26, 1986.
Our witnesses were Elizabeth Longford, Anne, and Brian.

With the psychoanalyst Carole Morgan on my first Los Angeles lecture engagement
in 1987. The police were called to investigate a death threat.

Signing copies of the French edition of *Melanie Klein*, Paris, 1991.
After my lecture to the Parisian psychoanalytic elite,
I was chided for mispronouncing Freud's name in French.

A valued supporter, the psychoanalyst Dr. Victor Smirnoff,
at our last meeting before his death in Paris, 1992.

With Ruth Rendell in front of her Aldeburgh house, 1993.
My research for *Byron* would not have been possible without her generous offer
of accommodation at her London residence.

Sipping champagne with Mavis Gallant, Christmas 1995, in Paris.
Her conversation is eclipsed only by her brilliant short stories.

Peter Dyson in his usual place at our table.
We shared many interests, including Continental travel and university politics.

Visiting my cherished mentor, the psychologist Dr. Mitzi Jahoda,
in her Sussex home, 1996. Undaunted by advanced age and failing eyesight,
she still reads voraciously and travels widely.

Speaking at the John Addington Symonds Symposium at the University of Bristol in April 1998, held in the house in which Symonds grew up.

Unveiling the plaque on Symonds's Bristol home in April 1998.

Hard at work in Venice with the biographer Rosemary Sullivan
and the Canadian literature specialist Branco Gorjup, May 1998.

At a party at the home of the writer Barry Callaghan, November 1998.

started snapping pictures of the control towers at the border, followed by miles of rusting tanks. On our return journey guards held vicious Alsatians who sniffed under the train for escapees.

We reached Berlin in the late August heat, three months before the fall of the Wall. The first time I had heard that this momentous event was in the wind was from Matthias when we arrived in Speyer. At that time we still had to cross at Checkpoint Charlie; like everyone else we were stunned by the contrast between the two parts of the city, particularly after marvelling at the sumptuous food hall in the Kadawe on the west side. Outside the incredible Pergamon Museum on the east side a young man attached himself to us and told us how much he longed to visit the Prado and other museums in the West. I wonder where that young man is today. We also ran into the parents of Daniel Goldhagen, from whom we learned about the research their son was doing on the part German civilians had played in the extermination of the Jews. Naturally we had no idea that his research would result in the highly controversial book *Hitler's Willing Executioners*, in which he suggested that the entire German population was complicit in the Final Solution.

In December 1990 when the manuscript of *The Secret Ring* was completed, I went down to New York to work with Jane Isay on the editing and brought Anne over for a week. When Anne arrives in an interesting city she seizes it and greedily devours its sweetness. She sat close to Bobby Short in the Hotel Carlyle, listening in a state of entrancement as he belted out Cole Porter tunes, and the same joy lit up her face at the Metropolitan Opera the next night when we went to see *Salome*.

All these experiences are recorded in a diary I started that year. I had always wanted to keep a regular journal, and now that I was approaching sixty-five, I thought it about time. At first I handled it warily and the entries were terse, but gradually I became so dependent on this daily companion that I looked forward every morning to opening that firm leather volume and having a self-discussion about what was concerning me. It was and still is a means of priming the pump before I get to work, and when I am not writing, it keeps the creative juices flowing. It has been particularly useful as a means of working out problems connected with the later books. The whole process and publication of *The Secret Ring* and the work that followed it are contained in its pages. Occasionally when I flip back to check a date, I am amazed at how upset or incensed I was by something long forgotten. Among other things, my journal replaced Bob's "worry notes," which he had kept during the first years after our return to Canada.

I reappeared as the Difficult Woman when I was made to retire from the University of Toronto in 1989, particularly as my pension was less than half my salary. (Ironically, the following year the university gave women faculty a considerable increment to bring their salaries up to those of the men.) Retirement was a narcissistic blow as well. It struck me as absurd to leave when my teaching was at its most confident. I took my concerns to George Connell, the president, who gave me a chilly reception. Several colleagues nominated me as a University Professor, a position of distinction, but, ignoring my credentials, Connell turned down the proposal; from what my supporters later told me, he considered it a ruse for me to stay past the mandatory retirement age. I was permitted to keep my office and continue teaching the psychoanalysis course for a further seven years for a small stipend, helped by a superb teaching assistant, Laurette Larocque. By then I was deep into research for the next biography and I wanted to commit myself more fully to this new life, if not the financial restrictions it entailed.

My experience of university politics, especially the tenure battle at University College, possibly enabled me to understand the group psychology of Freud and his colleagues. My recollection of the neurotic dependence of Mother and her sisters on my strong grandmother must have also contributed to my comprehension of the committee, who addressed one another as "Brother," sometimes between clenched teeth. These early pioneers exhibited the same envy and aggression towards each other as similarly rivalrous groups.

There was yet another controversy with the publication of *The Secret Ring*. This time I offended the Freudians. I was really quite stupid in failing to realize how strongly people who idealize certain figures prefer to leave their mythologized form undisturbed. When I addressed a group of analysts in Rome in 1992, one woman said plaintively, "We just aren't ready for this yet." In response to a piece I wrote for the *New York Review of Books,* an analyst wrote to me that he was sure I had had a bad analytic experience. My critics describe me as a "revisionist" or, sometimes, as "a Freud-basher," which in actuality means that I have ignored myth in favour of fact. If I am a "revisionist" I am glad to be in the company of scholars like Frank Sulloway, for whom I have the greatest respect. I also admire the wit of the iconoclastic Frederick Crews, although I think he tends to throw out the baby with the bathwater. "Do you really want [that Freud]?" he recently asked at a conference at Yale. "The fanatical, self-inflated, ruthless, myopic, ruthlessly devious Freud who has been unearthed by independent scholarship of the past generation? Or would you prefer the Freud of self-created legend, whose name can still conjure the illusion that 'psychoanalytic truth' is authenticated by the sheer genius of its discoverer?" As for myself, I consider Freud one of the great thinkers, sometimes breathtakingly perceptive, but I am critical of his views on women, and I agree with Crews that he was not a particularly nice person. But then, why did he have to be? I also agree with Sulloway that he raised some extraordinarily interesting questions about our psychic lives.

The British launch party for *The Secret Ring* was held in the Freud Museum in Hampstead, and I felt very uncomfortable in that room where I had once discussed Marie Bonaparte with Anna Freud. The book did not reflect particularly well on her father. Professor Tillotson had instilled in me that every fact must be documented – but the fact that things were true didn't endear the truth-teller to the Freudians any more than it had to the Kleinians.

Many of the negative reviews were painful, and I was no better equipped to cope with the experience than I had been with the Kleinian reaction. The way I generally handle bad reviews is to read them quickly, cut them out, stick them in a scrapbook, and never look at them again. That doesn't mean that I'm not pretty bruised. "The biter bit," Bob sometimes remarks, recalling that I had written some tough reviews myself when I was in my forties.

THE LECTURE CIRCUIT

During those years Bob and I worked on a project that he had dreamed up while I was still writing the Klein book. I had collected a great many photographs connected with Klein and the early history of the psychoanalytic movement, and he suggested that I organize these as a slide lecture. The presentation proved immensely popular, and I couldn't count the number of times I have presented it. The first time was at the University of Tennessee at Knoxville in 1987, when we did it as a team. By then Bob knew almost as much about psychoanalysis as I did and could carry his own in any psychoanalytic group. (I often tell him he would have made a good analyst.) Over the years he accompanied me on speaking engagements if we could combine the lecture with an interesting trip.

Confident in my knowledge, I now had self-assurance light-years beyond that of the nervous woman who had once stood quaking in front of a classroom of students. "Okay, showtime," I'd say as we set off on one of these gigs. Just before I was to give a lecture in Philadelphia at the University of Pennsylvania, my leather skirt slipped to my ankles. Quickly securing it, I stepped to the podium without a moment's hesitation. Being regarded as the Expert brings a pleasurable, narcissistic satisfaction. I enjoyed fielding questions, and I wasn't particularly fazed by hostile responses. The greatest pleasure of all was in meeting intellectuals with whom one could have challenging discussions, a far different travel experience than being led around by a tour guide. The danger is that the temptations of being wined and dined can become an addiction.

We crisscrossed Europe by car the way my family used to travel across America. The first place in Europe to which I was invited to give the slide lecture was Geneva, in 1990. Jorge and I had seen each other sporadically through the years, and I gave his name to my host, Dr. André Haynal, as someone who might be invited. I looked over the audience – but no Jorge. When I had finished he suddenly appeared at the door. He said he couldn't bear to sit through the lecture because of the memories it would stir up, but he had listened from the hall. Bob behaved impeccably, offering his hand with a warm smile. As we walked down the hall together, a small vivacious woman appeared. Jorge introduced her as Elvira, a Chilean who was his new wife. André urged them to join us for lunch, but they could not be persuaded. In none of my later visits to Geneva did I ever attempt to contact him. What's past is past.

From Geneva we went on to several cities in Germany. The whole experience was exciting, but it was also stressful, and occasionally we had what we call "the snappies." Some tiny incident sets them off. In the art gallery in Stuttgart, Bob blew up when I contradicted him by saying that its restaurant was not a cafeteria. I glowered almost all the way to Munich, broken by a truce in Tübingen where I spoke at the venerable university founded in 1477. Here we had one of the most stimulating of all our evenings. *The Secret Ring* was about to be

217

translated into German, and there was much discussion about the title because the word *geheim* (secret), with its sinister Gestapo connotations, had disappeared from the language. We met a young analyst, Baron von Stauffenberg, nephew of the one-armed colonel who had failed to assassinate Hitler in 1944 at his headquarters in East Prussia. He seemed astonished that we knew about the plot, little knowing that we had seen innumerable films and documentaries about it on late-night TV.

The way this charming young man kissed my hand was a truly sensuous experience, which brings me to a slight digression about hand-kissing. I hope the delightful custom doesn't become as obsolete as local currency in the new Europe. In France I have had my hand imprinted on many occasions, but apart from the incident in Tübingen, Venice is my all-time favourite. Here aristocrats gently lift the hand almost to the mouth, then drop it with a graceful gesture.

Our final destination was Munich where we arrived on a Sunday evening and were put up in a hotel on the edge of the Englischer Garten with which I immediately fell in love. A group of extremely nice analysts took us out to dinner and later strolled around the city with us. It was one of those magical evenings I shall never forget. A sad aspect of these tours is that one meets people whom one would love to have as friends, but physical distance makes this impossible. The next day we visited Dachau. The experience left me in such a state of distress that I didn't think I could lecture the following night. I still have difficulty in reconciling these enchanting people with the horrors that co-existed in the lives of some of them.

On our return we stopped off in Paris, where I suggested to Dr. Alain de Mijolla, my editor at the Presses Universitaires de France, that I do the lecture tour in France the following year. At first Alain was reluctant, but he then agreed on the condition that I give the lectures in French. During the following winter I prepared myself by reading the French edition of my book and by having a teacher from the Alliance Française come to the house twice a week. I had really taken on a challenge this time: there would be questions and discussions in which I would have to speak with some authority in a different language.

The first lecture took place in a large auditorium on the rue Georges V the night after our arrival, when I was still suffering from jet lag. For the first time in years I had a highly visible ladder running down one leg. The place was filled with the cream of the French psychoanalytic world. I thought, If I can get through this, I can get through anything. At the conclusion Alain rushed up to the platform, bursting with complaints. Did Pheeleese not realize that Freud was pronounced "Frud" in France? Even my adorable Victor Smirnoff (who had not been able to attend) told me that he had heard that I spoke "haltingly." The content seemed of secondary importance.

Alain had made splendid arrangements for a ten-city tour and we started off the following day. My nervousness had manifested itself on that awful first occasion in a fumbling with dates. All the way from Paris to Nantes Bob rehearsed me – 1889, 1902, 1935, etc. By the time we reached Nantes I was more confident. The people were welcoming, totally unlike the patronizing Parisians. And so it continued throughout the provinces. Gradually my French improved to the point that I could bluff my way through a *table-ronde*, occasionally catching the eye of Bob, who looked highly amused after someone had made a long peroration and sat expectantly waiting for me to reply in kind.

Unfortunately Alain and I hadn't made a firm agreement about how and when I would be paid, simply that I would receive a lump sum out of which we would pay all our expenses. Nantes, Bordeaux, Toulouse – no sign of any money. After I had finished speaking in Marseilles, a gentleman handed me a bulky envelope and asked me to sign a receipt. When we returned to our hotel we opened the envelope to find more cash than we had ever seen in our lives – the total sum for the entire trip. We counted the large notes and I tucked them into the zippered section of my outsize handbag, Bob stipulating that from then on we would pay for everything with cash.

My journal for the following day begins, "*Quel jour!*" The bell captain tucked us solicitously into the freshly washed car and saw me place the bag on the floor between my feet. It was a beautiful late May morning and we set off for Geneva in high spirits. Just outside Aix-en-Provence we stopped at a red light. My elbow rested on the open window. Suddenly a black leather arm reached down and across me and seized the bag from the floor. I struggled and screamed but was constrained by the safety belt. All Bob could do was hold his hand on the horn. The bag vanished with the thief who ran down a grassy verge that separated the dual carriageway, then jumped on the back of a disappearing motorcycle.

It happened so quickly; was I dreaming? My first thought was: I worked so hard for that money! A passing woman comforted me: "*Du courage, Madame.*" I could not go to pieces because I had to make a clear report to the police. Fortunately Bob had our airline tickets and passports, but in addition to the money, I lost my reading glasses, itinerary, and all our credit cards. Once I had travelled to Grenoble by bus many years earlier and passed through Sisteron, which struck me as a picturesque town to which I would like to return one day. Now we spent the night there, frantically making telephone calls about our credit cards.

For about a day I was silent and depressed, but then I thought, My God, we're in France — which we both love — so let us salvage something from this situation. In Geneva André Haynal and his wife, Véronique, greeted us warmly. André has a great joyous smile that radiates comfort. Do people with generous smiles realize how much they can ease a heavy heart? It is a gift of grace, like any other talent. Reinvigorated, we continued through Strasbourg to Brussels, all at our own expense. I had regained my spirits so much that one night as we were walking along the Meuse, where a series of houseboats were moored, I was all for joining in a rowdy party taking place in one of them. Bob had to restrain me in the way my father had done when I was three years old. Then back to Paris for a final appearance. This time I acquitted myself respectably, determined not to let the Parisians think they had defeated me. I was, however, desperately hurt by Alain when we met at Le Chat Grippé. He was totally uninterested in hearing anything about the incident of the theft, seemingly absorbed in his *amuse-gueule*, an eggshell that had been filled with a scrambled egg concoction which apparently required intense concentration to extract.

The last occasion on which Bob and I did our dog-and-pony show together was in Rome the following year. By then Bob had built a splendid new life for himself. I have long felt that he is more of a throwback to his missionary grandparents than to his capitalist father because it is a real necessity for him to help others. In England he had been a volunteer for Abbeyfield, a venture in small civilized homes for elderly people as an alternative to large institutions. In 1984 he had founded Abbeyfield in Canada, and it has become particularly strong on the West Coast. In a few short years he had established diverse interests for himself, although I still discuss all my work with him.

The last big "psychoanalytic tour" I did on my own was to South America in 1995. I had always wanted to visit it, and the experience was in many ways unsettling – as travel sometimes should be. In São Paulo I was stunned by the magnificence of the homes I visited, all heavily guarded, in contrast to the acres of squalid favelas, where the poor lived in subhuman conditions. Armed sentries guarded the intersections of residential areas. In São Paulo I spent time with a group of young women analysts, trying to learn as much about their lives as I could. They lived lavishly behind high walls, all had full-time housekeepers, but they were in constant fear that their children would be kidnapped or they would be attacked in their cars. It was strange: we dressed alike, we could exchange ideas, yet our daily lives could not have been more different.

Then in Rio, while we sat in Marius, an expensive restaurant on the Copacabana, a young career woman turned to me. "You do realize that we are in a state of civil war in this country? It's between us and them." My Brazilian agent, Lucia, took me to dinner at the yacht club with her mother, the widow of an admiral. Lucia had grown up believing that she lived in the most beautiful city in the world, and now they were distressed and bewildered about the ever-expanding favelas. Both of them were indignant about the reputation Rio had acquired for crime. Senhora Admiral, in her Chanel suit, brushed aside the idea of danger: she said that when she left her luxurious apartment, she simply carried an old handbag so that it wouldn't matter much if it were snatched. All this terror existed side by side with the most spectacular scenery I had ever seen.

I was also invited to lecture in Argentina – a nation that has more analysts per capita than any other country in the world. Like most other Latin American countries it was, until fairly recently, solidly Kleinian. (Jorge, for example, had had a Kleinian analysis.) Considering the hostile reaction of the British Kleinians to my book, one might wonder why the invitation was extended, but I found that in other countries (not dominated by Dr. Segal) the book was regarded as celebratory of Klein.

When I arrived in Buenos Aires, my hospitable hosts asked what I would like to see, fully expecting that I would answer: the tango. Of course I wanted to see the tango – and did so on my last night – but I replied immediately: the Madres. These were the women whose sons and daughters had been rounded up in the middle of the night and carted off as enemies of the state, thousands of them ultimately to be dropped by plane into the Atlantic. My hosts looked stunned. They didn't think anyone else was interested, they said. Dr. Noemi Buchsman's eyes filled with tears: "There isn't a single one of us who hasn't been affected."

I had come down with some mysterious illness, but I insisted on getting up on Thursday afternoon, the only time in the week when those dignified women circle the Plaza de Mayo, with photographs of their lost ones hanging around their necks. In reproachful silence they move slowly in full view of the pink presidential palace. No one will ever return their children to them, but they must make some symbolic gesture of respect and protest. Jorge's mother might have been among those who passed me.

Despite experiences like this, the excitement and challenge of the psychoanalytic world had begun to lose its edge for me, particularly as I saw bitter feuding almost everywhere I went. Analysts have a particularly rich vocabulary with which to rubbish an opponent – paranoid schizoid, psychotic, narcissistic personality disorder, etc., etc. Academics, on the other hand, say, "He hasn't produced much of any quality." And writers? "How's the book going?" "Fine, I'm just about finished." Glowering disappointment, whereas "Terrible, I seem to have writer's block" will bring delighted smiles of relief. But analysts win hands down in invective.

I was beginning to decline more invitations than I accepted. There were opportunities to go to Australia, to Russia, to other parts of South America. Many people urged me to write a biography of Sandor Ferenczi, the most human of the psychoanalytic pioneers. He would have been a fascinating subject, but I felt that this phase of my life was coming to an end. After writing a long and difficult piece on psychoanalysis and feminism for the *New York Review of Books* I told Bob Silvers, "That's it." He agreed, and suggested that I should be writing intellectual history, although I believe my real inclination is for psychological analysis.

I had long been interested in the phenomenon of exile. Since a great part of the world is in a perpetual state of dislocation, how do people cope? I recalled those family trips to Muskoka when we sometimes stopped for a fried egg sandwich (something we were never allowed at home) at a Chinese restaurant in Orillia. I could see small children about my age in the background, and I wondered if they had friends. Many years later my own family, on an Easter motor trip, found itself on a miserable Sunday night in Aberystwyth, where the only restaurant open was Chinese. Surely these people must live in an enclosed world of their own, just as a small group of Welshmen do in Patagonia.

I started to plan a book, to be modelled roughly on the structure of Lytton Strachey's *Eminent Victorians*, about different types of exiles at different periods of history. Harvard University Press was willing to draw up a contract. But I began to look realistically at the problems involved. Each of these profiles would entail as much work as the biography of a single person and would require years of research and considerable funding.

We spent Christmas of 1992 in London. One evening, just before dinner with Jacqueline Korn and her husband, Ralph Glasser, she told me that a publisher had approached her about my writing a biography of Carl Jung or Lord Byron. Jung – definitely not! But Byron? Here was my quintessential exile. I rang my friend William St. Clair, who had succeeded Ian Scott-Kilvert as president of the Byron Society, to ask his reaction. He had spoken frequently about the need for another biography of Byron since so much new material had turned up in the years since Leslie Marchand had published his magisterial three-volume work in 1957. I was well aware of the suspicions that are aroused when one changes disciplines, but I was game – as well as desperate – to turn my energy in another direction.

It took several months for a three-country deal with publishers to be worked out. The details were finalized just about the time I received an invitation to address the British Psycho-Analytical Society in the spring of 1993. I was fully aware that the aim of many of the members was to attack and humiliate me. Now that I had made up my mind that I was walking away from these people and certain that I knew more about their own history than they did, I stood my ground. The chairman later told me that it was the most difficult meeting over which he had ever presided. I was extremely critical of their former president, Ernest Jones, to which one woman responded angrily, "To think we are hearing this in the Ernest Jones Room!" When I had finished what was in effect a defence of my work, Bob jumped to his feet, two thumbs up.

The next morning I told Ruth Rendell that I felt as though I had crossed a river. With her quick wit, she asked, "The Rubicon or the Jordan?"

"The Jordan," I replied.

9

A BARONY VIOLATED

Nineteen ninety-three was a good year, a very good year indeed as years go. I had been worried about Anne, who was having a difficult second pregnancy, but on February 9 she produced an adorable son, Robin. I now had five grandsons, two British and three Canadian. But I am no competition for Elizabeth Longford, who has twenty-six grandchildren and fourteen great-grandchildren. She wants to live long enough to see them all grown, and she is doing pretty well, approaching her ninety-third birthday on August 30, 1999, as I write.

I began the new year by immersing myself in Byron's life and work, collecting rare editions secured mainly through my old friend Timothy D'Arch Smith. I was reluctant to tell anyone except a few close friends about the project before the publishing contracts were signed. That didn't occur until June, when we were staying with the Rendells in Aldeburgh, on the Suffolk coast. The four of us were about to set off on a walk when Ruth came running out excitedly to say that Jacqueline was on the line. Hodder & Stoughton made up the final unit in the trio with Houghton Mifflin in the U.S. and Macfarlane Walter & Ross in Canada. I strongly suspected the hand of Elizabeth Longford in this since John Curtis of Hodder had long been her editor. Her magnanimity when I told her that I was planning to write a book on Byron (after criticizing hers on the same subject) was typical of her. Frequently when a tricky ethical situation arises, Bob and I say to each other, "How would Elizabeth handle this?"

In April I travelled to Victoria, B.C., for the first time in over thirty years. I stayed with Mary Earnshaw, an old friend from college and naval days. The city looked lovely, familiar and yet alien, so peaceful that it would probably make me as restless today as it had done in the past. By now Mavor was living there, but I didn't look him up. Mary drove me around looking for the house in which I had lived with BG and our children before moving to Ottawa in 1958. My diary entry reads: "I feel like Rip Van Winkle. Wherever we lived has been torn down or subdivided or disappeared off the face of the earth. Perhaps it is just as well because that is where our marriage effectively ended … yet I feel sad because I expected to find it exactly as we had left it."

When I did find familiar landmarks, such as the gate of another house out of which Brian had escaped as a toddler, causing me the most frightened anguish of my life, I could feel no connection with them. The past, I was beginning to realize, cannot be recaptured through places, by trying to rediscover houses in which one has lived, but only through the memory of how one felt at the time.

In October I started out in earnest on the Byronic research trips. In Paris I visited Brian and his wife, Ting Chang, also an art historian. Brian took me around the Louvre, pointing out the Delacroixs and Géricaults that had been influenced by Byron's poetry. Peter Dyson and I arranged to meet in Paris and drove to Provence, where he was staying in Roussillon for a few months. Marc had died of AIDS in 1991 and it was an enormous step for Peter to return to a place where he and Marc had been so happy. The night before we left, we took Mavis Gallant to dinner at La Coupole. She arrived bearing a first edition of Edward Trelawny's *Recollections of the Last Days of Shelley and Byron*. I was extremely touched because she had clearly treasured it for many years.

Peter was a wonderful travelling companion. At Valence we dined at the three-star Pic, and around Roussillon we revisited places familiar from my last visit in 1976, when he and Marc had given me comfort during a difficult time. It was so sunny that we could sit on the balcony and gaze at the Lubéron swelling beyond the tiled roofs. Peter was well known in the village, and in the evenings we visited his friends and sat cozily around a roaring fire.

Bob was waiting for me in London, where we spent a few days before I set off for Oxford. We made a trip to Brocket Hall, the country seat of the Melbourne family in Byron's day. It had strong associations with Byron's egregious lover Caroline Lamb, who was married to the man who became Queen Victoria's first prime minister. The present Lord Brocket, a man in his early forties, had turned the beautiful house into a conference centre. He was an old Etonian, tall, handsome, and very arrogant. The house had sumptuous flower arrangements and many family photographs of his glamorous American wife and their children.

Lord Brocket took us around, telling us outrageous stories about Caroline Lamb and how she had jumped naked out of a soup tureen. I didn't mention that the dating made this impossible, but I am sure such stories must have impressed a group of American orthopedic surgeons who were arriving by helicopter just as we were leaving. Some weeks later I received a batch of newspaper clippings from Ruth Rendell. Lord Brocket was in jail for defrauding an insurance company by claiming that his collection of vintage automobiles had been stolen when he had in fact hidden the dismantled parts in the lake on the property. The following week his wife was arraigned for forging prescription drugs. Lord Brocket, clearly, was not the most reliable of sources.

In London we stayed in Ruth's pied-à-terre in Cornwall Terrace Mews, just off Regent's Park. Without Ruth's generosity in placing this house at my disposal I could never have afforded to embark on the Byron biography. Instead of dwelling on the attacks I have experienced in Britain in the past fifteen years, I should always think fondly of the wonderfully supportive friends who have helped me through those times. One of these was William St. Clair, president of the Byron Society, who had promised to help in any way he could. At the time he was a Fellow of All Souls, Oxford, and he invited me to stay there as his guest while I worked on the Lovelace Papers in the Bodleian Library, to which I had been given access by Lord Lytton, Byron's direct descendant through his daughter Ada.

This was a truly glamorous experience. Professor Roger Hood, the eminent criminologist, was concerned about the spartan room I had been assigned and arranged to have me move into Lord Hailsham's suite where, the porter teased me, the taps were solid gold. The first evening I said to William, "Let us just sit here on either side of the fireplace and savour the moment." All Souls has a reputation for fine food, great scholars, and incredible snobbery. A college with no students and only one female Fellow, it is undoubtedly sybaritic, but I could not have been treated with greater kindness. High table was set on a dais in a splendid hall where we dined one evening on soufflé aux moules, pintade de Drôme et aux olives noires, followed by withdrawal to the Dessert Room, where the Fellows joked about A.L. Rowse and old *Carry On* films. Isaiah Berlin was now so old that he seldom attended high table. One afternoon I was sitting on a bench outside the porter's lodge, where I was to meet William, and found Sir Isaiah sitting next to me, waiting for his driver. I was so shy I couldn't think of anything to say to one of the world's great conversationalists.

At breakfast I would stand, holding my orange juice, and gaze across at the golden Radcliffe Camera which, to me, is one of the most exquisitely proportioned buildings in the world. It was a fitting prelude to a day spent in some of the most exciting research of my life. The material was brought to me in large cardboard cases held together with cotton tape which I would untie with trembling fingers. These were the Lovelace Papers, all the correspondence and papers connected with Byron's marriage to Annabella Milbanke. They had been deposited in the Bodleian by the Earl of Lytton in 1976 – some years after Leslie Marchand had published his life of Byron. On this first exploratory trip I realized what a gold mine this archive was and that I must be prepared to return for a long stretch of time. In the short term, I had to vacate my sumptuous quarters at All Souls because Lord Hailsham was returning for a gala celebration of the ninetieth birthday of my old friend and adversary A.L. Rowse.

The winter was spent at home in Toronto in intense reading to prepare myself for a prolonged return visit in the spring. Odd little details associated with each book linger in the memory. One connected with this period was of the late afternoon sun touching the red brick of the house across the street as I raised my eyes from my book. The mellow softness of it was so beautiful that I waited expectantly each day, just as the rising tides on the Thames will always be a reminder of the time when I was writing *Havelock Ellis*.

It was during this period that I learned in a telephone conversation with the author Phyllis Rose in New York that another woman, Benita Eisler, was writing a book on Byron's women (as Phyllis recollected it), commissioned by my former publisher, Alfred A. Knopf. Eisler had been given an enormous advance, had started about ten months before me, and had a full-time research assistant working for her in England. Was I now faced with another Marie Bonaparte situation? No; this time I could not fade away. All I could rely on was my tenacity and my experience.

John Murray, the publishing house still in the hands of the descendants of Byron's publishers, had amassed a considerable amount of material pertaining to the poet. Benita Eisler had been working there and apparently had become good friends with Mrs. Murray (wife of the current John Murray), who was in charge of the archives.

When I applied to Mrs. Murray for access, I was told that the papers had been put away after Eisler's visit and there was no plan to bring them out again in the foreseeable future. It was made clear to me that she considered Eisler's book would be the definitive study.

Knowing what treasures lay in the Bodleian and elsewhere, I pushed this setback to the recesses of my mind. In the spring I worked for a time in Byron's baronial seat, Newstead Abbey, followed by a prolonged stint at Oxford, from which I would return to London every weekend to see Anne and her family. In Oxford Larissa Haskell had found me a room in the house of a kind Russian émigré. It was a beautiful spring, and early each morning I would set off with my laptop computer for the Bodleian. I could not stay indefinitely in England because I was on a tight budget, so every minute was precious. Making notes on the laptop was a far cry from the laborious copying by hand I had done for the Symonds biography thirty years earlier.

I was completely caught up in those amazing letters. They had the breath of life in them, and, unlike most libraries, the Bodleian allowed readers to handle them. This is my idea of sheer heaven. Holding a letter in one's hand, one can actually see where someone has underlined a word in anger so vigorously that the paper has been torn. To find blots where tears have fallen over words of anguish – that to me is the way to enter the still-living past. Constantly my sympathies were to change according to the letters in which I was immersed at the time.

At noon I would rush across the Woodstock Road to grab a sandwich at a pub. I had to force myself to break off in mid-afternoon to take a walk around the beautiful Oxford quads. As the shadows lengthened I would glance apprehensively at the clock on the wall. At seven, the last manic scholars still there were forced out of the building. I would emerge, dazed, into the Oxford evening, so dizzy with fatigue and excitement that I was often almost run down by cycling undergraduates.

In the first week I ran into a serious technical problem. Whenever I would go out for lunch I would press "save" on my laptop, and when I returned everything I had typed that morning had disappeared. The same thing after my afternoon walk and at the end of the day. I began to feel jinxed. Each evening I made an hysterical call to Bob's son John, who is a computer whiz. He would ask a series of patient questions as though I were an imbecile child. At the weekend I rushed down to his house in Wimbledon. The poor man had not yet showered or shaved but he immediately set to work – and eureka! He retrieved the lost material from a lower level of memory. Has anyone ever compared a computer to Freud's model of the preconscious and the unconscious?

I had many hospitable friends in Oxford and I was still sometimes invited to high table at All Souls, but most evenings were lonely and it was difficult to sleep. After my experience with the Kleinians I had decided to avoid the Byron Society (probably a mistake), but one Saturday I joined their annual expedition to Byron's old school, Harrow – an expedition I had made with Ian Scott-Kilvert many years before. It was an odd coincidence that like Symonds, Byron was an Old Harrovian. As I sat waiting for the group to assemble at Byron House in Chelsea I glanced through the list of people expected – and there was the name of Benita Eisler. An elegant woman in an expensive suit – very Upper East Side – entered and I knew immediately who she was. I believe my first words to her were, "I hope you don't regard me as a rivalrous competitor?" "Not at all," she replied. "Besides, you're working on the early Byron, aren't you?" "No, I'm doing the whole life. And you are doing Byron's women?" "No, I'm doing the whole life." At this point Mrs. Elma Dangerfield, the *éminence grise* of the Byron Society, tactfully intervened. "Ladies, would you like a Campari?"

Benita and I boarded the bus. We sat together on the way, talking of mutual friends in New York. At Harrow we went our separate ways, although from time to time I would catch her regarding me appraisingly. We travelled back together. Mrs. Murray had given me the impression that Benita's book was almost completed, but I somehow began to doubt this. Shortly before we parted I said, "Look, let us regard our situation this way. Our books are bound to be very different and they are going to enhance each other." She gave me a big spontaneous hug. I hurried back to the London mews house and telephoned Ruth in Suffolk. "All right," she said, "you are going to put this right out of your mind. Agreed?"

Elizabeth Longford was my confidante through the whole process of producing the book. On the afternoons when I visited Elizabeth for tea in her Chelsea flat I always bought roses from a flower stall opposite Chelsea Town Hall. Each time I would choose some exotic variety – pale pink with scarlet tips, yellow with tangerine edges. It is very comforting to know in advance exactly what to expect – a door opened, arms extended in a welcoming embrace. I have never fully analyzed our friendship but undoubtedly I have seen in her the ideal mother, someone who has a heart large enough to include one more surrogate child. I once read a description of what it was like to be with Gandhi – like the feeling of waking after a good night's sleep. That is exactly how it feels to talk with someone as serene as Elizabeth Longford.

Once the tray was set on the low table between us, we would scrutinize my latest discoveries, analyzing Byron's character as it unfolded. Elizabeth's open-mindedness was remarkable in view of the fact that she had already produced her own book on the subject. She had always tended to idealize Byron a little, but gradually she began to see him as more complex.

Sometimes on my way back to Sloane Square I would walk via St. Leonard's Terrace, pass Ian Scott-Kilvert's house with the blue plaque announcing that Bram Stoker had once lived there, and then stand for a while across the road from our old house. I would marvel that I had once spent four years running up and down its stairs, making Mont Blanc in the kitchen, scolding Christopher for teasing the younger children. Was this the house in which I wrote my Ph.D. thesis and my first book? Lost in my reflections on one such occasion, I realized that a passing man was regarding me suspiciously, as though I were planning a burglary.

In the spring of 1995 I made a final research trip to Oxford, and on this visit Mrs. Murray at last agreed to let me into her closely guarded archives in Albemarle Street. She stipulated that I would be permitted to examine only ten sets of correspondence and would be charged £25 a day access fee. (Benita, on the other hand, had been allowed to see anything she liked.) Fortunately I had written the major part of the biography by then and knew exactly what I wanted to examine.

Working against time, I hardly had a moment to appreciate the fact that I was sitting in the very room where Byron would frequently drop in to join Murray's literary circle. There was the fireplace where Murray and Byron's protective friends had fed the pages of his memoirs to the flames after his death. The loss of the memoirs was unfortunate, but I have never considered it a disaster because Byron wrote constantly and frankly about his life.

My impression was that Mrs. Murray – rather to her surprise – approved of me. She agreed to my returning at Christmas to finish the work. Closer to the time I bought a plane ticket and faxed her, asking what day would be convenient. I was surprised to receive a reply from her husband: the archives were now closed because the English biographer Fiona McCarthy had been commissioned by Murray to write a biography! William St. Clair and other biographers were outraged: the reversal of the agreement Mrs. Murray had made with me was in fact a breach of contract. They urged me to write an indignant letter to the *TLS*, but I had been through so many battles that I couldn't face another. Besides, I felt confident that I had more than enough material to finish the book. I have often thought that some biographies are overburdened with detail. Northrop Frye once asked me how I knew when it was time to stop researching and start writing; I replied that it was simply a matter of instinct.

Experiencing a great sense of liberation after the stringent confines of psychoanalytic history, I was enjoying the freedom of writing on a literary subject again, especially one with such a dramatic story. As always I produced the first draft in pencil, usually in bed as I had originally done in England in order to keep warm. I then transferred this rough draft to the computer, revising continually, often incorporating suggestions from Bob.

The book also entailed a good deal of travel, not only to libraries, but to places where I could retrace Byron's steps. Since I had already been through Portugal and Spain, I concentrated on Byron's Italy and Greece. Doors were opened to me in Italy through the kindness of Francesca Valente, then director of the Istituto Italiano di Cultura in Toronto. In Venice Donatella Asta, the present owner of the Palazzo Mocenigo, showed us through the great building where Byron had lived in exile on the Grand Canal, and in Ravenna I was given access to the Gamba Papers in the marvellously baroque Biblioteca Classense. There I felt that the atmosphere was very much the same as in Byron's day – he too must have been attacked by mosquitoes when he went riding in the Pineta. Ravenna struck me as a rather sad backwater – as indeed it was in Byron's day – but Pisa is now full of tourists swarming around the Leaning Tower, which never seems to have made any impression on Byron. He had complained about the noise of traffic outside his palazzo on the Arno, but he would have been driven mad by the constant stream of cars passing the building which today houses the municipal archives.

In Greece the following year the sense of place was even stronger, particularly in the rugged terrain of northern Epirus, where the youthful Byron and his friend Hobhouse had felt like intrepid explorers in 1809. Sailing from Ithaca to Cephalonia and then to Patras gave me a sense of the distances Byron covered and the dangers to which he had been exposed. I was delighted to find that it was raining in Missolonghi because I was seeing that desolate place under conditions much as they were during Byron's last terrible days. The Greeks have idealized Byron into a national saviour, and a large statue of him stands in the Park of Heroes. In every town of any size there is an *odos* (street) named after Byron. People need their myths, and they don't welcome biographers who tell them that in actuality Byron was exasperated and contemptuous of the unruly Greeks.

On each of these trips I stopped off in Paris. I had not seen my friend Victor Smirnoff since 1992, when we were returning from a trip to Morocco and took him, Mavis Gallant, and some other friends out to dinner. Each subsequent time when I rang he seemed remote, and I was hurt when I could not entice him to meet me. The last time we spoke was in 1995, when I said I would walk over from my hotel and pay him a visit. He seemed delighted. It was a beautiful day and I decided instead to make a long-deferred expedition to the Buttes-Chaumont, associated with Proust's account of Marcel's jealousy over Albertine's unexplained excursions. For years I had been curious to see this quarry converted into a park. I gave Victor some feeble excuse. Some months later I received a letter from his friend Marie-Claude Fusco, saying that she had been going through his papers and realized that I didn't know that Victor had died suddenly of a heart attack. Apparently he had had open heart surgery in London two years before and had told no one. And all I needed to do that day was to walk across the Luxembourg Gardens to the rue Duguay-Trouin! I had put literature ahead of friendship. Dear, dear Victor, forgive me.

When I had written about two-thirds of the manuscript, in early 1996, I sent it off to Peter Davison, my editor at Houghton Mifflin in Boston. Peter is a poet of considerable talent, which I believe has never been sufficiently appreciated. He travelled from Boston to New York in 1993 to meet me when I was doing research at the Pierpont Morgan Library. Barely fifteen minutes after introductions, he startled me with the revelation that he had had an affair with Sylvia Plath. I subsequently learned that he offered this information to a great many new acquaintances.

I expected Peter would share my excitement about all the dramatic material I had found in the Bodleian and incorporated into the manuscript. At the beginning of March I was invited to New York to see the American production of *Mrs. Klein* and to give some lectures at various places such as Albert Einstein University. On the night of my arrival, just as I was leaving for the theatre, I was handed a long fax. It was from Davison. I sat in the lobby reading it in a state of bewilderment. Peter couldn't have been more blunt. The manuscript, he declared, required a lot of work. He said I hadn't assimilated the material properly, there were too many women so that the storyline became confusing, etc., etc. He could not help me, he emphasized: I would have to work it out for myself.

As a poet himself, Peter is highly conscious of language, and this letter read as though he planned to include it in his collected correspondence. I stumbled out into the night. The rain was coming down in sheets. I boarded the Second Avenue bus and got off without any idea where I was. After the play Uta Hagen and I finally met, and in a picture taken of us together my strained smile reveals the shock I was feeling. In my journal that night, in an effort not to be discouraged, I wrote: "Thought of starting all that work again daunting. He could have done a little stroking, but realize have much to learn from him. A long time since I have had a serious blow, will handle it with courage, common sense, & humility. Forget about Benita – concentrate on best book can possibly write."

The following night I had dinner with old friends, the sociologist Gertrud Lenzer and her husband, the nineteenth-century scholar Steven Marcus. I was feeling dejected about Peter's fax. They suggested that Steven read the controversial sections of the book. I gratefully accepted, and when Steven rang me about ten days later from his office at Columbia, he assured me that the book was marvellous and that I could tell Peter he had said so. All it needed, he advised, was some signposts for the reader. He gave me just the kind of advice I should have been receiving from my editor.

Several years before, when I was working on the Melanie Klein book, I had had a furious row with Bob Gottlieb over what I perceived as editorial censorship of remarks critical of Freud. (For example, I had a footnote that Marilyn Monroe had left a considerable sum to Anna Freud's nursery, and this was taken out because, I was told, it reflected on the dignity of Miss Freud.) I was determined to use more restraint this time, whatever the provocation. In April I went to Boston with the lightly revised manuscript and told Peter frankly what Steven's reaction had been, and nothing more was said about the necessity for immense rewriting. Yet it was very offputting, working with a man who never once smiled. He kept bemoaning the state of the publishing world and seemed eager to get away from it.

Other pressures were imposed on me. Houghton Mifflin became extremely edgy about the strong possibility that Benita's book would appear before mine, and since publishing was in such a parlous state, this would be a financial disaster for all of us. With the Symonds book I had had to work furiously to finish it lest we return to Canada prematurely; the Ellis had to be completed before the cancer operation; and now I was in a race to get to market before Benita. And Peter insisted, rather late in the day, that the finished book must be under 500 pages, a cost-saving measure that meant I had to cut about 100 pages from the manuscript. Bob had a shirt made for me on which he had inscribed: "All My Life I've Worried About Ending Up in the Workhouse. My Home *Is* the Workhouse."

The strain of the effort was too much, and by the time the book appeared in the spring of 1997 my health had suffered. Nevertheless, trying to pace myself, I had to go through the publicity campaign surrounding the book's publication within three months in the U.K., Canada, and the United States. All that had been allotted for the book's American promotion, I was horrified to learn, was the cost of an ad in the *New York Review of Books*.

COLONIAL GRANNY

I dedicated *Byron: The Flawed Angel* to my three Byron friends – Elizabeth Longford, William St. Clair, and the late Ian Scott-Kilvert. Both Elizabeth and William read the entire manuscript. William had some differences in interpretation, but on the whole seemed to like it very much. Elizabeth finished it in her Sussex garden and immediately sat down to write me an excited letter of praise.

The first British review appeared in the prestigious *Literary Review*, where Jonathan Keates wrote admiringly of the book. The second, in the *Daily Mail*, was equally appreciative – and I thought all was going to be well. Bob knew about the third one before I did. He received a call from Elizabeth telling him that a devastating review had appeared in the *Sunday Times* and to keep the news from me. All day he debated about whether to tell me. I was stunned the next day to read Miranda Seymour's bitchy, scornful, supercilious dismissal of a colonial granny who had the cheek to try to pull herself out of her rocking chair.

By the time I arrived in England I had to face a reaction I had shoved to the back of my mind – namely, that the British perceived Byron as their personal icon and that when I wrote my book, in Edward Said's phrase, "a barony had been violated by a crude trespasser." I do not think the reaction would have been so intense if people had not known that "one of them," Fiona McCarthy, a member of the close-knit London literary circle, had been commissioned to write The Biography. A well-known Cambridge academic wrote to Peter Davison that she knew which of the three biographies she was going to prefer – even though Benita's had not yet been published, and Fiona had only just started her research!

One of my worst ordeals was with Hermione Lee, the biographer of Virginia Woolf. She interviewed me on the BBC from Manchester, and I could sense her barely concealed hostility. Later when we heard the heavily edited tape followed by a discussion with some critics, I was outraged by the sadistic way she acted like a ringmaster, whipping the others to say exactly what she wanted to extract from them. In the morning we laughed: it had been like a skit out of Beyond the Fringe.

What was abundantly clear was that among those critical of the book there was no consensus about what was wrong. Few detractors actually addressed the content or interpretation of Byron that I had presented. Yes, there was one thread: I was putting Byron on the couch. No one said exactly how, but the fact that I had written on psychoanalytic subjects was enough. In fact I had always deplored a psychoanalytic model imposed on a subject, such as Bruce Mazlish had done with John Stuart Mill, and had sedulously attempted to avoid any hint of this. But what would be considered psychological insights if given by a British author were in my book unacceptable, especially when applied to a national hero. John Addington Symonds had been a hitherto unknown subject, but everyone had his own idealized Byron – and how dare a Canadian suggest that he was a self-indulgent manic-depressive?

The book received even greater coverage than *Symonds*, and friends kept reminding me to count column-inches. I had defenders, of course, such as Peter Ackroyd in the *Times*. The Irish reviews were good, which I think is rather revealing. Jacqueline later told me that I was a real trouper, that I didn't betray any of my hurt in public. It was a very odd experience to go to dinner parties and be treated as a celebrity when I saw myself as an object of humiliation. I once broke into tears at Nussteads, where Bob and I were spending the weekend with the Rendells. Elizabeth was totally bewildered by the negative reaction, but neither she nor Ruth could accept my theory about the anti-colonialism behind it.

England had given me my first opportunity as a writer, so it was disconcerting to find myself growing antagonistic towards the British. Then Jacqueline had a publication party for me, and as I looked around at my friends, some of them dating back more than thirty years – Noël Annan, Francis Haskell, Francis King, Michael Holroyd – I realized that all these people were there to support me. In my speech I tried to make a joke about the uproar, saying that I refused to accept complete responsibility for it – also responsible were Jacqueline, Lady Longford, William St. Clair, the Rendells – all of those who had been so good to me.

Lord Lytton wrote me that he had received letters asking him to denounce the book, but he had refused. As far as he was concerned, he told me, my portrait of his ancestor was the best he had read. His public support would have made a great difference. On reflection, I think that as chairman of the Byron Society, he might have felt that it was more statesmanlike not to become embroiled in the controversy.

The strain took a further toll on my health. I returned to Canada and was cheered when Elspeth Cameron praised the book highly in the *Globe and Mail*, and even more so when Terry Castle gave it a marvellous review in the *New York Times*. The differing reactions in Britain and America were extraordinary. Even more surprising was that when the book came out in paperback in England, the reviews were unanimously splendid. I was invited to the Cheltenham Festival and fêted like a star. I asked Mavis Gallant what she made of it. "It is the journalists and the general readers now, not the special interests."

On this visit, in October 1997, I addressed the Byron Society at St. Ermin's Hotel in London. It reminded me of the evening when I had had to face the British Psycho-Analytical Society. Most of the members regarded Byron as a demigod, not the complicated human being I had depicted. Many of the elderly ladies had the kind of crush on him that was not unlike that of the Elvis fans. Ruth insisted on being present. Elizabeth was in the chair and defended me vigorously, as did William and, for that matter, John Murray. Michael Foot and others actually boycotted the meeting, a childish and cowardly thing to do. (I have always considered Foot a silly, vain man, a terrible choice when he was made leader of the Labour Party.) When someone mentioned that Foot had stayed away, Elizabeth sprang to her feet. "The trouble with Michael Foot," she shouted in the voice she had used when on the hustings as a Labour candidate, "is that he has always regarded Byron as a card-carrying member of the Labour Party!" With the help of such friends, I managed to get through the evening.

What one must remember is the joy of actually writing the book. Once it leaves my hands, it no longer belongs to me. That is why I hate saying goodbye to books and old friends. One's books are what Mary McCarthy called one's "mind-children"; once gone, they become "products" or "commodities." Nevertheless, the attacks were directed against what I had originally written. It has been far more painful to write about the furor caused by the Byron biography than about the attacks by the Kleinians more than ten years ago, but the only way to put it behind one is to get on with something else.

I sometimes think how much easier it would be if only my talent lay in novel-writing. For one thing, in Canada the novel seems to be regarded as the true art form, and non-fiction as decidedly inferior. In a novel I could write about my own life in a disguised form, and could manipulate facts artistically. But my talent, if such it is, has to be accepted gratefully as something that has enriched my life.

It seems to be my fate to be drawn to controversial biographical subjects. In each case I have been the outsider invading jealously guarded territory. Do I, one might ask, deliberately seek subjects that are going to cause me pain? The subject of the Symonds book was one that I knew would disturb my parents, and it was perhaps a form of long-postponed rebellion, but I did not write it specifically for that purpose. I chose it because it interested me. I started the Melanie Klein out of desperation, but in the course of writing the book I saw how contentious the material was and ultimately I realized that it would cause consternation among the Kleinians. With *The Secret Ring* I knew from the beginning that it would be disturbing to those who idealized Freud, but I couldn't resist the subject. I was slightly nervous about the Byron, but certainly did not anticipate the subsequent uproar. If I have to suffer the consequences of writing on figures about whom people have strong feelings, so be it. I would find it impossible to write about pallid, safe subjects. Nor can I sidestep incendiary material, although I observe that many British biographers do precisely that. And the truth is that the next biography will undoubtedly be just as controversial as the others.

EPILOGUE

For years my friend Mitzi Jahoda Albu has been telling me that old age is the most difficult challenge one will ever have to face. She first announced this in her Sussex garden when we were both twenty years younger. I had always been interested in old people, and her remark alerted me to observe them with closer attention. Perhaps I could learn something from them.

What I have learned is that they are wonderful role models. Mitzi herself, at ninety-two, has had some rough patches but is managing remarkably by dint of wry humour and, above all, curiosity. Her eyesight is bad yet she still writes learned articles on psychology and not long ago was given the freedom of the city of Vienna. She patiently read this book in manuscript, chapter by chapter, just as she had done with *Havelock Ellis* in 1978-79. Elizabeth Longford has just completed a shorter version of her biography of Queen Victoria. (She was so busy with her own book that she had to give up on this one.) True, these are extraordinary women, but my observations have led me to the conclusion that most people cope with age amazingly well. *On se débrouille.*

There are, however, insidious and unexpected hazards that face one. On a recent trip I made to Mexico, a two-man electronic band played something (I don't even know its name) that pierced a vulnerable chink in my defences. My whole body was flooded by its beauty. And I wept a little – for something unremembered, something lost during the bumpy ride. More than likely, common sense says, it never existed in the first place, it was simply a wisp of a dream – but I tend to believe that it was a piece of lost youth. As my husband comforted me, I said through my tears, "I feel so young *inside*."

I hope I don't lose curiosity about the unknown, but I do find that best of all is the reassuring familiarity of home. Bob and I have lived in our Victorian workman's cottage for nearly eighteen years. I have produced four books and countless reviews and lectures within its walls. We have had wonderful evenings with friends around our dinner table. The toy box that was pulled out whenever the grandsons visited has long since been relegated to the basement. The small garden is a place of enchantment for me, and I watch every year for the return of the red cardinal. (It must be a grandson of the original by now.) Our house is old and needs repairs. So do we.

I occupy a house in a neighbourhood within a large vibrant city which, despite its familiar landmarks, bears no resemblance to the overgrown colonial town in which I grew up. I love to walk the quiet surrounding streets, especially in the morning, when occasionally I pass someone with a dog. People are a little reluctant to say "Good morning" since this is the way Toronto still is. As Northrop Frye remarked, Toronto is a good place in which to mind your own business. Yet I know by name the local butcher, the dry cleaner, the pharmacist, the fishmonger, the florist, the man who develops my film.

On my walks I pass along the ridge of the high hill above the Don Valley where Joan and I planted a Schubert cherry tree to commemorate our parents. Ironically, we had fulfilled their ambitions for us: Joan as a librarian, Virginia as a political scientist, and I as a biographer.

For a long time I had difficulty recalling my parents' features, but for the last year or so I have been able to envision them very clearly. Once Mother and I sat on the crest of this very hill after a visit to the zoo. Two cheeky boys, catching sight of her fashionable hat, serenaded her: "Lady, where did you get that hat?" Leaning back on her elbows, she laughed delightedly. It is a good memory.

I think I have accepted the fact that one of these days I shall have to move out of my house. Marcus Aurelius says that our life is a brief sojourning in an alien land. In the meantime, brief or not, I am happy being home.

INDEX

The text in this book is set in Bembo, a typeface produced by Stanley Morison of Monotype in 1929. Bembo is based on a roman typeface cut by Francesco Griffo in 1495; the companion italic is based on a font designed by Giovanni Tagliente in the 1520s.

Book design by Wioletta Wesolowski/James Ireland Design Inc.
Typesetting by Marie Jircik